UNDER
THE
KAPOK
TREE

About the Author

Alma Gottlieb is an associate professor of anthropology at the University of Illinois at Urbana-Champaign. Since 1979, her major research has been with the Beng people of Côte d'Ivoire (West Africa). She is the coauthor (with fiction writer Philip Graham) of the memoir *Parallel Worlds: An Anthropologist and a Writer Encounter Africa,* which won the Victor Turner Prize for 1993; coeditor (with Thomas Buckley) of *Blood Magic: The Anthropology of Menstruation;* and coauthor (with M. Lynne Murphy) of a Beng-English dictionary. A contributing editor of the *American Anthropologist,* Gottlieb has published articles in many edited collections and scholarly journals, including *American Ethnologist, American Anthropologist, Man, Anthropology Today,* and *Africa.* Currently she is at work on a new book about Beng infant-rearing practices.

UNDER

T H E

KAPOK
T R E E

Identity and Difference in
Beng Thought

ALMA GOTTLIEB

THE UNIVERSITY OF CHICAGO PRESS
Chicago and London

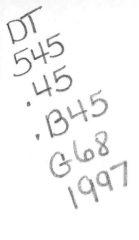

The University of Chicago Press, Chicago 60637
The University of Chicago Press, Ltd., London

© 1992 by Alma Gottlieb

All rights reserved. Originally published 1992 in the series
African Systems of Thought, edited by Charles S. Bird and Ivan Karp,
Indiana University Press.
University of Chicago Press Edition 1997
Printed in the United States of America
03 02 01 00 99 98 97   6 5 4 3 2 1

Library of Congress Cataloging-in-Publication Data

Gottlieb, Alma.
    Under the kapok tree : identity and difference in Beng thought /
Alma Gottlieb.
        p.   cm.
    Originally published: Bloomington [Ind.] : Indiana University
Press, 1992. (African systems of thought)
    Includes bibliographical references and index.
    ISBN 0-226-30507-4 (pbk. : alk. paper)
    1. Beng (African people)—Ethnic identity.   2. Beng (African
people)—Psychology.   3. Philosophy, Beng.   4. Identity
(Psychology)—Côte d'Ivoire.   5. Difference (Psychology)—Côte
d'Ivoire.   I. Title.
DT545.45.B45G68   1997
306'.089'9634—dc20   96-26356
                                                    CIP

To Philip
devoted husband, friend, and travel companion

and to my Beng family, hosts, hostesses, and friends
eci ka kwã sí

The close relation of identity and difference . . . [is] that which gives us thought.

Martin Heidegger, *Identity and Difference*

CONTENTS

FIGURES

MAPS

Preface

This book proposes an interpretation of Beng life that is oriented toward two principles that on some occasions appear complementary, on others oppositional. I gloss these principles as "identity" and "difference," following Beng phrases that occur in speech quite regularly. In recent years in the social sciences and humanities, there has been much discussion of the issues that follow these terms. The debates generally revolve around questions of morality: Is it possible to maintain justice in the face of difference? Or is identity the necessary condition for the long-term creation of justice? These questions have become especially pressing in considering the interlinked spheres of race, gender, and class in the modern world.

This ethnography aims to address issues raised by the questions of identity and difference in a rather different arena from the Western orientation of current discourse. It focuses on how one group of people in the West African rain forest have constructed a society and live out their daily lives in relation to an interconnected series of meditations on the notions of identity and difference. In Côte d'Ivoire, Beng people continually consider, play with, and become entangled in the paired notions of identity and difference. In this study, contradiction becomes a central concept as I explore how these two notions are frequently at logical loggerheads with one another. Through the book, I consider the workings of the two ideas in diverse realms of Beng life and thought, from religious worship to daily life.

The first chapter places the Beng world in the larger world of ideas and theoretical issues. In the second chapter, I discuss Beng Earth worship, which is the cornerstone of traditional Beng religion. The kapok tree is analyzed as a central symbol embodying the fundamental duality of identity and difference. At one level a symbol of difference between village and forest and all that those two domains represent, at another level the tree provides the means to achieve an identity between those realms. Thus the kapok tree confounds the very distinction I will be emphasizing.

Chapters 3 and 4 look at the linked themes of identity and difference in the context of issues relating to kinship. Chapter 3 concentrates on descent. A first look at the two types of clans reveals a general association of matriclans with the principle of identity and patriclans with difference. But at deeper levels this set of associations does not hold up, and once again the absolute dichotomy is challenged.

Chapter 4 looks at alliance systems. Here, further complexities present themselves. Both endogamy and exogamy are ideal principles—endogamy for the matriclans, exogamy for the patriclans—once again revealing associations with identity and difference, respectively. But these associations are not inviolable. In this case, the matriclan is ideally endogamous but only to a certain degree: clanmates should marry relatives who are close, but not too close. The entire alliance system indeed hovers unresolvedly between a sociological understanding of proximity and distance.

In Chapter 5, I return more explicitly to issues deriving from cosmology by focusing on myth and ritual. Specifically, I turn to several levels of attitudes and daily practices concerning dogs and hyenas. Here Beng thought is seen as dealing with the themes of identity and difference in a variety of complex ways, posing dogs as beings that lie somewhere between allies and traitors to the human cause and hyenas as beings embodying the notion of the Other—a notion that is alternately amusing and terrifying. Thus this chapter explores the ambiguity of that which lies between identity and difference.

Chapter 6 looks at how Beng cosmology has confronted material stimuli from the West. I highlight both the ambivalent reactions that the Beng have had to imported commodities and technology and the ambivalent meanings that these foreign goods have come to embody. Identity and difference here speak to the very construction of ethnicity as envisioned by the Beng.

In short, the current work may be taken as a reading of Beng culture. Another outside observer—for example, one with a more explicitly political or economic orientation—would have written a radically different book. And of course, Beng people themselves naturally have their own understandings of their society. While the sort of anthropology that I practice relies heavily on indigenous statements and attitudes, ultimately it is my own interpretations that I offer in this work.

These interpretations are based on sixteen months of fieldwork among the Beng (fourteen months living in one village in 1979–80 and two months living in another village in 1985) and on regular correspondence with several Beng friends while I have been in the United States. A few brief words here should help to position my field situation and enable the reader to better judge this work.

Thinking back on my immersion in Beng lives, it is hard to imagine myself as the detached observer posited by a previous rhetorical age in anthropology. As Rosaldo puts it (1989: 169), there is no Archimedean point to which the fieldworker can revert. While in the field, I continually tried on a series of identities, each of which on given days felt more comfortable than the previous one both to me and to my hosts and hostesses. Some days I shucked corn, drank palm wine, and danced at all-night funeral dances; other days I treated infected cuts, wrote letters home, and typed up field notes. More to the point, my relationships with my Beng neighbors oscillated constantly between exclusion and inclusion; even concerning the latter, it was rarely predictable whether my inclusion in particular events would be in the role of fictive equal, addressed as Amwe (my Beng name) and asked to wail for the dead or to hold the crying baby, or as high-prestige guest, addressed as White Person (*sō pú*), seated among the male elders, and given the choicest chunks of meat from the stewpot. My own attitudes varied proportionately to these decisions about me made by others: when I felt included in the social world around me as a fellow villager, I imagined staying in the field for years on end; when I felt excluded, I counted calendar pages and thought longingly of all-news radio, autumn leaves, popcorn at movies. As time passed I came to be included more and more, but to the end there always remained activities from which I was excluded. I suspect this is true of all fieldworkers, though few dwell on the point in print.

Indeed, unlike the impression of fieldwork that one gains from most of the now voluminous literature on the subject (for the paradigmatic piece, see Geertz 1973a), my fieldwork role did not take the typical unilineal trajectory from threatening stranger to awkward visitor to adopted daughter. In fact, for the first six months, fieldwork in many ways became more and more challenging, as my Beng hosts and hostesses came to understand the depth and breadth of my presence among them and to feel increasingly beleaguered by some of my questions. By the end of my first stay, I had made several friends with whom I felt as close as any friends back home, and I had a wide network of people with whom I was less intimate but on friendly terms. Nevertheless, there were more than a few people who continued to resent my presence to the end, for reasons I consider elsewhere in my sections of a fieldwork memoir I am now coauthoring with my husband, the fiction writer Philip Graham, who accompanied me to the field on both trips (Gottlieb and Graham n.d.). In my sections of that book I also discuss several personal struggles that continually preoccupied me while in the field but that I do not have space to take up here—struggles with the Beng language, which I learned as I studied the culture; with tropical diseases, which are responsible for the utterly delapidated state of my copy of *Where There Is No Doctor*; and with my doomed attempts to fairly compensate my Beng hosts and hostesses for the abundant information they continually offered—doomed insofar as the small efforts I was (and am) able to make to help a few individuals can be no more than stopgap measures, however well meant, with no structural effect on the wider injustices the world has inflicted on minority, Third World populations such as the Beng.

No matter whether I felt more or less included or excluded by my Beng hosts, there is no doubt that the sixteen months I have spent in Beng villages were overwhelmingly involving—in a sense, my own "total social institution," as Goffman would put it. This fieldwork immersion accounts for my use of the classic ethnographic present in this work. As Hastrup has argued (1990), the continued rhetorical use of the ethnographic present is justified not on the grounds that local social life never changes—an absurd proposition that is hardly supportable any longer—but that the intense involvement of the anthropologist in the field renders the experience a sort of "time out of time," and it is this that the rhetorical use of the ethnographic present indexes.

In sum, our Beng neighbors put up graciously with two uninvited foreigners even if the motives for our continual curiosity and rounds of questions were at times incomprehensible. For those Beng people who have an opportunity to read this book, now or in the future, I hope that they might see the relevance of the proverb that one Beng friend, trying to explain the earlier suspicion of a few villagers toward my work among them back in 1979–80, offered me during my 1985 visit: *ā ɣra kpandri o, na ā ta sra mɔ blɛ lu* ("We threw it out into the darkness but we retrieved it in the moonlight").

Acknowledgments

Much of the information in this book was shared with me by three people: Mme. Véronique Amlan Akpoueh, M. Kouassi Kokora, and M. Yacouba Kouadio Ba, to all of whom I offer my profoundest thanks for their friendship, and respect for their wisdom. At different points, while I was learning the Beng language, several other people served as translators and assistants, including Jean Kofi Kona, Pascal Kouadio Kouakou, Noël Kona Kouadio, Bertin Kouakou Kouadio, Yao Yapi, and "Baa" Hubert Akpoueh. Countless other Beng people took an interest in my work, telling me of their lives for rewards that, to many, must have seemed nebulous at best. I do not cite them by name and I mask their identities in the genealogies and texts that follow, as was their preference, but here record my deep gratitude to them.

While in the field, my husband, Philip Graham, was a constant and comforting anchor for what was often a storm-tossed ride. His contribution to this book suffuses every page not only with his continual challenging and intelligent reading of my ideas but also with the constant encouragement he has provided me wherever we have been. Our young son, Nathaniel, born after our last field trip, has inspired me by his own example, plunging me into another kind of fieldwork and showing me all over again what a joy it is to see the world from another's radically different perspective.

While in Côte d'Ivoire, my stay was made possible by the kind support of several governmental agencies, to whose officials I am especially grateful: M. H. Leroix and M. J. Michotte of the Ministère de la Recherche Scientifique; the Ministère de l'Intèrieure; Professors Moustapha Diabaté and Daniel Kadja of the Institut d'Ethno-Sociologie at the Université Nationale de Côte d'Ivoire; the Department of Housing at the Université Nationale de Côte d'Ivoire; M. Cheikhou Badio of Citibank; Mr. Terry Schroeder, then American Ambassador to Côte d'Ivoire; Ms. Harriet Elam and Mr. Bill Parker, then U.S. Cultural Affairs Officers; the Préfet of Bouaké; Commandant Camara Mory Dienl, then Sous-Préfet of M'Bahiakro; the staff at the M'Bahiakro Infirmary; and in Washington, D.C., M. Kakoubi, then Chargé d'Information at the Côte d'Ivoire Embassy.

Before setting out to the field, I profited greatly from the sage advice of several learned Ivoirianist scholars: Ariane Deluz, Mona Etienne, Philip Ravenhill, Judith Timyan, and Susan Vogel. I am grateful for all their counsel.

In Abidjan, as two very bedraggled fieldworkers, my husband and I often showed up with no notice and were received with the kindest of hospitality by our dear friends Esti Votaw and her late husband, Albert Votaw, as well as by Philip

Ravenhill and Judith Timyan. In M'Bahiakro our friend Lisa Sammett, then a Peace Corps volunteer, was always a cheerful hostess and friend during our mail sorties.

My initial fieldwork among the Beng was supported by a predoctoral grant from the Social Science Research Council. Dissertation write-up grants were provided by SSRC, the American Association of University Women (Constance L. Tomkies Endowed Fellowship) and the Woodrow Wilson Foundation (Program in Women's Studies). My 1985 trip was supported by a United States Information Agency Linkage Agreement between the National University of Côte d'Ivoire and the University of Illinois at Urbana-Champaign, ably administered on the Illinoisan end by Professor Donald Crummey and on the Ivoirian end by Mme. Rose Eholié. Several units at the University of Illinois at Urbana-Champaign also supported this trip: the Center for African Studies, International Programs and Studies (William and Flora Hewlett Award), and the Research Board. In addition, historical research on the Beng at the Overseas Section of the French National Archives was funded by the National Endowment for the Humanities (Travel to Collections Grant). A semester relieved of teaching duties offered by Professor Thomas Riley, head of the Department of Anthropology at the University of Illinois at Urbana-Champaign, gave me the time necessary to complete the manuscript. I am indebted to all these people and institutions for their various forms of support.

I presented earlier versions of several chapters of this book as talks at Indiana University (Center for African Studies), the Johns Hopkins University (Department of Sociology), the University of Illinois at Urbana-Champaign (Department of Anthropology and the Social History Group), and Southern Illinois University at Carbondale (Department of Anthropology), and at Annual Meetings of the American Anthropological Association and the African Studies Association. I am grateful for all the invitations, for I profited greatly from the very helpful questions and suggestions offered by members of all those audiences. Some chapters of this book have been published elsewhere in quite different forms: a short portion of chapter 2 appeared in expanded form in Buckley and Gottlieb, eds. (1988); chapter 5 is a fusion of two articles printed in *American Ethnologist* (vol. 13, no. 3, 1986; and vol. 16, no. 3, 1989); and a rather different version of chapter 4 appeared in *Man* (vol. 21, no. 4, 1986). I am grateful to the American Anthropological Association and the Royal Anthropological Institute of Great Britain and Ireland for permission to reprint the reworked articles here.

I am fortunate in having a large number of colleagues, friends, and mentors, both local and distant, who have offered astute comments on various pieces and stages of the manuscript. I hope I have dealt with their suggestions in ways that have deserved their attention. The original members of my doctoral committee at the University of Virginia—J. Christopher Crocker, J. David Sapir, and Roy Wagner— have continued to offer a welcome blend of support and challenge through the years as my ideas have evolved beyond the dissertation they first read. Others who have generously commented on portions of the manuscript include Charles Bird, Mona Etienne, Gillian Feeley-Harnik, Eric Gable, Adam Kuper, Joseph C. Miller, Jennifer Nourse, Thomas Turino, and James Wilkerson. I am especially grateful to Ivan

Karp and to Janet Keller, both of whom read the complete manuscript and offered their usual perspicacious comments at particularly hectic times in both their lives.

For help with references, I am thankful to Thomas Bassett, Josephine Kibbee, Yvette Scheven, and Curtis White. M. Lynne Murphy was an ace last-minute assistant tracking down obscure references. Sandy Huss originally drew the maps and house drawings in the book, and Gary Apfelstadt was originally responsible for the meticulous genealogies. Chuck Stout and Inni Choi redrew all the maps and figures on computer with great technical panache. Barbara Cohen was a thorough and patient indexer, especially in the face of my own buddinsky behavior. William and Florence Gottlieb have been a source of support in ways I am sure that I, like other children toward their parents, barely recognize.

Folktales told to me by the Beng are printed as extracts in smaller type. Some have been edited slightly for this volume. The original Beng texts of these stories, with word-by-word French and English translations, are available from my field notes to interested scholars.

CHAPTER ONE

The Beng in the World of Ideas

Do I contradict myself?
Very well then I contradict myself,
(I am large, I contain multitudes.)
                    Walt Whitman, "Song of Myself"

WHO ARE THE BENG?

"The Beng" is the kind of phrase that is now problematic in anthropology. In Africa in particular, a large group of works by anthropologists, historians, and political scientists has shown convincingly how fluid the "ethnic group" has been in many parts of Africa (e.g., Salamone 1975, Schultz 1984). These works have also shown that the social boundaries we scholars have relied upon, even held dear, are complex constructions with heterogeneous origins (e.g., Arens 1975, Nurse and Spear 1985), in some cases quite recent ones at that (e.g., Kopytoff, ed., 1987; Weiskel 1976, 1978; Zilberg 1989). In all likelihood, most Third World populations in Africa and elsewhere were far less isolated from one another before Europeans set foot in their lands than we in the West have tended to assume. With contact and trade often came deep mutual influence through intermarriage and active circulation of social and religious customs, including dances, healing practices, individual spirits, and occult arts. Yet in Africa, European colonial officers were all too eager to divide their subject populations into tightly bounded groups the better to rule them. The current South African situation demonstrates all too devastatingly how destructive to the lives of Africans our own reified Western categories have been (Gordon 1988).

Does the revelation of the precolonial openness of certain social groups, coupled with the pernicious colonial insistence on discrete groups, render the notion of ethnicity in Africa wholly irrelevant? I think not. While ethnicity in all likelihood was, and in many cases still is, far more fluid in most of Africa than anthropologists have until recently depicted, nevertheless it is an important feature of the mental and political landscapes today. Not only is Western journalistic discourse singlemindedly oriented toward the exotically ethnocentric notion of "tribalism," but African governmental officials periodically issue declarations against the divisive forces of that same "tribalism." Even more importantly, African villagers themselves speak of their own ethnic groups in a variety of ways, ranging from pride to self-conscious ambivalence, that attest to the staying power of the concept itself. "Members" of different groups may point to different factors that for

1

them constitute the most important criteria in distinguishing their ethnic identity from their neighbors'—customs such as mode of reckoning descent or determining postmarital residence, initiation rituals, dress or scarification style, house style, language. None of these factors constitutes an "objective" index of ethnicity. Indeed, my own position approaches the radically relativist notion that an ethnic group is any group of people who consider themselves one, for whatever reasons they adduce and as a means of contrasting themselves with some postulated Others (compare, e.g., Poyer 1988).

By this standard, the Beng of Côte d'Ivoire "are" an "ethnic group."[1] It is true that they offer different responses to a question such as "Are the Beng a separate people?" depending on the questioner and the context. For instance, in government offices, when asked their race for noting on their national identification cards, Beng often answer "Baule"—the name of the ethnic group that is not only numerically important (with a population of about 1.5 million) but that in many ways dominates Ivoirian affairs and has high prestige, due in good part to President Houphouët-Boigny's Baule origin. In this official context, the Beng affiliate themselves to another group because in their own country, as well as in the anthropological literature, they are an extraordinarily obscure people who, as we shall see, have endeavored in many ways to keep to themselves. One modern mode of doing so has been essentially through social chameleonism: blending into the colors of the local ethnic foliage. But paradoxically, this attempt at superficial ethnic melting has as its deeper aim the preservation of what is conceived by many Beng as a bedrock of ethnic differentiation. I do not take the indigenous emphasis of the Beng on their own ethnic identity to indicate that "the Beng" as such have existed as a homogeneous ethnic unity since time immemorial (cf. Lehman 1967). Yet I do think that their own contemporary perspective needs to be taken seriously as a valid one. At least in their own view and at this historical juncture, the Beng "are" an ethnic group (cf. Lehman 1979:233).

In their statements, language is generally adduced as the bottom line: Beng speak their own language, which, while it contains lexical and other elements from surrounding languages (including Jula and Baule), is nevertheless a coherent language that the Beng recognize as such. Indeed, while I was conducting my initial research among the Beng in 1979–80, a cultural revival of sorts was occurring that centered quite self-consciously on language. Young men had begun composing songs in Beng for the first time; previously the Beng sang songs in Baule and Jula. One such song, often sung as the opening of an evening's entertainment, proclaimed:

> They say there are no songs in Beng,
> They say there are no songs in Beng.
> But they lie that there are no songs in Beng.
> The world says there are no songs in Beng.[2]

The audiences at these events beamed and often hummed along with pleasure at this song, and the day afterward I often heard villagers of all ages listening to tapes of the previous evening, rewinding frequently to that first tune. In view of this, it may not be surprising that to the degree that I was accepted by the Beng, that acceptance was based initially on the fact that I was studying their language, which is rarely learned by any outsider, let alone a Westerner. And of my works on the Beng, the one that has generated the most excitement has been a Beng-English dictionary (Gottlieb n.d.).

Still, there are serious theoretical difficulties with using the criterion of language as a simple index of ethnicity (see Lehman 1979). In the Beng case, for instance, some villages that border on Baule territory are now "going Baule," as the Beng put it, by which they mean that only a few old people in those villages still speak the Beng language. In other villages in which the Beng language remains paramount, most Beng are at least trilingual, speaking both Baule and Jula quite fluently (and often Ando and some Jimini—and sometimes French as well). In ways such as this, language and ethnicity shade into one another quite actively.

If the possibility of self-definition by means of language is less than crystal clear for the Beng, this too is the case for their general vision of their ethnic identity. Indeed, a fundamental paradox lies at the base of Beng visions of their own ethnicity. On one hand, Beng see themselves firmly as an ethnic enclave. They now claim (with probably only partial accuracy) that formerly there was no ethnic intermarriage (indeed, as we shall see in chapter 4, one ideal of their alliance system is endogamy within the heart of the matriclan). Yet, considering that the Beng have a population of only about 10,000 (Côte d'Ivoire 1984), this scenario may not be far off the mark.[3] In any case, until very recently, Beng generally did aim to keep a healthy distance between themselves and the modern Ivoirian world. Both young and old people readily conceded to me that they have been far more conservative about maintaining their traditional life-style than have members of many other Ivoirian ethnic groups with whom they are familiar.

Despite this, in precolonial times the Beng were hardly an ethnic island with no bridge to the surrounding shore. In fact, as we shall see in chapter 6, they had a large network of relations with neighboring ethnic groups. The traders who came to their villages must have carried news as well as commercial goods with them. And it is likely that at least an occasional marriage took place between the Beng and the traders. In short, the Beng were hardly isolated in fact, despite a certain mental outlook that still stresses ethnic insularity.

Nor are the Beng frozen in some precolonial time warp. As we will also see in chapter 6, the wider world has affected all Beng to varying degrees, though some enthusiastically extol the advantages of Western influence while others roundly bemoan it. This variation in individual reaction also reflects a structural ambivalence concerning Western imports, as we shall explore.

Considered ethnologically, Beng culture appears an interesting hybrid. Those who have studied, or are members of, neighboring cultures—the matrilineal Jimini (a Senufo subgroup) to the immediate north, whose language is in the Gur family; the patrilineal Jula farther to the north, whose Northern Mande language is distantly related to Beng, which is a Southern Mande language; the matrilaterally inclined Baule to the west and south, whose language is in the Twi family; and the matrilaterally inclined Ando (once thought to be a Baule subgroup but now

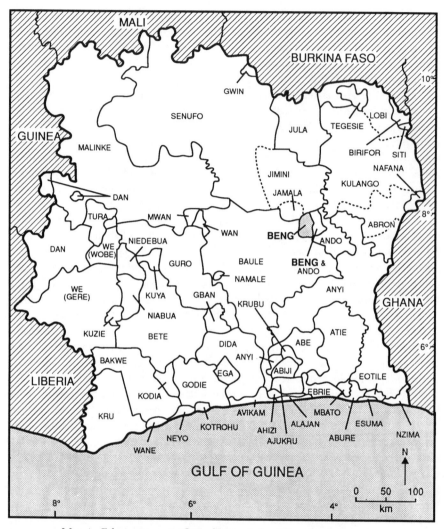

Map 1. Ethnic groups in Côte d'Ivoire (after Côte d'Ivoire 1971).

considered a related but independent ethnic group)—such people will doubtless recognize striking similarities to specific Beng customs and beliefs (see map 1). By no means do the Beng offer a "pure" culture all of whose customs are created and produced by them alone.

What is known of Beng history that might shed light on this situation? Unfortunately, tantalizingly little. To the Beng themselves, history appears to play a far less determinative role in daily life than it does, say, in the well-organized, expansionist states found in other parts of Africa in which an endogamous group of oral historians (for example, the *jeliw* or griots among the various Northern Mande peoples) is responsible for remembering and reciting the kingdom's illustrious past, especially the military exploits of its famous leaders (Vansina 1965). In contrast to such societies, the Beng of M'Bahiakro are avowed pacifists and have done all they could to avoid war.[4] Their history is of a much quieter sort. If told by them, it would emphasize events that are no less significant in the lives of the individual but that perhaps lend themselves less readily to recital in a formal context by a professional "historian."

Most Beng living today are content with the seemingly stereotyped version of their history that is current among them. It postulates an origin in Ghana and a western migration into Côte d'Ivoire, including a traumatic crossing of the Comoe River. This myth, which is corroborated in other published accounts of the Beng (e.g., Person 1971:n.p.; Salverte-Marmier and Salverte-Marmier 1966:18), is widely known in the Baule world, where it is accepted as the orthodox version of that group's history (for a critical analysis of it by a Western historian, see Weiskel 1976, 1978). Other peoples in Côte d'Ivoire have begun adopting at least parts of the myth because of the general prestige it seems to add to one's personal and group history, owing to the generally valued place that the Baule now occupy in contemporary Ivoirian affairs.

As for the Beng, such an understanding of their history may indeed be "legitimate" (accurate from the Western historian's point of view) for at least a portion (perhaps a recent portion) of their history, but from linguistic evidence it is unlikely that this myth tells the whole story. The Beng language is part of the Mande family of languages, and this fact would suggest that at some point in the very distant past, the Beng lived closer to the Mande heartland, which was on the border of present-day Mali and Guinea. The linguist Charles Bird (personal communication) estimates that the Beng, like the other Southern Mande groups, must have split off from this Mande heartland no less than 2,000 years ago (and see Welmers 1960, Loucou 1984:72–73), and it is thus understandable that this phase in their history is quite lost to the current generation. Still, if they could not account for their linguistic relation to the Northern Mande-speaking peoples, some Beng elders did account for their linguistic relation to the other Southern Mande groups in Côte d'Ivoire, who live in the western portion of the country (see map 2). One oral history I collected outlines a circuitous series of migrations beginning in Ghana, as with the more commonly claimed route, but then moving northwest to Guinea, Mali, and Liberia, then doubling back east to Côte d'Ivoire, where the Beng are said to have first stayed a short time with the Guro, another Southern Mande group, before finally moving farther east to their current location (see map 3).

In pondering the several versions of such migration routes that I was told, mutually contradictory as they are on the geopolitical specifics, I have detected a common thread: hints that the Beng may have been refugees at several points—perhaps even most—of their history. They say they are pacifists in that when faced with attackers, their reaction is to flee. Elders told me that this was the response to both African and European aggressors. For instance, during the last three decades of the nineteenth century, the Guinean Muslim crusader, Samori, endeavored to

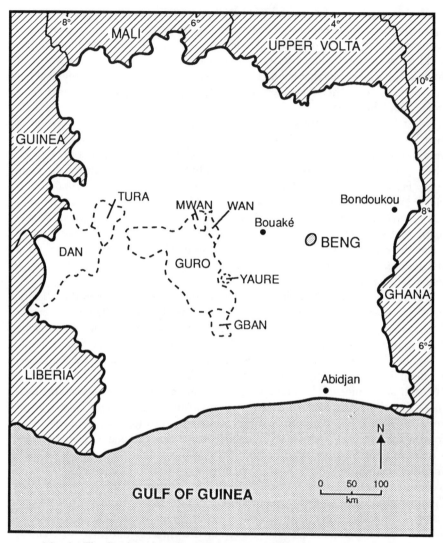

Map 2. The Southern Mande groups in Côte d'Ivoire (after Le Saoût 1976).

build a vast Islamic empire in West Africa (Person 1968a, 1968b, 1975). As the Beng recount it, at one point Samori's soldiers reached the northern border of the Beng territory and announced that they would attack the Beng villages the next morning. The Beng elders prayed to their most powerful shrine to be spared, and they fled successfully into the forest.[5]

Likewise, according to older Beng, French administrators looking to recruit laborers for "public works" projects in a campaign of forced labor were often faced with the same response. There was no armed resistance against the French, as, say,

Map 3. Proposed migration route of the Beng.

the neighboring Baule offered (Weiskel 1980). For the Beng, the reason must be found in traditional religious ideology: an act of homicide performed by a Beng person is said to bring death swiftly to the perpetrator, as punishment by the Earth for the sin. Once having killed another person, the only way to avoid this fate is to engage in a year-long series of arduous rituals of atonement. The fact that this taboo against killing is considered by the Beng to be relevant even for acts of defense in the face of group aggression against them would seem to suggest a refugee mentality that accords somewhat with the oral histories I collected. In at least one stopping place in the migratory circuit just described, the Beng were said to have tried to make peace for the Guro. (The very name *Beng*, according to a king I spoke with, means "meeting," an appropriate ethnonym for the Beng who, he said, at an earlier time lived in a multiethnic area where they convened meetings as mediators and peacemakers for the other groups when the latter had affairs and disputes that needed to be judged.) But having failed in this particular effort, they fled east.

In short, the previous paragraph aside, given the difficulty I had eliciting anything but brief, stereotyped historical sketches of only very recent history, my impression is that there is a general lack of developed indigenous historiography that is noticeable among the Beng, in comparison to other ethnic groups that do have highly developed institutional historical traditions. Assuming this is accurate—and not an artifact of my own relationship to Beng elders who, it is always possible, may have had their own reasons for concealing Beng history from me—it may speak to an overall "this-worldly" focus that is in fact quite prevalent. This is most obviously revealed in the striking emphasis on the Earth itself—which, as we shall see, is the focus of Beng religion.

THE WORLD OF IDEAS

My first impressions of the Beng were full of contrasts and contradictions. While the people seemed poor, and embarrassed in my presence by their poverty, they also seemed dignified and self-possessed. If at times they were irrepressibly curious about my husband and me, at other times they appeared distressingly aloof toward us. Most villagers spoke no European language and in general seemed as distant from a Western consciousness as I could imagine; yet our newly proclaimed host, André, who did speak French, the national language, was moved to ask us on our first day about a bizarre radio report he had once heard that America had sent people to the moon.

I saw no signs of those vibrant plastic and other visual arts traditions for which Africa is so famous in the West. The buildings were not decorated; I saw no major sculptural collections; and people's daily dress consisted of once-bright factory fabrics that, in the face of their poverty, had necessarily faded from hundreds of washings—there were no signs of looms (or, for that matter, of pottery kilns). Yet the urge to decorate was apparent in one unexpected place: on the human body—in fact, babies' bodies. Every baby I saw was decorated elaborately with what I initially assumed were bright-colored paints on both face and torso, and most sported jewelry as well—not only necklaces and bracelets but also waist bands, knee bands, anklets. These babies were so beautiful that I shot several rolls of film on them during my first week alone. I soon discovered that what I took for adornment was in most cases not that at all, but was in fact applied as medicine: symbolic means for warding off a host of diseases to which babies were considered particularly vulnerable.

Those bright babies' faces lit up villages that to me seemed otherwise rather drab. The short buildings were made of brown mud brick, and they seemed almost to disappear into the brown ground, which had obviously been deliberately cleared of all vegetation. These villages could not have been further from my own Western images of lush tropical vegetation that I must have expected to see duplicated. But in this short, brown village a lone enormous tree—a kapok, I was to discover— towered prominently above the main plaza. The kapok tree that first caught my eye soon caught my anthropological imagination, for it was clearly a center of social life. With its enormous flying buttress roots providing natural benches and the bright, spreading leaves on its tall trunk giving a wide circle of shade beneath a hot tropical sun (Whitmore 1981:267), the tree was a place under which adults could relax and chat when they were not working in the fields, and children could laugh and chase each other noisily. Not only that, but I soon noticed that trials, dances, and even sacrifices were held under that enormous tree. How could a single tree bear so much social and symbolic weight? Pursuing the answer to this question, which occupied much of my first few months in the field, led me ultimately to see in the kapok tree a symbol of some of the basic contradictions that I have observed in Beng life and Beng society (see chapter 2).

For as the weeks passed, the diverse and conflicting images of the village that my husband and I were settling into did not resolve themselves; rather, they multiplied and deepened. Ultimately, after struggling in vain to integrate them all into a single synthetic vision, I took them as a sign of structural complexity at the heart of Beng society—complexity that could not be reduced to a monothematic analysis. After I returned from my first long stay among the Beng, the extent of such complexity became clearer to me, its ramifications more impressive.

Current directions in anthropological thought have further stimulated my consideration of complex models. These directions, though varied, all position themselves in one way or another in relation to the paradigms that dominated anthropological discourse before the late 1960s. While these earlier paradigms were multiple, they shared several crucial assumptions. Most obviously, they all tended to point mercilessly to a hypothesized sociological homogeneity (for reviews and critiques, see for example Giddens 1976 and Kuper 1983). In my view, the most welcome challenge to this set of models came initially from Turner, Geertz, and others who sketched out the foundations of an interpretive model for anthropology (Ortner 1984:128–132). In their own ways, Turner and Geertz asked a series of questions that enabled a new emphasis to be given to cultural constructions, with richly structured yet ultimately plastic symbols serving as the cornerstones of meanings that people derive not only from communal ritual experiences but also from their daily lives.

Turner (1967b) insisted on the malleable and multivocalic nature of symbols, while Fernandez (1974) and Sapir (1977a) later focused on similar characteristics of the related notion of metaphor. Given these important theoretical developments, it now seems inevitable that a focus on symbolism would pave the way for a considera- tion of heterogeneity and multiple layers of meaning and structure in society. This focus had already been present in Ortner's extended elucidation (1973) of the "key symbol" and some subtypes of symbol that she carefully delineated. Most importantly, for our discussion, Ortner warned against a simplistic misapplication of her analysis:

> I am not assuming that there is only one key symbol to every culture; cultures are of course a product of the interplay of many basic orientations, some quite conflicting. (Ortner 1973:1339)

In her own later work, Ortner has made use of this cautionary note. For example, in her controversial but celebrated essay recounting theoretical trends in anthropology since the 1960s, Ortner acknowledged that the notion of "practice," which she identified as a key symbol uniting several strands of contemporary theory, was not the only such symbol that she could have chosen to emphasize (1984:159).

Other writers, however, have not always provided such important caveats, and the notion of "key symbol" has often resulted in analyses of a single "summarizing symbol" that is presented as a sole theme defining all discourse within a given society (e.g., Peters 1982). This is in keeping with the earlier rhetorical emphasis on holism that not only marked virtually all anthropological writings until very recently but, as Thornton (1988:290–291) pointed out, has long been a hallmark of Western thought in general, from philosophy and religion to science. Yet tempting as it may sometimes be to try to "fit" all the miscellaneous components of a society into such a theoretical model, this quest has proven too problematic for implementation (e.g., Appadurai 1988). And so, as we have come slowly to relinquish our long-held grasp on the assumption of homogeneity in small-scale societies, the possibilities of contradictory, oppositional, and counterhegemonic forces within such societies have begun to be considered seriously. Here the legacy of Marx often joins, via Gramsci (notably 1971), with symbolic anthropology to produce a group of important studies both within and outside anthropology (e.g., de Certeau 1980, Hall 1985, Ong 1987, Taussig 1980). Indeed, there is now a salubrious trend in many fields of contemporary scholarship, in both the social sciences and the humanities, emphasizing a consideration of ambiguity, contradiction, and paradox as well as "ever changing contexts of interaction" (Marcus and Cushman 1982:45). As early as fifteen years ago, Sally Falk Moore presciently summed up this heightening trend in noting that among anthropologists there was already

> an intensified awareness . . . that "ideological systems" as well as "social systems" are frequently full of inconsistencies, oppositions, contradictions, and tensions, that there is much individual and situational variation, and that cultural and social change is continuous, though it may take place at a more or less rapid rate and be more or less radical or pervasive. (Moore 1975:216)

In recent years, the set of issues that Moore identified has gained prominence in diverse theoretical branches of anthropology. Taking stock of contemporary trends in anthropology as related to those in a large variety of other fields,[6] Marcus and Fischer have recently written (1986a:14–15):

The only way to an accurate view and confident knowledge of the world is through a sophisticated epistemology that takes full account of intractable contradiction, paradox, irony, and uncertainty in the explanation of human activities. This seems to be the spirit of the developing responses across disciplines to . . . a contemporary crisis of representation.

Contradiction, paradox, irony, uncertainty: the very terms of our analysis have changed dramatically as we now include these modes in our working vocabulary. Attesting to the growing recognition of the importance of these issues, a multitude of compilations of articles have been published recently that utilize these general perspectives in analyzing a variety of topics. For example, in introducing a collection of anthropological approaches to texts, Bruner (1984:13) has written:

> One way in which these papers open up anthropology is that they avoid monolithic interpretations. The metaphor of opening up appeals to me: I picture a huge "soft" rock filled with cracks, faults, and fissures. In the past, we have tended to gloss over the irregularities; but present-day anthropology stops to reexamine the cracks, probe the faults, and penetrate the fissures. We move into the open spaces of soft rocks . . . to explore new complexities of meaning.

More simply, Clifford has introduced another collection with the statement, "Culture, and our views of 'it,' are produced historically, and are actively contested" (1986a:18). The notions of fissure and contestation speak refreshingly to a sense of the possibilities now present in anthropological writings. Indeed, the "creative crisis of reorientation and renewal" of which R. Rosaldo writes (1989:28) now permeates much contemporary work in anthropology, injecting a refreshing balance of doubt and hope into our writings.

In working out the implications of the ideas responsible for this "creative crisis," new questions are being posed that require radical rethinking of the very terms through which we view and define our data. Symbolic analyses may explore how key symbols and cultural scenarios not only reflect social and political structures—the classic Durkheimian view—but how they may themselves actively organize experience (e.g., Arens and Karp, eds. 1989, Sahlins 1981, Schieffelin 1981). At the level of the individual, we can now ask how dominant symbols are interpreted differently by different actors (e.g., Keesing 1987:163), who may directly contest the meanings of such symbols for use in their own (often political) agendas (e.g., Bruner and Gorfain 1984, Hall 1985:293 and passim, Newman 1986:248). In a wider sense, the possibility of intracultural variation is now regularly being investigated, enabling us to inquire to what extent the hegemonic system of knowledge in a given society is accepted and internalized as meaningful by members of subgroups, including disenfranchised minorities, of that society. For example, Garro (1988), in analyzing beliefs held by a group of Canadian Ojibway Indians concerning their own diagnosed high blood pressure, has found those ideas to be significantly at variance with the Western biomedical explanations of their condition that are available to them from the local medical community treating them. Equally striking is the work by Stromberg (1986), who focused on significant variations in religious experience, including conversion, among members of a single, small congregation of Swedes belonging to the Pietist-derived Immanual Church in Stockholm.

Related to this emphasis on intracultural variation at the individual level is a group of works that emphasizes similar issues at a more structural level. I see Lévi-Strauss's work on the nature of intellectual oppositions in culture as a precursor of sorts to this approach. In some ways a harbinger of more recent Marxist trends in anthropology as well, Lévi-Strauss was one of the first anthropologists to deal extensively with contrasting forces in society by pointing to the branch of linguistics dealing specifically with phonemics as a powerful model for anthropological analysis of intellectual oppositions in society.[7] An important corollary for Lévi-Strauss was that such oppositions were considered unstable; accordingly, he postulated that they could not be left to their own devices. Much of Lévi-Strauss's subsequent work on myth therefore focused on acts of mediation, which he considered as required to connect those unstable oppositions (e.g., 1967, 1969b, 1973, 1978, 1981).

Several more recent works have been inspired very loosely by Lévi-Strauss while challenging the posited inevitable centrality of mediation. These authors have suggested that a given society may in fact be organized around two or more complementary or competing premises, and that this fact may obviate an inexorable need for constant mediation. To the authors of these works, a given society may reveal more than one founding intellectual principle, each of which may have its sphere of influence. Societies (like people) may permanently embody mutually contradictory principles that are in constant dialectical relationships with one another. This dialectic may provide the impetus for social change (as in some Marxist models of society), but in these works, potentially revolutionary movements are not necessarily the outcome of a combination of mutually contradictory principles within a single society. In other words, the existence of intellectual complexity and even paradox, far from being either superfluous or contingent, can be viewed as potentially central to the human condition.

Gregory Bateson's Naven (1936) was an extraordinarily precocious example of this general approach to social life. Offering a flexible and multifaceted vision of a particular ritual and of society in general among the New Guinean Iatmul, Bateson's perspective was fundamentally grounded in paradox and contradiction.[8] Recently, several authors have followed Bateson's early lead in exploring the multiplex nature of social reality. One of the clearest full-scale analyses of this sort of approach is Geertz's Negara (1980). Writing of traditional Bali, Geertz proposes that there was a central paradox at the base of the classic and enduring political system of Bali: a still center, in the form of the king, around which a dynamic world turned, in the form of rival lords trying to approach the king. The tension between these two models of political action is seen by Geertz as endemic and irresolvable (1980:132).

Similar perspectives have been taken by a number of other recent scholars. For example, writing on the Bororo of Brazil, Crocker (1977) highlighted two different but complementary principles as forming the basis for much social interaction. Among the Bororo, *aroe* represents the principle of timeless identity created by the life of clans, while *bope* embodies the principle of mutability and ultimately death. Crocker's subsequent work (e.g., 1985) explores in admirable detail the ramifications of these complementary philosophical principles for Bororo society, especially in the continual round of rituals traditionally enacted by the Bororo. In a somewhat similar vein, M. Rosaldo (1980) used a related perspective as the intellectual framework for her analysis of social life among the Ilongot of the Philippines. In particular, she identified the two contrasting notions of "knowledge" (*'amet*) and "passion," especially "anger" (*liget*), as opposed but equally central modes of being and orientation that lie at the intellectual base of Ilongot society (for a somewhat parallel model for Africa, see Shaw [1985] on the Temne of Sierra Leone). Similar issues placed in a political setting have been explored by John Comaroff in South Africa. Writing of the Barolong boo Ratshidi, a Tswana chiefdom, Comaroff centers his analysis around the "contradictory tendencies toward hierarchy and egalitarianism" that were indigenous to the society (1987:68). He is careful to note that among the precolonial Tshidi, there was no Kachin-style "regular oscillation" between the two forms of social organization (78), for each managed to assert itself at the expense of the other, while both "coexisted" as "partial representations of the manner in which the everyday world was constituted" (71).

The sorts of perspectives employed by these authors is not only well suited to small-scale Third World societies; it is appropriate—perhaps even more obviously—to the West as well. To cite just one example, Gaines (1982) has used an analogous approach in writing on a group of psychiatrists who consider their Christian beliefs to be integral to their professional practice. In analyzing this unexpected combination of factors, which might appear to be mutually exclusive, Gaines focuses specifically on how two key symbols, seemingly in opposition, can be paired within a society to form a powerful and surprisingly stable combination.[9]

Aside from the specific ethnographic writings just mentioned, a broader influence on the chapters that follow is the work earlier this century of Mikhail Bakhtin, who has stretched our understanding of literature as well as social action to include multiple models and heteroglossic encounters. In writing about heteroglossia in the novel (Holquist 1981:xxi), Bakhtin (1981) speaks of language as inherently multivoiced, with speech (*parole*) being integral to, not separable from, the linguistic system as such (*langue*). Those multiple voices exist in juxtaposition, creating a lively (and possibly tension-filled) dialogue throughout any given novel. "The novel," Bakhtin writes, "is the expression of a Galilean perception of language, one that denies the absolutism of a single and unitary language." Outside of fiction, multiple voices exist in opposition to the official, "centripetal" language against which they are constantly, and "centrifugally," pitted and which they often parody (Bakhtin 1981:273).

This view of language and the novel has been applied profitably to culture at large. Bakhtin (1984) himself used this approach in his analysis of medieval French culture, as perceived through the writings of Rabelais. In the Bakhtinian perspective, culture does not display a "single and unitary" view of the world but has multiple voices, much as language and the novel do. As Clifford notes, "[D]ialogical processes proliferate in any complexly represented discursive space (that of an ethnography or, in his [Bakhtin's] case, a realist novel). Many voices clamor for expression" (1986a:15). Such voices can take several forms: male and female, commoner and aristocrat, child and adult, and so on. These voices may be heard singly, but far more complexity can be accommodated if they are heard in pairs (or even multiply). This is so because the voices are not mutually redundant; rather, each offers its own distinctive model of reality.

Anthropologists have been intrigued by this approach and the possibilities it offers for understanding both the messy crevices and the structural contradictions of society. In this work, I join several colleagues in making my own use of Bakhtin (for other interesting anthropological uses of Bakhtin, see for example Bruner and Gorfain 1984, Handelman 1984, Limon n.d., Trawick 1988). While my discussion of myth in Beng society (chapter 5) makes explicit reference to Bakhtin, his influence is more pervasive at less obvious levels. Inspired by Bakhtin's celebration of complexity and diversity within a single society, I will be exploring for the Beng how a traditional system of thought is premised on two basic propositions that are opposed but in some ways complementary. Specifically, I will be suggesting that Beng society is organized around a dominant pair of principles that I gloss as "identity" and "difference." The Beng phrase I gloss as "identity" is à sé do, which means literally "we are all one." Its antonym is à tɔtɔ, which means "we are different." The semantic field covered by these phrases is large and its contexts varied. I explore the specific dimensions to these various contexts in the chapters that follow. For now, what I want to emphasize is that the Beng make continual use of these two principles in ordering and living their lives. While the principles appear to be irrevocably opposed, the Beng do not see them as wholly incompatible—far from it. Thus they do not combine to constitute a full paradox in that each does not exclusively posit a state of being that the other absolutely denies (Quine 1962). Rather, each serves as a principle around which certain aspects of society are organized. Together, they offer two quite distinct visions of how the world can be structured.

At a general level, we will see the complementary nature of these two principles, as their scopes are mostly discrete. Yet following Dumont (1979), it is also possible to observe an element of hierarchy in their relationship, insofar as in the Beng context, the principle of identity is in some respects valued above that of difference, as we shall see especially in chapters 3 and 4. Still, for the Beng, identity does not provide a final framework to fully "encompass" difference, as Dumont might have predicted. Rather, the two principles provide their own possibilities whose relationships are multiple; among the Beng, no absolute ranking of them is accomplished.

Furthermore, unlike Lévi-Strauss, I do not discuss mediators between the two principles of identity and difference because I do not believe that mediators are important for the Beng when it comes to this issue. [10] Rather, as I understand Beng thought, two intellectual statements exist as alternative models—equally active—for how to organize society and how to think about that organization. Moreover, the influence of the two organizing principles among the Beng is not confined to rituals or other special occasions, as it is in some other societies, but rather emerges with equal force during daily social life.

Although I do not focus on process and indeterminacy at the individual level per se, what I do stress is contradiction, albeit at a structural level. What I suggest is that in the Beng case, individuals do not need to exist in opposition to the wider structure of authority, providing a counterhegemonic set of voices, precisely be-cause that structure of authority itself provides for the possibility of its undoing, insofar as it offers two models—in some ways complementary, in other ways contradictory—for how people in the world should behave. Thus for the Beng, contradiction lies not in relation to unstable, class-based contradictions (Beng society is relatively homogeneous insofar as class is concerned) but at the very core of social order itself.

Still, if formal acts of mediation between identity and difference (such as Lévi-Strauss would expect) are not present in the Beng case, the relationship between the two terms is nevertheless not one of an absolute chasm. Rather, there is some intrinsic relationship between the two. Indeed, at a philosophical level, as Heideg-ger has stated, identity itself posits a certain form of difference within it, as it is not properly defined as "mere sameness" (1969:25):

> Sameness implies the relation of "with," that is, a mediation, a connection, a synthesis: the unification into a unity. This is why throughout the history of Western thought identity appears as unity. But that unity is by no means the stale emptiness of that which, in itself without relation, persists in monotony . . . since the era of speculative idealism, it is no longer possible for thinking to represent the unity of identity as mere sameness, and to disregard the mediation that prevails in unity.

This view of identity is certainly relevant to the Beng, as we shall see in chapters 3 and 4 especially. But the relationship between two (or more) Others that Heidegger sees as inherent in the principle of identity is not confined to identity for the Beng. Rather, the relationship between Others is highlighted for them in the principle of difference, which the Beng acknowledge and make use of equally.

Contemporary philosophers have matched Heidegger's interest in the conjoined notions of identity and difference, to the point where the notion of difference has been elaborated by the new term *différance*, which combines meanings of difference and deferral (Derrida 1973). My interest in the topic is spurred by this body of work. But the difference, if I may be pardoned the word, is profound. Derrida discusses "difference" (as well as *"différance"* and "identity") in a universal sense, implicitly assuming a cross-culturally valid set of meanings to the terms. In con-trast, my intention in this work is to probe the indigenous meanings to the sets of Beng phrases that I am glossing as "identity" and "difference." On at least one point, however, there is a significant convergence between Beng and Derridean philosophy. Derrida sees difference as existing from the beginning, rather than deriving from a unified state.[11] Likewise, the Beng, in their more sociological way, do not postulate an ur-form of identity from which difference later emerged. Rather, in their view, identity and difference exist, and very likely have always existed, side by side. In other words, Beng culture attests to the position that the existence of difference is intrinsic to the business of being human. They would likely agree with Stephen Tyler's statement, written in a more general context: "Identity and difference are correlatives, the one unthinkable without the other" (1987:13).[12]

Writers in other fields have also recently stressed the importance of difference as a field of study not only in the Third World but in Western society as well. Western feminist writers, for example, have been significantly influenced by Third World women's writings, whether or not the latter explicitly identify themselves as "feminist," to question the earlier model of Western feminism as universally applicable. Influenced as well by the lessons of anthropology, whose hallmark is a celebration of difference, these writers have begun challenging the seductive notion of sisterhood, for example, instead acknowledging the locally situated nature of women's lives as defined by race, class, and cultural practices, and thereby producing feminisms of difference (see, for example, Haraway 1988; Kirby 1990; Milan Women's Bookstore Collective 1990; Przybylowicz, Harstock, and McCallum 1989, 1990; and the journal *Differences*). Indeed, not only gender but other factors—sexual orientation, religion, and language as well as race and class—now combine to "pervade modern everyday life in urban settings" (R. Rosaldo 1989:28). Our own encounters of "difference" in the West are daily, and academic musings about the situation are in good part playing catch-up to this longstanding fact.

In this regard, the Beng material that follows offers its own perspective on difference. As we will be exploring, Beng life is intimately tied up with the notion of difference but in conjunction with its opposite number, identity. The daily lives of individual Beng people are in good part a working out of their own encounters with difference and identity, albeit in a much smaller field than is the case in the urban West. How they understand and negotiate their own local definitions of difference and identity, producing in effect an indigenous discourse on these fundamental issues, is the focus of this book.

At a more general level, the overall aim of this work is to offer an indigenous view of the meanings that Beng society holds for its members by focusing on the conflicting ideological constructions that underlie the society. In taking this approach, I do not see ideology as the superstructural paint on an iron scaffolding of political economy, as in what has come to be called the classic interpretation of Marx and Engels' work (see Bloch 1983:30–31, Hall 1986). Along with Foucault (1980:118), I find problematic the common assumptions that ideology invariably occupies a place secondary to economic realities and that these realities are (as in the classic Marxist scheme) inevitably oppressive. For in many societies, power itself is far more subtly defined than it can be using purely economic or even political terms (Foucault 1980:122). Indeed, among the Beng, as among many African peoples, power differences are in good part based on access to resources that are defined in spiritual terms rather than economic terms (Arens and Karp 1989:xvii). Accordingly, and at a more general level, in this work I treat ideology as itself fully determinative, if not uniquely primary (Augé 1982, Lan 1985).

Furthermore, unlike the classic Marxists, I do not assume that ideology by its nature promotes "false consciousness," nor that it necessarily "mystifies" hegemonic arrangements rooted in power inequalities. With Foucault, I reject the notion that ideology by definition "always stands in virtual opposition to something else which is supposed to count as truth" (1980:118; for a discussion of Foucault on this point, see Rabinow 1986:240). Rather, I take the notion of "truth" as always contingent, itself shaped by ideological and other forces. As Foucault writes,

> Truth is a thing of this world. It is produced only by virtue of multiple forms of constraint and it induces regular effects of power. Each society has its regime of truth, its "general politics" of truth: that is, the types of discourse which it accepts and makes function as true; the mechanisms and instances which enable one to distinguish true and false statements, the means by which each is sanctioned; the techniques and procedures accorded value in the acquisition of truth; the status of those who are charged with saying what counts as true. (1980:131)

To this I would add that there are inevitably many "truths" within a given society, depending on one's social locus within (or outside) that society. Given all this, positing ideology as a medium of mystification becomes problematic, insofar as there is no single, absolute truth that could be masked by a given ideology. This position is close to the perspective now being taken by those in cultural studies and others influenced by this new discipline, with its intriguing blend of Marx and symbolic anthropology (e.g., Hall 1985:294). In particular, those Marxist writers, inspired by Gramsci, are grappling with ideology as a central, determining force in society (e.g., Hunt 1985:13, 20–22; Larrain 1979; Sumner 1979; on Gramsci, see Boggs 1976, Hall 1986).

As Weber showed forcefully long ago (1904–5; see Weber 1976), ideas have as much to do with the construction of society as do economic and political factors. Indeed, ideas may shape economic and political forces as much as they are shaped by them. Another way of putting this would be as Geertz has boldly written: "The real is as imagined as the imaginary" (Geertz 1980:136). In this work I take this general premise as implicit.

In so doing, a more submerged but specific aim is to explore how the combination of identity and difference defines the conceptual basis of two broad aspects of social life: kinship on one hand, ideology (which I am defining as cosmology and world view in their broadest reaches) on the other. In the Beng case, I aim to show that both "domains" are informed by the same pair of contradictory principles. Indeed, I hope to explore how the very notion of separate "domains" is itself problematic, often taken for granted in Western anthropological models of non-Western societies. I endorse the recent work of Schneider (1984), who argues that kinship has all too frequently been inappropriately depicted as the primary domain in anthropological analyses of small-scale societies. Paralleling in some ways an early proposition stated by Needham (1971), Schneider makes the radical suggestion that kinship may not even exist as a separate domain for analysis at all.

John Comaroff (1987) has ably summarized and evaluated several lines of analysis in this direction that have been offered over the past fifteen years. While working from theoretical frameworks that range from transactional analysis (Barth) to Marxism (e.g., Meillassoux), these works have in one way or another all challenged the universal applicability of the analytical distinction, come down to us from Maine (1864) to Meyer Fortes, between the public domain, which is classically equated with the political lives of men and may to some extent be defined by achieved status, and the private domain, which is typically associated with the domestic lives of women and is defined in great part by ascribed ties of kinship. While the distinction is clearly relevant to contemporary state-level societies, including modern nation-states, the anthropological proclivity to read, Malinowski-style, from the society one knows best to the rest of the world is in this case entirely unjustified, as the analytic dichotomies are of greatly varying utility—in some cases nonutility (e.g., Moore 1986:7–8). Yanagisako (1987) has even shown how in America itself, among contemporary second- and third-generation middle-class Japanese-Americans, the public–private dichotomy, while still present, takes on a vastly different burden of meanings from the one it had a mere generation ago. Likewise, John Comaroff (1987) offers a superb analysis of the intricate ways that gender relations have been constituted and have changed in a Tswana chiefdom over the past two centuries in ways that seriously confound the simplistic binary opposition that typically isolates kinship from politics.[13]

My own analysis of the Beng explores and aims to challenge a related set of analytic boundaries: the supposed "realms" of kinship and ideology. I hope to show that these two categories—artifacts, clearly, of a Western imagination—are for the Beng utterly interpenetrating. Far from masking kinship (or some other structural "level"), ideology defines, and is in turn defined by, kinship, in the Beng case in such a way that the postulate of discrete "domains" becomes inappropriate in the extreme.

I turn now to the Beng world of ideas.

CHAPTER TWO

Of Kapoks and the Earth

The kapok tree is the head of the village. It's in the head that a
person begins, so the head is like the center of the body.
Beng Master of the Earth

Traveling around Beng country during my first few weeks in the field, I couldn't
help but notice that all the villages I was visiting, like the village in which I was
staying, had one, and only one, kapok tree *(Ceiba pentandra)*. And this one
kapok—usually the only tree in the village—towered over the one-story houses
and the carefully swept and weeded ground. In asking about this image, which was
soon becoming predictable, I discovered that the presence of the tree was no
accident of nature. Indeed, I was told that a cleared space cannot be considered—
or called—a "village" *(gbe)* unless and until a kapok tree has been ritually planted
there by a Master of the Earth, a priest of the tradition religion.[1] In trying to
impress upon me the symbolic centrality of the tree, one Beng friend explained
that the village kapok tree is "the beginning of all things in the village." In
response to this, a Master of the Earth who was also conversing with us added that
the kapok tree is "the head of the village" *(gbe a ŋru nyɛ)*.

   Why is the ritual planting of this tree so crucial to the establishment of a
village? The Beng answer would be to invoke the perceived consequences of
ignoring the requirement that each village have its kapok. Without a ritually
planted kapok tree, any adult Beng would point out, no human sexual relations may
take place, and so the group could not reproduce itself. In a literal sense, perhaps
this is what was meant by my friend's remark to me that the village kapok tree is
"the beginning of all things in the village." Should a couple foolishly have sex in a
space where no kapok tree has been ritually planted—whether in the forest or a
newly cleared spot for a future "village"—the consequences for them are serious, as
we will see. The Beng themselves consider this taboo against what we may term
"forest sex" the most important of all their spiritually based rules. Considering the
emerging centrality of the kapok in the village, let us look at what happened when
an already standing village kapok tree was obliged to be chopped down.

   In the village of Asagbe, the ritually anchored kapok tree was felled in 1979
owing to government pressure. In the 1960s local representatives of the government
working in the nearby town of M'Bahiakro had encouraged the Beng to have their
villages undergo *lotissement*: dividing the village into rectangular lots, each of which

would be owned by a single nuclear family. Running through the future lots would be paths sited at right angles to one another in an even, gridlike pattern (for further discussion, see chapter 6). It happened that in Asagbe, one of the planned house lots was situated on the spot on which the village's kapok tree stood, and the Beng—having agreed to the reorganization of the village but having had no input into the actual design—had no choice but to cut it down.

The current Master of the Earth told me a story to explain how it happened.

Planting a New Kapok Tree

Before chopping down the old tree, I planted a new kapok and let it grow a bit at first, so people could still have sex in the village. First, I put a bit of gold into the hole that was dug for the new tree. The village chief gave me the gold—he got it from the village treasure *(koye)*. Then I said some prayers and killed a chicken and a she goat, and poured ten liters of palm wine. The chicken, the goat, and the gold are like a sacrifice *(pɔgbali)*; they're for the spirits that live in the village and the forest. I kept a little bit of the gold as payment for my services, but I gave it to the chief of my matriclan since he's the elder. It's mine, but the clan chief holds it for me. In any case, it's just a small amount of gold, not a fortune.

When I planted the tree, all the male elders came to watch. It was morning, not too early—about 8:00 or 9:00 A.M.—because you need some sun up in the sky, to see a shadow. But when you're planting the tree, the shadow can't be between you and the tree—otherwise you'll die. If your shadow falls across the hole that's been dug for the tree and you plant the tree in the hole, it's as if you've buried your shadow [= soul] *(neneŋ)*—so you'll soon die.

This shadow taboo exists for the kapok tree because this tree belongs to the whole village *(gbe nā ŋo se kpa pɔè)*. But the shadow taboo also exists for planting two other kinds of trees: the kola nut tree and the palm wine tree. All these three kinds of trees are valuable *(trõwé)*—from the kola and palm trees, you can make money by selling the fruits or the wine of the trees. [The kapok, as we shall see, is valuable symbolically.]

Now, kapok trees grow fast in a tropical climate; after only a year, the newly planted sapling had grown sufficiently. Only then, in 1979, was the old and majestic kapok tree by its side toppled. The government sent in a bulldozer for the purpose, but while the large machine and its operator struggled with their enormous adversary, the village Master of the Earth, accompanied only by a few male elders of the village, conducted a ritual. One of the men blew an animal horn and another brought out some statues, all to request that the spirits in the tree leave peacefully. Without this, the tree, in being felled, would have fallen on someone, probably a child.

Once the old tree was felled, it was inconceivable to haul it off, dead as it was. And so it still lies fallen, only a few meters from the new tree, which is still growing. "Modernization" Western style succeeded in disrupting the traditional religion, but in the end a central symbol of Beng religion was restored, and a new kapok stands, vital, in the village.

The kapok tree is not only at the heart of the social life of the Beng; it is intimately connected to their religion as well. Why is a Master of the Earth obliged to oversee its planting and, if required, its demise? To understand this, I must first mention that the kapok tree, while located in the village, has deep ties to the Earth, which the Beng say is anchored in the forest. Thus to appreciate the place of the kapok tree both in thought and daily life, I must unpack several layers of meaning that the Earth—which is the focus of worship—holds for the Beng.[2] In exploring this, we will encounter spirits and ideas about those spirits intertwined, revealing a profound spirituality on the part of the Beng coupled with a reflexiveness about that spirituality.

THE BENG EARTH

As with the West, the Beng view of the Earth is a culturally specific interpretation, not a universally valid understanding. On one level, the Beng stress that all the soil on which humans walk is unified, a single "Earth" *(ba)*. This conception is perhaps closest to the Western environmentalist's vision of the earth (itself akin to several Native American groups' visions of the earth): a nourishing force to be treated respectfully. But there are cultural differences that cannot be glossed over. For one thing, where the Western and Native American views designate the earth as female, often further specifying an association of earth as mother, the Beng conception of the Earth is as a male entity.[3] Second, in the Beng vision, the protecting Earth can give way to a vengeful one if its rules are violated; a very large proportion of human deaths are attributed by the Beng to such punishment.

The Beng Earth is not only animate, it is omniscient. In that sense, it is the ultimate object to be personified (Ellen 1988).[4] "One cannot lie to the Earth," a Beng friend told me, "because the Earth likes the truth," which is to say that it can discern "the truth" and distinguish it from lies. For example, my husband had once promised the Earth of our village a sacrifice (Graham 1989); he wanted to offer the sacrifice, but circumstances intervened and caused him to postpone the offering. We worried that the Earth might be offended by the delay, but our friend consoled us by explaining that the Earth "knew" our good intentions, and that was what mattered. (In this sense, perhaps Beng religion, in its emphasis on motivation rather than action, has more in common with Catholicism than with Protestantism; this may in part account for the higher conversion rate of the Beng to the former than to the latter.[5])

The Earth communicates its knowledge about the motivation of a supplicant at the time of a sacrifice. After an animal is ritually killed, the Master of the Earth butchers the carcass and immediately investigates the genitals: the testicles or ovaries must be white, indicating that the Earth has accepted the sacrifice. Black is a sign of rejection. Typically the reason for rejection is that the person making the offering owes another sacrifice or has violated a taboo and has not yet confessed or offered the necessary atonement.

While the Earth keeps track of outstanding sacrifices, it punishes only those who make no effort to pay their debts. It happens frequently that deaths are blamed on such outstanding religious obligations.[6]

The Son, the Mother, and the Egg

As a young man, Ali went off to the city for a short period to make money. His mother Amwe had prayed to the Earth, offering a sacrificial egg, that he return safely, and soon, to the village. In such a rogatory sacrifice, the petitioner enters into a contract with the Earth: in three years' time, she or he is obliged to thank the Earth with a second sacrifice of more value than the first (the usual pairs of offerings are egg–chicken, chicken–goat, goat–sheep, sheep–cow).

But in this case, Amwe failed to offer the required animal, feeling grieved and perhaps even betrayed: her son had been killed in a bus accident on his way back to the village. Soon after the three years had elapsed since the woman's first prayer, she too died. Her death was blamed on the Earth, said to be angry over her neglect of the sacrifice.

In this case we see how thorough and unrelenting is the Earth in its accounting measures, unyielding even in extreme circumstances.

Moreover, unpaid debts to the Earth are inherited by one's heirs. If they continue to go unpaid, they may cause bodily afflictions, in a manner common through much of Africa.

Akissi and the Chicken

Akissi had a certain sickness off and on for a few years: her whole body ached, and her head spun so that she could not see clearly and she became dizzy. Her husband consulted a diviner, who pronounced that Akissi was ill because her father, now deceased, still owed a sacrifice to the Earth. Many years ago, he had offered a chicken to ask for the well-being of his children, and he should have later sacrificed a goat to thank the Earth. But he had not done so before he died, and now the Earth was causing his daughter Akissi to fall ill, as a reminder of the debt.

A few days after the diviner revealed this situation, Akissi found the necessary goat and gave it to the Master of the Earth to sacrifice.

This case reveals the long-term nature of Earth debts and the ready acceptance by villagers of diviners' pronouncements concerning them. Another case illustrates how financially onerous such debts may become.

Bernard and the Two Cows

Bernard had a large debt: after first sacrificing to ask for something major, he had promised two cows to the Earth as thanks. But he died with the debt unpaid. His son, Kwame, inherited the debt and should have bought the necessary two cows, but these were a major expense and he did not have the requisite money. After Kwame died, it was Kona who inherited the debt. Because of the great cost of a two-cow sacrifice, a series of formal trials were first conducted before the members of Bernard's matriclan agreed to help Kona raise the necessary money with which to buy the cattle.

From these stories, one can see that the Earth in effect keeps track of the many sacrifices that are owed it, and it is viewed as impossible, ultimately, to "cheat" where Earth debts are concerned.

In addition to being omniscient, the Earth is seen as omnipotent. Indeed, for the vast majority of Beng, the Earth provides a sense of reality that is quite literally grounded. In a historical sense, the Beng view their very survival as a minority group as due to their powerful Earth. Assuming compliance with its taboos, the Beng rely on the spiritual strength of their Earth to see them through hard times. This is evident in their own view of their history. As we have seen in the previous chapter, the Beng seem to have been refugees at several points in the past. The elders I spoke with insisted that the pacifist response of the Beng to outside invaders has always had its foundation in religious faith: fleeing into the forest to hide, they prayed to their Earth shrines to be spared.

The French never directly invaded Beng territory nor, to my knowledge, did they threaten to do so. However, they did forcibly conscript some young men into the army to serve in World War II (a Beng elder estimated the number of such conscripts at approximately fifty to one hundred). Beng elders prayed to their Earth for the safe return of these young men, and according to them, not one of them was killed in action, in contrast to many of their compatriots of other ethnic groups. Many similar miraculous tales are told by the Beng as proof of the omnipotence of their Earth. They cite further support in the fact that Ivoirians from other ethnic groups scattered around the country come regularly to the Beng villages to pray to their Earths, which do have a wide reputation well beyond Bengland as being powerful.

Moral ties between the Beng and their Earth are strong, but are not uncomplicated. If Beng have faith that their Earth will protect them in times of need, they also fear that their own frailties may leave them open to the Earth's wrath. For this reason, many people are reluctant to accept positions of political responsibility, which are directly tied to the Earth's powers.

Yaokala: The Reluctant Clan Chief

Several years ago, the male chief of a certain matriclan died, but since then no one has been formally chosen to replace him. As the chiefship revolves between branches of the clan, it should be the turn of the men in a certain clan segment to contribute a candidate. Ideally this should be the oldest man in the lineage. So the elders informed this person, Yaokala, of his duty. But he refused to accept the position. Reluctant to pass on to a younger man, or another segment of the clan, the clan elders asked Yaokala again, but again he refused. All told, he was asked four times and four times refused.

I asked Yaokala's younger brother, Yaokro, why his elder brother had kept refusing what in other societies would be an honor. He explained: "Yaokala is afraid of the Earth. The chief of a matriclan has to judge many affairs and preside over trials. It's possible that one day he might be bribed by a defendant with, say, a bottle of beer, and he could judge the case wrongly. Ultimately, the Earth would know this, and would punish him: he'd get a headache and would die immediately. This is what happened with the last clan chief. And this is why Yaokala is reluctant to take on the chiefship. If he makes a mistake and judges wrongly and the Earth is angered, it will kill him."

While the Earth overall is seen as powerful, the Beng also divide up the Earth into smaller Earths—also called *ba*—that are localized, named, worshiped, and situated in the forest.[7] Some of these Earths are seen as more powerful than others. Although each Beng village sits on at least one such Earth (some sit on two or three of these Earths), the Earths are fundamentally associated with the forests that surround the villages. For instance, the boundaries of the various Earths are drawn through the forests, and the main shrines dedicated to the Earths are situated in the forest. It is here that most sacrifices to the Earths are offered.[8]

To attain the blessing of the Earth, humans use the mediation of Masters of the Earth. Each named Earth has its own Master of the Earth (who usually has at least one assistant to substitute for him if he is ill or absent). This priest regularly worships the Earth through sacrifices of animals, eggs, palm wine, and water, and through prayers (which accompany all sacrifices).[9]

Each Earth is worshiped most frequently at a designated shrine that is located in the forest. Such shrines, being symbols of the Earth, seem to take on metonymically some of their powers; hence the areas surrounding them are considered "strong" (grégré) and subject to taboos.[10] As for the shrines themselves, no one but Masters of the Earth may touch, regard, or address them. All children and adults know the shrines' locations in the forest, and when they walk by them while going to the fields, Beng are careful to look straight ahead and generally speed up their pace. Polluting the Earth shrine (by gaze or touch) pollutes the Earth itself: the transgressor will be judged and must pay a series of heavy fines, in the form of expiatory sacrifices to the Earth. Given these circumstances, it is not surprising that I could not enlist any friends to point out the shrines to me, and photographs were clearly out of the question. Descriptions of the shrines were offered to me in whispers.

Despite this secrecy about the actual shrines, there are nevertheless many occasions on which discussions about the Earth in its other manifestations are appropriate. Though the Earth may be talked about in either its unified or its subdivided aspect, it is clear from the context of discussion which level of Earth is meant. For example, the localized, named Earths are said to have certain powers with which the Earth in its unified aspect is not endowed. Thus during a dispute, an individual may invoke the name of his or her village's Earth to curse someone.[11] Such speech acts in relation to the Earth have an illocutionary force that, barring certain actions, is seen as automatic (Ahern 1979, Austin 1962). If the speaker is found to have been at fault in improperly invoking the Earth in a curse, he or she must then apologize by offering an animal (usually a chicken) as a sacrifice to the Earth that was invoked. This sacrifice would then have the effect of "lifting" the curse. Without this, the accursed person would inevitably die.

The Stolen Palm Nuts and Afwe's Curse

One day in 1980, Afwe discovered that a bunch of palm nuts that she'd left in the forest to bring back the next day to the village had been stolen. Outraged, she invoked her village's Earth to "catch" the person who had stolen her palm nuts. As it turned out, the thief was Au, a young woman from another village. Because the particular Earth that Afwe invoked was an especially powerful one, Au's family mobilized very quickly to organize a group apology to Afwe, Afwe's family, and their village's Earth.

During the ensuing trial, Afwe's village elders insulted both Au and her mother and they argued among themselves heatedly about the case. But Au and her contingent endured the difficult trial with only token complaint, terrified of the Earth's curse. In the end, they agreed without protest to pay the hefty fine of a goat, a chicken, and a case of imported wine, so as to lift the curse and save Au from untold misery.

Despite what may appear to be a heavily mystical vision, the Earths are not conceived of amorphously as vague sources of intangible power. Rather, they are said to be the locus of powerful forest spirits that inhabit them. When I asked a Master of the Earth which came first, a given Earth or its resident spirits?—or another version to that question, is an Earth powerful because of its spirits, or vice versa?—he was quite baffled because, as he explained, an Earth and its spirits are really coterminous: one cannot be conceived of without the other. The only answer he could provide was to offer the absurd scenario that if the spirits were to leave their Earth, then that Earth would leave as well. With this reply I understood the inappropriate framing of my question, grounded as it was in a Western insistence that a place and its occupants must be fully dissociable. Recent efforts to reveal— and overcome—our own ethnocentric biases in struggling to understand other people's conceptions of place have produced notable analyses by anthropologists (e.g., K. Basso 1984, 1988; *Cultural Anthropology* 1988). My own stumbling attempts in 1985 to approach a Beng feeling for place finally compelled me to ask questions that permitted the priest to explain his own vision of sacred space in a way that made sense to him. He revealed that the place of spirits in the forest is very much an actively inhabited one, with the spirits living their lives in much the same way that the Beng live theirs.

The Earth spirits are said to live in their own villages within the forest area of their proper Earth. Beng say that the spirits should normally confine themselves to their forest villages, and likewise people should avoid trespassing on the soil of the spirits' villages. The two realms—village inhabited by humans, and forest Earth inhabited by spirits—are seen as quite discrete.

Once, in mythic times, spirits and humans lived together. But that age has passed, and as a result of the mythic break between them, contemporary Beng must now separate themselves from the spirits (for the text of the myth, see chapter 6). Thus in historic times, when looking to settle into a new village, the Beng must seek a territory that is free, or potentially free, of spirits. This would be determined by a diviner, who would be consulted on this question. If a site is found that does have spirits but is otherwise attractive according to the cultural-ecological require- ments—is relatively flat, has adequate water nearby, and so on—then the would-be village founder would offer a sacrifice of a chicken and perhaps a sheep to any local spirits to request them to vacate the premises, leaving the area free for human occupation.

In the case of one village, although such a sacrifice was performed, the local spirits nevertheless remained and caused trouble. My informant explained, "The village was never cold"—which is to say that there were many cases of illness plaguing the villagers.[12] A diviner was consulted and explained the problem, and the decision was made to move the village to a new site entirely, to escape the resident spirits.

Not only are the spirits now distant from human habitation; if a person were to encounter spirits in the forest, he or she would not see them: spirits should properly remain invisible to humans. My Beng friends could only speculate that if a human were to catch sight of a spirit, the result would undoubtedly be instant death for the unfortunate person. But this is considered a hypothetical possibility that can only be talked about in a heuristic sense, as a myth recounted to me by a Master of the Earth demonstrates.

A Man Meets a Spirit

An old man was friends with a spirit. But whenever the spirit came to visit, he changed into a man with black skin. One day, the old man asked the spirit what color his real skin was. The spirit said, "Don't ask this or you'll die." The man said, "I want to know." The spirit said, "Wait for another day."

One day the man went to the spirit's place. He knocked on the door and entered: there he saw the spirit. He was unbelievably white, much whiter than "white" people. The old man chatted with the spirit and then left. But as soon as he left, he died!

Citing this myth, Beng explained to me that it is now said that one should not try to know the real skin color of the spirits—that is, one should not try to see them. Indeed, it is impossible for a person to ever see a real spirit. If someone says he has glimpsed a spirit, Beng know that the image was really a witch who changed into the form of a spirit to do the person harm.

While the spirits remain in the forest during the day, for a short time every night, from about 11:00 P.M. to 3:00 A.M., they enter human villages. Adults should not make love during this time, for if they were to conceive a child when a forest spirit was nearby, the baby would not be a "good child," being too shaped by the spirit. Lovemaking should thus be confined to the early part of the night, between 7:00 and 11:00, and the early, predawn hours between 3:00 and 5:00. Thus we see that while humans and spirits should do their best to avoid each other, there are inevitably some unfortunate possibilities for contact.

Furthermore, while people may actually see forest spirits, it is possible that as they are working in their forest fields during the day they may accidentally bump into a spirit. Everyone knows where the spirits' villages are located deep in the forest, and people try to avoid these areas. Should someone knowingly or un-knowingly trespass such a spirit village, she or he will be punished severely. "Trespassing" includes defecation. Beng may choose to defecate at any convenient spot in the forest, but should they do so in an invisible spirit village, the spirits may send illnesses into the village, including children's diseases such as chickenpox, or they may cause a village fire.[13]

A fire caused by humans in the spirits' village may provoke revenge by the spirits as well. The story of one woman involved such an incident.

Afwe's Insolence,
Her Father's Curse, and the Spirits' Revenge

As a child, Afwe was rather rebellious and often talked back to her parents. One day she actually hit her father. This is a serious offense, and her father responded by cursing his daughter. Now it is said that a mother's curse is retractable but a father's curse is not. In this case the father's curse operated in the following manner.

Many years later, as a woman, Afwe went into the forest to burn the underbrush to make way for a new cornfield. She was with several other women engaged in the same activity. The fire went out of control and burned down a larger section of the forest than planned—a rare event, for Beng women are normally quite adept at this potentially dangerous skill. The other women blamed Afwe for the fire, although she denied it. They returned to the village and consulted a diviner. He confirmed that Afwe was to blame for the fire and added the disastrous news that the fire had burned down a spirits' village in the forest. The spirits were incensed and cursed Afwe with madness. Soon after, she indeed started slowly losing her mind; within several months she was mad. At the time of my fieldwork in 1985 Afwe was a sad, broken woman who barely spoke, rarely fed her children, regularly destroyed her own granary, and generally lived a wasted life. It was widely believed that her negligence in letting her forest fire go out of control was the working out of her father's curse years earlier.

Because of the threat of such punishments by spirits for impinging on their territory, people endeavor strenuously to maintain their distance from the places they consider to be inhabited by the forest spirits.

Accordingly, the occasional presence of spirits in the village is generally considered dangerous. Spirits are said to travel in the wind—indeed, in the Beng view, the wind is the movement, or "footsteps" (*be*), of spirits traveling invisibly through the air. Thus a windy day is feared, and people take cover inside their houses if they are in the village. If one is near spirits when they are passing through the village, the effect is immediately known. One woman, Akissi, described it this way: "My body got very heavy and I couldn't move or talk. I wanted to call my husband, but I wasn't able to. The spirits were sliding over the thatched roof." The wind produces an impossible contradiction: the introduction into the village of just those spirits that must remain in the forest. To the extent that this conceptual anomaly is untenable, then Akissi's reaction is poignantly apposite: she has created a kind of temporary rigor mortis that immobilizes her until the danger—at once empirical and conceptual—has passed.

A LÉVI-STRAUSSIAN INTERLUDE

Given the dualist division of Beng space as I have outlined it into "village" and "forest," or "Earth," one might be tempted to associate these two spheres with "culture" and "nature," respectively, following the Lévi-Straussian scheme. But I would caution against such a strict association, for I would argue that Beng do not perceive or experience the forest/Earth area as anything akin to *nature* as Western culture understands that term. When I first arrived in the Beng region, the villages appeared to me as dramatic round clearings in the tropical forest, which appeared formidable, chaotic, dangerous. But Beng do not experience the forest in this way at all and were amused at my early fears of going into it. For the Beng, the forest is not a vast, undifferentiated mass, as the West views nature in both its wild and pastoral versions (e.g., Chiappelli 1976, Manuel and Manuel 1972, L. Marx 1964, Onians 1951, White 1972, Williams 1962). Rather, it is quite orderly; in fact, it has been meticulously classified by the Beng into zones: zones for spirits, for planting, for hunting and gathering, and so on. In keeping with this, Beng herbalists were quite certain that all the forest plants have names, whether or not any given individual knows all those names. This urge to name speaks eloquently to the humanizing impulse that the Beng have adopted toward the forest. Not surprisingly, a large proportion of forest plants are used as herbal cures by healers, who know exactly where to find whichever plant they need for a given treatment.[14]

Beng not only pick forest products for medicinal purposes; they also work in the forest every day: the fields for both edible crops (yams, rice, fruit trees, assorted vegetables) and cash crops (coffee, cotton, rice, cocoa, kola nuts) are located in the forest itself. Moreover, adult men hunt in the forest (more so in the past than nowadays), and women regularly gather edible wild plants in the forest, including mushrooms, leaves from the kapok and other trees, wild berries, and so on. In short, the Beng have daily and intimate contact with the forest, which nourishes them in both literal and spiritual ways. Indeed, given their deep experiential familiarity with the forest, the French colonial officer Binger even appears to have mistakenly thought that the Beng actually live in the forest (1892, vol. 2: 224; cf. Tauxier 1921:369).

While they certainly do not do this, the two spheres of village and forest/Earth are hardly perceived by the Beng as mutually exclusive and antagonistic, as "nature" and "culture" are in the West; rather, they are seen as inextricably tied to one another. Indeed, if one zone could be said to dominate the other in Beng thought, it would have to be said that the forest/Earth ultimately defines and dominates the life of the village, and not vice versa. This will be strikingly evident when we consider in the next section the taboos that the Beng say the Earth requires them to observe. All this, of course, is the converse of the Lévi-Straussian model in which culture (which might seem to be associated with the Beng village) inevitably triumphs over nature (which might seem to be associated with the Beng forest/Earth). For these reasons, I resist the temptation to make the structuralist analogy between the Beng forest/Earth area and "nature," on one hand, and the Beng village and "culture," on the other.

Having considered this issue, we can now turn directly to the taboos concerning the Earth. Here we will see how practice links with ideology in such a way that Beng religion, which perhaps has seemed a bit abstruse until now, in fact shapes the daily lives of Beng people in the most intimate and far-reaching ways.

TABOOS OF THE EARTH

A stereotyped description of non-Western societies often invokes phrases such as *taboo-ridden*. Perhaps as a legacy of Lévy-Bruhl's work (e.g., 1966, 1985), misunderstood as it has been (see Littleton 1985), rural, Third World people are still often seen by Westerners as severely constrained in their behavior, which in turn is seen as "automatic," with no individual meaning other than the weight of custom and, correlatively, no possibility of rebellion. While criticized severely, this vision of rural, non-Western peoples still lives on in many places, not the least in popular Western journalists' accounts. The Beng challenge it in important ways. For example, individual Beng have a very clear notion of why they observe particular taboos: it is out of personal and meaningful respect for the Earth and its powerful spirits. And individual Beng may choose to reject these taboos for any of several reasons: a waning respect for the Earth due to "conversion" (to Islam or Christianity—see note 5); disillusionment due to failure of the Earth to grant specific desires; general laziness about maintaining the local version of moral rectitude, combined with optimism that the Earth will overlook negligence; or financial constraints leading to a demotion of assigned Earth sacrifices to the lowest priority.

Still, Lévy-Bruhl is relevant to the Beng in one sense. In keeping with Lévy-Bruhl's insistence that non-Western people focus their lives around spiritual concerns, the Beng do in fact make a good many decisions concerning their day-to-day activities in relation to their knowledge of the Earth's taboos (só pɔ́). This is certainly not to say that individual Beng are "taboo-laden" to the point of inability to act practically in the world. But the meanings that they impart to those daily, "practical" actions are profoundly molded by their religion. What they do, where they do it, with whom, and when—all these are shaped to a great extent by the ways that they understand the taboos that they consider have been laid down for them by the Earth. In looking at the most important of these taboos, we will see how thoroughgoing is the Earth's shaping of people's consciousness. And, paradoxical as it seems, we will see how the Earth at once demands vigilant attention from people, while requiring them to keep a healthy distance from the spirits that animate the Earth. I group my discussion of the Earth's taboos into two sections: those relating to time ("Earth Days") and those relating to space (sexual taboos).

EARTH DAYS

A basic set of taboos revolves around the days on which the Earths should be worshiped. The traditional Beng calendar is based on a six-day week (lɛ). In each six-day week, one day is set aside for worship of the Earths.[15] In addition, apart from the wider, regional rest days, many agricultural fields have their own days of rest. In these cases, the particular days are said to have been determined by local spirits who live in the fields (as revealed by a diviner).

On these various rest days, no one is allowed to work in the forest or fields. In particular, hard labor in the forest or fields is absolutely forbidden. This includes women chopping down trees for firewood or burning the forest to make new fields and men chopping down trees to prepare new fields. The day before a rest day, women must bring into the village enough wood with which to cook the next day's meals. Light work, such as collecting crops for that day's meals, is discouraged but permitted.

Rest days are seen as directly accommodating the forest spirits: on these days, the Earth's spirits, who are said to eat only once a week, leave their villages in the forest and venture out into people's fields to eat some of the crops that are growing there. It is because the spirits want to maintain distance from humans that they forbid the latter to work in the forest on those days. Should a person encounter a spirit in the fields, the spirit would flee in anger and the person would have to offer a chicken sacrifice by way of apology.

To show respect to the forest spirits, village activities are also curtailed on rest days. For example, men may not make bark cloths (traditionally a product that Beng men produced and traded). More significantly, during the beginning hours of each Earth day—which extends from sundown to early morning, as the Beng day begins at dusk—no one may make loud noises. This includes speaking in a loud voice—in the old days, I was told, adults spoke in a whisper during this time. And as young children could not be trusted to control their voices, in at least one village they used to be stuffed into large ceramic pots (ordinarily used as water jugs) during the evening hours before going to bed! No one may beat drums or play other instruments; nowadays, radios are still not played in at least one village. Moreover, after sundown women may not use their large wooden mortars and pestles with which they pound *foutou* (a dietary staple dish made from cooked and pounded yams); hence many people either eat dinner early on the evening of the Earth day or, if they eat past sundown, they dine on rice, boiled yams, or some other starch staple that does not require pounding in the large mortars. In contrast, the next afternoon—the last hours of the Earth day—most everyone does eat *foutou* for dinner, and this is seen as a weekly celebration, the successful end of a day dedicated to the Earth.

If speaking loudly is prohibited in the early portion of the Earth day, one can imagine how strictly arguments would be curtailed. In 1980, I observed what happened when this taboo was violated.

Co-wives' Fight on Earth Day

Kona's two wives, Au and Nakoyā, were having a dispute. To conclude her arguments, Nakoyā hissed at Au menacingly, "You'll see when we go to the fields together tomorrow!" Such anger between the two women was not unusual, as they were less than happy co-wives. But a fight on the Earth day *was* unusual. It degenerated to the point that Nakoyā went to strike Au while Au's baby was tied onto her back, and the baby fell down and began wailing. Hearing the cries, Kona came over, observed the scene, left and came back with a belt with which he began to beat Nakoyā. This made matters more serious, as physical violence is seen as far worse than the verbal violence of shouting, as far as the Earth is concerned. Now in a small village, news of such fights travels instantly, and Kona's maternal uncle, Yao, soon came over to investigate.

"What happened?" he asked Kona, disturbed.

"Well, Nakoyā and Au haven't been talking to each other for two months," Kona began by way of preface.

"What? Why didn't you tell me earlier!" Yao jumped in. "We could have discussed it and settled the problem, and this public fight could have been avoided!"

"I'm sorry, uncle," Kona said, with some shame added to the misery already noticeable on his face, but Yao left the compound in disgust.

Two weeks later, on the eve of another rest day, Kona was informed by a

village elder that he must offer a sacrifice of two white chickens for his wives'
fight, as well as for his own participation in having beaten Nakoyā. The outcome
was all the more ironic as Kona himself is a devout Muslim and could barely be
said to "believe" in the Earth. Yet he had no choice: if he wanted to continue to
live in the village, as a Beng he had to abide by its laws; in this case, laws dictated
by a religion he had all but discarded. He grumblingly contributed the chickens.

During the time that quiet must be maintained for the Earth, the Master of the
Earth is working. During the evening of a rest day, those who plan to offer sacrifices
to the Earth the next morning come to the courtyard of the Master of the Earth. If
there are many such people, they in effect stand in line in front of his house,
bringing the animal they will be sacrificing and explaining the reason for the
offering. The Master of the Earth listens and remembers each of these cases. While
he is making mental notes of his next morning's work, the spirits to whom he will
be sacrificing the items are listening in, too. For after dusk, these spirits are said to
leave their usual forest spot and enter the compound of the Master of the Earth, so
that they know what to expect the next morning. Then, around 10:00 P.M., when
everyone has gone to sleep, the spirits return to the forest. This is one of the few
occasions on which forest spirits' entry into the village is auspicious.

About 6:00 A.M. of the rest day, the Master of the Earth and his assistant walk
into the forest with all the eggs and animals to be sacrificed. At the shrine, they slit
the throats of the sacrificial animals while uttering assorted prayers explaining to
the Earth spirits who is offering what, and why; then they carve up the animals.
While in the forest, they may cook and eat their allotted share of the meat, but they
bring back the rest of the meat to the village where they divide up the carcasses,
donating a portion to the head of their matriclan.

Midmorning, when the sacrifices have been offered and the quiet time for
respect to the Earth is over, the villagers may speak in normal voices and the village
once again becomes noisy. But the most important taboo must still be observed: no
one may perform heavy work in the fields or the forest at large. For the rest of the
day, people generally pursue an assortment of activities in the village—hairdress-
ing, visiting, craft work, sitting in on trials, drinking palm wine, napping—or they
may choose to visit relatives or friends in other villages.

The Earth not only makes stringent demands of its followers on days designated
as Earth days; during the rest of the week, the Beng must observe certain behavior
that is also specifically dictated to them by the Earth. As the Earth is said to be
omniscient and omnipotent, violation of these taboos relating to daily life can be
grave, resulting in misfortune, illness, or death. In the following section I consider
the most important of these taboos, those that pertain to sexual activity and
notions of fertility as they emerge in space.

Sexual Taboos and Notions of Fertility
Five taboos are said to be laid down by the Earth pertaining to human sexuality:

1. Menstruating women may not perform any kind of labor in the forest nor,
   indeed, may they set foot in the forest for any reason other than to defecate.

2. Couples may not have sexual intercourse in the forest or fields.
3. Men may not engage in sex the night before they will be eating meat from animals that were sacrificed to the Earth.
4. Pregnant women may not eat food while walking on any paths into or out of the forest.
5. Women in labor may not deliver in the forest or fields.

All five of these taboos circumscribe various aspects of human sexuality in a manner that carefully defines appropriate spaces for conducting the various activities. In every case, the distinction between forest/Earth and village is highlighted. In what follows, I explore the implications of these taboos: what results when they are violated, and the means for atoning for the sin of violating them. I conclude by discussing their wider relevance to Beng cosmology as it has been presented earlier in this chapter.

Menstruation and the Earth. One of the most important aspects of her daily routine that changes when a young woman is married is that she may no longer go into the forest or fields when she has her menstrual period.[16] Associated with this change is a sacrifice of chickens or goats offered to the Earth. The purpose is to apologize for the girl's having previously entered the forest to work in the fields (or to chop wood or draw water), and to promise the Earth that she will never again repeat that offense, now that she is married.

If this necessary sacrifice is not performed by the time she becomes pregnant, the young woman will later have a very difficult childbirth. If the infant survives, it will become sickly. Likewise, should a married or previously married woman go into the forest during her menstrual period, one result is the same: she too will have a very difficult delivery during her next childbirth. Another consequence is that the crops in the field in which she was working while menstruating will die. Thus the entire family of that field owner would be affected.

This set of rules is endowed with an aura of reality for all individuals, including those who violate them. Even transgressors seem to internalize the reality of the causal chain concerning the taboos and the consequences of their violation. When confronted with test cases, diviners manage to present the evidence in such a way as to convincingly make such hidden connections manifested, as the following case shows.

Akissi in the Yam Field

One day Akissi was in the forest, working in her husband's yam field. Two days later all the leaves of the yam plants in that part of the field fell off and the yams died. Akissi herself developed bad stomach cramps. She consulted a diviner to discover the cause of her cramps. He revealed that two days earlier she had been working in the forest while menstruating. Akissi confessed, but she explained that her period had come while she was in the fields and she hadn't wanted to return immediately to the village before finishing the work she had come to do. However, as a result of her misjudgment, the whole year's yam crop in that field was spoiled and the Earth was polluted (*e ba zozona*: she polluted the Earth).

To rectify the pollution, a sacrifice was necessary. In this case, a female goat was required, indicating the seriousness of the offense; a lesser offense would have required a mere chicken. The goat was sacrificed by the appropriate Master of the Earth at the forest shrine associated with the specific Earth that was polluted. This done, the Earth was no longer polluted, and the following year, the Earth allowed the yams to grow in the affected field.

If a required necessary sacrifice to the Earth is for some reason withheld, members of the guilty woman's family might be punished by the Earth, as the following story reveals.

Amwe and the Spitting Cobra

One day Amwe went to work in the fields while menstruating. Soon after, she confessed to the deed. The Master of the Earth who was associated with the Earth of her fields said that to lift the pollution of the Earth that she had caused, she must offer as a sacrifice a goat, a chicken, and an egg, plus ten liters of palm wine. Since the transgression had occurred in the fields of Amwe's father, Sã, it was he who was responsible for providing the egg; but for reasons that I never found out, Sã held out. Soon after, Amwe's brother went to the fields, where a spitting black cobra spit in his eyes. Their father took this disaster as convincing evidence of the Earth's power and anger. That very day Sã went to the Master of the Earth to donate the necessary egg.

Both these examples attest to the lived quality of the Earth's taboos, to the way they shape even skeptics' consciousness and determine their daily actions.

I note that these data also offer a counterpoint to comparative analyses of menstrual taboos that are now abundant in the anthropological literature (see Buckley and Gottlieb 1988). Most writers on the subject have taken taboos relating to menstruating women as a sign of women's lower status (e.g., Kessler 1976:72–74; Meggitt 1964; Ortner 1974; Sacks 1974; Young 1965:155). But Beng people do not view their taboo against menstruating women entering the forest in this way, nor should we. When I asked a Master of the Earth why menstrual blood pollutes the Earth, he could only answer my question in a way that revealed how far from a model of female oppression Beng notions of menstruation are:

Menstrual blood is special because it carries in it a living being. It works like a tree. Before bearing fruit, a tree must first bear flowers. Menstrual blood is like the flower: it must emerge before the fruit—the baby—can be born. Childbirth is like a tree finally bearing its fruit, which the woman then gathers.

This poetic statement contains in it profound ideas that are quite relevant to the argument I have been introducing. It reveals that menstrual blood is conceived as a symbol of human fertility. Separating it from the forest constitutes a ritual statement that human fertility must be separated from the kind of fertility that the Earth-forest creates: crops. It is fitting that the transgression of this rule results in aborted fertility in one or both realms: the woman's own offspring and the crops may die.

The remaining four taboos that we will explore further illustrate this principle.

Each insists on a separation between village fertility (human sexuality) and forest or fields fertility (crops).

Sex and the Earth. Although contact of menstrual blood with the Earth pollutes the latter, it is by no means the sole nor the severest cause of such pollution (see Gottlieb 1990a). Another action is considered the gravest of all the possible offenses to the Earth, causing it the severest form of pollution and in turn posing the worst threat to humankind: the act of human sexual intercourse in the forest or the fields. We have already explored one aspect of this in our discussion of the kapok tree, and its legitimation of village sexuality. Here I want to look into the rule as it affects individual people who do or do not follow it.

There are no exceptions to the rule: married and unmarried couples, legitimate, adulterous and incestuous liaisons, all are subject to it. The consequences of violating the taboo are various. Not only may the woman involved have a difficult time in her next childbirth (and in ensuing ones as well, if the sin is not expiated), but the couple's children and any close or even distant kinspeople (especially members of their matriclans) are imperiled. In one case I recorded, a married couple caused a major scandal by sleeping together repeatedly in the forest for a year. Six of their relatives died or suffered before the act was ritually punished, and these deaths and misfortunes were all widely attributed to the Earth as indirect punishment of the couple.[17]

In addition to endangering the couple's own relatives, the man and woman who have sexual intercourse in the forest or fields jeopardize the lives of all the Beng. For it is said that a general drought will ensue that, if the Earth is not properly propitiated in time, will result in the ruining of the entire year's crop and could ultimately cause the starvation of all the Beng.[18] Here the entire group of Beng people is being conceived as a single, interconnected moral community, each of whose members is seen as ultimately responsible for the well-being of the others.

In fact, illicit acts of forest sex seem to be common: one informant recalled at least five cases having occurred in three villages within her recent memory.[19] During my 1980 fieldwork, a minor drought in June was blamed on two separate couples having had intercourse in the forest. They were the subject of endless speculative gossip: Had the couples really done it, and if so, why? Did they know the consequences? (One couple was a pair of young, unmarried lovers.) Was there witchcraft involved? For the act of forest sex is so immoral that mystical motivation and mechanisms are often invoked as an explanation of the otherwise unthinkable.

Having sex in the forest is more shameful as one ages and presumably becomes responsible for one's actions. This is borne out by another case.

Forest Sex and Witchcraft

Kouassi, a middle-aged man, was bewitched to have sexual intercourse in the forest (presumably with his wife), but other witches of his matriclan were able to partly protect him by changing the spell so that it was Kouassi's son (about twenty years old) who committed the offense with a girlfriend. Although the cosmological result was the same—the Earth was polluted—Kouassi himself, while deeply ashamed that his son had engaged in forest sex, was less ashamed than if it had been he himself—a near-elder who should be a model of propriety—who had polluted the Earth in this manner.

The punishment meted out to a couple who have sexual intercourse in the forest or fields is considered drastic (*grégré*). They must return to the scene of the crime. There they repeat the act in front of a large, jeering audience of middle-aged and old men who brandish sticks and firebrands with which they beat and burn the couple during the act of sex. Then the Master of the Earth sacrifices a cow. The couple's clothes are taken from them and later given to the king of their region, and they are given new clothes to wear back to the village.[20] This punishment was endured by one of the two guilty couples during the drought that occurred during my fieldwork. Soon afterward the rains indeed came—which my Beng friends pointed out to me with the satisfaction of seeing their cosmology confirmed in the empirical world, much as a scientist breathes relief when she or he successfully replicates the results of a famous experiment.

A variation of this ritual punishment is possible in extenuating circumstances. In one case, a man who raped his wife in the forest was sent to jail by the woman's relatives. But since the Earth was still polluted and needed purification, the raped wife was required to perform the ritual in the forest and go through the motions of sex without her husband, all the while being beaten and burned by the old men present. (My informant could not tell me what might happen if only the guilty male were present during the ritual as she could not recall any such cases.)

The ritual itself might be interpreted in several ways. At the psychological level, the punishment, with its traumatic public shaming, is certainly likely to prevent future occurrences of the illicit act by either or both members of the guilty couple. At a more cosmological level, the ritual, by its repetition of the sinful act, partakes of a principle that is found frequently in Beng religion that "two negatives equal a positive."

A corollary to the prohibition against forest sex is the result for the individuals who transgress it. Both members of the couple are said to be permanently polluted (*zozoa*). This manifests itself in speech patterns. If one talks early in the morning to such a "polluted" person before he or she has eaten anything or rinsed out his or her mouth, one has bad luck that day (for further comments on this, see Gottlieb 1990a). For this reason, "polluted" people find it difficult to marry, as the following case shows.

Refusing a Polluted Co-wife

Kouassi was married to only one wife, Au. A few years ago, he began having an affair with Akissi, a divorcée from another village. But Akissi was "polluted": it was common knowledge that she had once had sex with someone in the forest.

When Kouassi announced to his wife Au that he'd been having an affair with Akissi and now wished to marry her as a second wife, Au was furious and refused to accept Akissi as a co-wife. She made clear that she wasn't opposed to the idea of a co-wife in general, but just to Akissi, who was polluted. Kouassi capitulated and gave up on Akissi.

Related to the prohibition on sexual intercourse in the forest is a rule that all adults must bathe in the morning to "wash off sex" from the previous night (whether or not they actually had sexual relations the night before). Should a man or woman have sexual relations one night and go into the forest or fields the next day without having bathed in the morning, the person runs a good risk of getting bitten by a snake in the forest. In this case it is said that none of the usual snake remedies would be effective and the person would inevitably die.

This rule about "washing off sex" clearly relates to the prohibition against copulating in the forest: both reveal that human sexual activity must be confined to the village in both action (the sex act) and the metonymic residues of that action (sexual odor and fluids). Moreover, both these taboos are clearly connected to the taboo against menstruating women's entering the forest. Just as menstrual blood, a symbol of human fertility, must be separated from the Earth, which produces forest fertility (crops), so too the sex act, the direct agent of human fertility, must be separated from the Earth and its crop fertility. The rule about daily morning bathing further emphasizes the separation between human and forest fertility that Beng cosmology demands.

"Earth Meat." As with sexuality, food also serves as a symbolic medium that carries the weight of religious value, in this case marking out appropriate and inappropriate zones for consumption. In particular, Beng classify meat as belonging to one of two types: meat from wild animals that men hunt for food (by trap or gun), and meat from domesticated animals that they slaughter ritually as a sacrifice to the Earth (called *ba soŋ*, or "Earth meat"). The two kinds of meat are further distinguished by strict social rules concerning the identity of the eater. While hunted meat is eagerly sought out by all Beng, Earth meat may only be eaten by men, and by boys who are no longer nursing.[21] Furthermore, Earth meat may not be cooked in ordinary pots nor eaten with ordinary spoons (wooden or metal) with which other food is handled. Instead, most men own a special pot and spoon that they store separately from their wives' pots and spoons. Earth meat has its own place as well: men cook Earth meat in the salon of the house, never in the kitchen.

The meaning of these restrictions becomes clear when another taboo is considered. Men (including Masters of the Earth) must refrain from having sex the night before they will be eating Earth meat. If they violate this rule, they will die. Here we see repeated the theme we have been following in diverse domains of behavior: human sexuality must remain separate from the Earth. This is seen more forcefully if we recall that the Beng day begins at sundown; hence having sex one night and eating Earth meat the next morning or afternoon would all be done on the same day, by Beng calendrical reckoning. Considering this, the taboo joins the ritual requirements that we have already treated, concerning the sex act and bathing, as another endeavor to keep human (village) sexuality apart from the forest-based Earth.

The injunction to restrict human sexuality, in act and association, from the forest is joined by a pair of taboos relating to the next stage of sexuality: fertility.

When they are pregnant and when they are in the beginning stages of labor, all women must keep this in mind and orient their actions accordingly.

Pregnancy and the Earth. As with the prior taboos already considered, practice and abstract taboo are intimately related in Beng women's reproductive lives. In particular, it is taboo for a pregnant woman to eat while she is walking on a path that connects the forest or fields and the village.[22] Should she violate this taboo, she will know soon after she has given birth, for it is said that the child that is born to her will not be fully human but "really a snake" in the guise of a human. This state of affairs is the result of a rather complex chain of events. When the pregnant woman ate food while walking on the path, it is supposed that she must have dropped some crumbs of whatever she was eating. A snake must have been nearby and enjoyed those crumbs so much that it became filled with a desire for human food. To assuage its longing, the snake entered the woman's womb and changed places with the fetus (releasing the latter to go to some undetermined place) so that, once born, it could continue to eat human food. During the woman's delivery, what emerges looked more or less like a human infant but is really the impostor snake.

However, as the baby develops there are certain telltale signs that reveal that the infant, whom Western psychologists would probably classify as mildly brain-damaged or perhaps retarded, is really a snake. It moves its body as a snake does, in slithering motions. Later the child is clumsy and does not learn human speech properly. For instance, one such girl of about ten years never learned Beng kin terms perfectly and made mistakes frequently, referring to an elder sister as her father, and so on.

If parents suspect that their child may really be a snake, they may bring the child to a specialist diviner who performs a ritual to test the child's species identity. The diviner leads the child (and, optionally, his or her parents or other interested relatives) to a certain spot in the forest. There, the diviner puts down a plate of food to which snakes are said to be particularly partial.[23] The child may look at the plate and do nothing, revealing his or her true humanity. Alternatively, the child may immediately go to eat the food. In such a case, after tasting the food, a remarkable occurrence is said to happen: the child's head will start spinning around on its neck and the whole body follows suit until it spins itself into a snake and slithers off into the forest, never again to be seen—unless it finds that it misses human food and returns to the same woman's womb during her next pregnancy, again replacing the human fetus, to be born as another "snake-person."[24]

The parents of a snake-person may not always elect to take the child to such a specialist diviner. For one thing, his services are quite expensive by local standards: one person estimated that for a young child, a healer might charge 15–20,000 CFA while the cost for an older child would be as much as 50,000 CFA (see note 20)—in addition to providing a chicken and palm wine to the healer as a gift. Then, too, the parents may be reluctant for emotional reasons to bring themselves to take the drastic step. In these cases, the child will be allowed to grow up and become an adult, though through childhood she or he will be teased and harassed by other villagers, who regularly pelt stones at him or her at the slightest provocation since, it is said, "snakes have no bones so they don't feel any pain." The cousin of a snake-girl once explained to me why the girl, about ten years old, always went nearly naked: "If you offer her a *pagne* [wraparound-style skirt], she'll try to eat it." A snake-person will learn to perform some work appropriate to his or her gender but rarely manages to be as self-sufficient as are normal adults. He or she may beg food from villagers and sleep anywhere in the village, with no regular bed. Such a person would invariably remain single for, as one informant asked me rhetorically in disgust, "Who would marry a snake?"

There are several aspects to the symbolism of snake-people that are noteworthy. First, it seems in some ways appropriate that brain-damaged or mildly retarded people are classified as snakes because of a certain resemblance to them: the body wiggles or slithers rather than walking firmly. Similarly, the snake-person is clumsy like a snake, which has no limbs. More to the point, there are also strong symbolic reasons why the snake encounters the vulnerable pregnant woman on a path. First, there is a level of visual similarity between the snake and the path: both are long, thin, and windy. Second, forest paths represent to the Beng a liminal area between forest and village (though to Western eyes they lie within the forest). Acting as a conceptual mediator between the two arenas of forest and village, they are bound to emanate a certain kind of danger, which is congruent with the danger that pregnancy, itself a liminal state, also represents.[25]

For as I have suggested, on one level the two spheres of forest and village are viewed as conceptually discrete, even mutually opposed (though as we shall see soon there are certain important parallels that symbolically link them). But the physical link between the two zones—the paths—are the most visible and concrete mediator between them, and I suggest that it is for this reason that they are the locus of a certain kind of danger—one associated in this case with pregnancy.

Then, too, we may inquire into the specific inclusion of eating food on the path that is deemed dangerous to pregnant women. To understand this, we must consider that people are allowed to cook and eat food in both the village and the forest. The latter is necessary because of the way the Beng have organized their farming space: some farmers build "camps" *(namwes)* where they stay overnight in their faraway fields and so they eat regular meals there. Given such an arrangement—which itself contradicts the logic of the seemingly thoroughgoing separation between village and forest that we have been tracing through this chapter—the only spot where it could logically be forbidden to eat food would not be in one of the two major realms—village and forest—but must instead be between them: on the paths.

In the taboo against pregnant women eating food while walking on a forest path, then, we find a symbolically rich statement whose ultimate logic revolves once again around the separation between village and forest.

Childbirth and the Earth. Like pregnancy, childbirth is an intense bodily experience for women that, while obviously a biological event, is also deeply shaped by cultural forces (e.g., Jordan 1983, Martin 1987). Beng culture has strictly defined the locale of the event, and this knowledge is part of every woman's mental repertoire. Consistent with the logical model concerning the space for reproduction that I have been developing, I note that just as it is forbidden to menstruate and to have sex in the forest, so too it is taboo for a Beng woman to deliver a child in the forest at large and in the agricultural fields in particular. If a woman feels the first contractions of labor coming on while working in the forest or fields, she must return immediately to the village to deliver the baby there.[26] Should she violate the taboo and deliver the baby in the forest or fields, the Earth will be polluted. She must then apologize to it by an animal sacrifice, offered by a Master of the Earth, whose action would lift the state of pollution from the Earth.

Occasionally an unmarried girl might deliver her child alone in the forest, from shame. (In the old days, a newborn delivered in this way would have been killed.) If the girl is even more miserable over her state, she might even abort in the forest early on in the pregnancy before anyone knows of her condition, to avoid the humiliation of an illegitimate birth (the reasons for such feelings of shame will emerge in chapter 4). But upon returning to the village, she should immediately confess her deed. The Earth would be polluted by the abortion, and a sacrifice of a goat would have to be offered to apologize for and lift the state of pollution. The same is true of an adult woman (married or unmarried) who, for whatever reason, terminates a pregnancy. If she aborts in the village, it is considered unfortunate and reprehensible but there are no cosmological consequences; in contrast, if she aborts in the forest, the Earth is polluted and must be apologized to and purified by a goat sacrifice. If a woman fails to confess a forest abortion, it is said that she will die either of severe diarrhea or of a snake bite. The taboos on abortion and childbirth in the forest are clearly related as they both reinforce the pattern we have been pursuing: human fertility in all its aspects, negative and positive, must be physically and conceptually separated from the Earth and its forest or field fertility.

Finally, it seems significant that snakes figure prominently in three of the five taboos that we have considered in this section. In violating taboos against "washing off sex" before entering the forest, against pregnant women eating food on the path through the forest, and against aborting in the forest, the transgressor risks dying of snake bite. All three activities involve crossing both conceptual and physical boundaries between village and forest and their respective modes of fertility. Certain distinguishing anatomical features of snakes suggest a liminal, "betwixt-and-between" status. These include their lack of limbs, their annual shedding of skin, and their fluid, slithering movements. Moreover, snakes are the one type of forest creature that do in fact move regularly from forest to village and back again. (I was all too aware of this in my daily rounds of morning and evening greetings, when I regularly saw snakes either being killed or newly dead. The Beng say that all local snakes are poisonous. My snake books came close to agreeing with them on this.) We can hypothesize that the combination of these features makes snakes appropriate for carrying the symbolic weight of punishing transgressors against symbolic boundary maintenance.[27] The snake thus becomes a symbol of threat to Beng thought caused by the violation of Earth taboos dictating separation between spatial and conceptual realms.

EARTH SPIRITS AND VILLAGE HUMANS:
IDENTITY AND DIFFERENCE

The taboos described in the previous section concerning the Earth all suggest a radical separation between humans' activities in the village and spirits' activities in the forest. I now want to backtrack somewhat to explore how the separation is by no means absolute. For despite the many-layered gulf that I have been analyzing between forest-dwelling spirit and village-dwelling human, the relationship between the two is a complex one that cannot in fact be characterized simply as one of identity or difference; rather, as we will see elsewhere in Beng thought, a combination of both principles is at work. In remarking on this complication, I am reminded of Stephen Tyler's statement that I cited in the previous chapter: "identity and difference are correlatives, the one unthinkable without the other" (1987:13). The remainder of this chapter seeks to show how this seeming contradiction works itself out in Beng thought. In exploring the issue, I hope to demonstrate the centrality of contradiction to a system of thought that is nevertheless coherent— though its coherence involves a firm adherence to contradiction.

We can begin this discussion with a consideration of the Beng Earth in relation to another entity: not the village, but the Sky. For in the relation between the two, a combination of the two principles of identity and difference is likewise found. On a superficial level, the Beng Earth exists in clear opposition to the Sky. For example, in its unified sense, the Earth is defined as male while the Sky is female. The Earth and the Sky are distinct, named entities, each with a radically different relationship to the human world: as we have seen, Beng venerate the Earth; but their relationship to the Sky is much more equivocal, less intense, for the Sky is very rarely the object of direct sacrifice.[28] Despite these radical conceptual differences that are postulated between the spheres of Earth and Sky, the two are said to be friends. Indeed, the Beng say they cannot know where one realm stops and the other begins, for there is no tangible or knowable boundary between them. I take this complex set of relationships as a model for the kinds of relations we have been discussing between village and forest/Earth: a relationship of both difference and identity. It is here that we can draw open the curtain to a window into Beng thought. For as with other domains of Beng life, this most abstract pair of major categories, human/village and spirit/forest/Earth, reveals a paradoxical combination of opposed principles.

If the ideal is for humans and spirits to live apart, nevertheless they need each other. As we have seen, humans need spirits for their mystical blessing as well as their moral sustenance. In myth, the spirits may have once fled the living quarters of humans in a mixture of shame and anger, but they still bestow benevolence on the Beng, so long as humans worship the Earth spirits regularly. People who neglect the Earth sacrifices required of them, or who violate the taboos dictated by the Earth, do so at their peril. Eventually they will suffer. Still, if the Earth is seen as all-protective and absolutely central to the well-being of the Beng, the latter must nonetheless keep their distance, quite literally, from the spirits.

If humans need spirits for their blessing, spirits need humans for their physical nourishment. The spirits are said to eat once a week, availing themselves both of meat that is sacrificed (they are said to eat the blood), and of the harvests that lie in the fields. If a farmer notices that some of his or her crop is missing, an accusation of thievery is rarely heard and would be ill-advised: it is assumed that it was spirits who took the crops, and no action against them is considered.

Forest spirits are thirsty as well, and their drink is palm wine. A male elder said emphatically that the spirits "love palm wine!" When a male farmer cuts down a palm wine tree for tapping, he offers a little new wine to the spirits, and each time palm wine is drunk—either on social or ritual occasions—a few drops are spilled onto the ground for the spirits. Without these frequent offerings by humans, the spirits would go thirsty.[29]

Many other connections exist between the areas that humans and spirits inhabit. The most obvious is not a metonymic but a metaphoric one: a visual parallel. The typical field area farmed in the forest by the Beng is pie-shaped. Now, the traditional Beng house was until recently also pie-shaped (though government regulation now discourages this, and there are no longer any viable round houses left, as we shall see in chapter 6). Indeed, the drawings in figure 1 reveal that the traditional Beng house was constructed to a design that was identical to that of the Beng field area. This visual identity between house and field shape was striking to me. When questioned, Beng seemed surprised by it; the only explanation offered was that the round shape of both field and house is "pretty," and that in general the circle is "prettier" than the square.[30] These aesthetic judgments aside, for our purposes what is significant is that the house and the field area are the single most important arenas for human design in the village and the forest/fields/Earth areas, respectively. Thus the major visual human imprint in both these domains is in the form of a single design motif.

Beng state that there is another kind of parallel between forest and village, this one invisible. According to a Master of the Earth, the spirits that live in the forest lead lives parallel to those led by the Beng: "They live like us," he explained. The female spirits become pregnant, though for a bit longer than human women's terms (one to three years). They have village chiefs and surely have matriclans, though the elder I spoke with about this was less certain that the spirits have patriclans. He did assert that the forest spirits get into fights and hold trials as the Beng do. On the rare occasion of their deaths, the spirits conduct humanlike funerals, complete with drumming, singing, and crying, all of which humans may hear far off in the forest. There are several "ethnicities" among the spirits. Yet they all understand the Beng language, as is evident from several facts: diviners regularly converse with the spirits

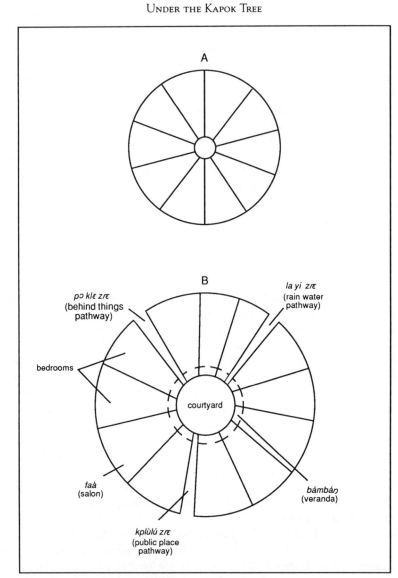

Figure 1. Circular field and house design. A. Plan for men's yam and kola
field areas. B. Basic room plan in traditional round houses.

during their divinations; the spirits listen in on human conversations on some
occasions, as we have seen; and at least one Master of the Earth often dreams of
spirits chatting with him in Beng.[31]

    A further mode in which the realms of village and forest are connected is that
an object in one realm is so placed as to ritually influence the other realm. This is
the case with all the sacrifices that occur in the forest with the aim of aiding

humans in their village lives. Furthermore, some of those forest sacrifices are specifically directed toward forest spirits with the goal of aiding human reproduction—that very principle that we have seen must otherwise be confined to the village.

For example, an expectant father may sacrifice an egg to the Earth spirits at a forest shrine to request that his wife's pregnancy be successful and her delivery easy. After the birth, he must sacrifice a chicken at the same forest shrine. Sacrificing in the forest to the Earth to ensure that a woman's village-oriented pregnancy and delivery go well certainly belies the proposition I have been developing that forest fertility and village fertility are conceptually distinct and must be kept ritually separate. Here we run straight into a contradiction that lies at the heart of Beng religion: the seemingly opposed principles of identity and difference combine in unexpected places to produce a more complex vision of the world. In this case, a woman's pregnancy, which is otherwise restricted to the village in the symbolically (and physically) significant ways we have seen above, is nevertheless regulated overall by the Earth spirits that inhabit the forest. In other words, responsibility for human village reproduction is taken by the forest Earth, crossing the conceptual boundaries that Beng cosmology itself so neatly sets up and otherwise rigorously enforces.

This exception to the pattern of separation between human and spirit domains is not the only one. Despite the fact that the Earth (and its spirits) is quintessentially seen as located in the forest, where its major shrines are kept, nevertheless there are occasions on which sacrifices (usually chickens but also goats and sheep) that are directed to the named forest Earths are performed not at the appropriate forest shrines but, rather, in the village. Moreover—and here is where the contradiction emerges in its fullest force—such a village sacrifice to the forest-based Earth is conducted at the foot of the ritually planted kapok tree: that very tree that, as we have seen, otherwise symbolizes the distinct identity of the village as a separate place and, as such, further symbolizes a conceptual separation of the village from the fields/forest/Earth. Despite this, the village kapok tree is sometimes termed *ba zyé*, the "Earth kapok," and any sacrifice offered to the Earth at the forest shrine could in unusual circumstances be offered at the foot of the kapok tree. How may we account for this symbolic contradiction, in which the kapok tree, as a symbol of difference, is used in a way that denies the distinction it otherwise makes? This is a true paradox in that it is essentially irresolvable, for it cuts "back and forth across terminal and categorical boundaries" (Colie 1966:7,12). Its meaning revolves around contradiction.

In taking this into account, we must now amend an earlier formulation. The ritual planting of the village kapok tree does indeed symbolize the ideological distinctness of the village as opposed to the forest. But in symbolizing that distinction, it also transcends it. The kapok tree thereby becomes both a symbol of difference and, simultaneously, the obviation of that symbolic difference, in the sense meant by Wagner (1978). Like many other powerful symbols, the kapok tree stands both for a certain concept and for the negation of that concept. Paradoxically, it becomes itself by going beyond itself, turning into its conceptual opposite: the idea of continuity between village and forest/Earth. If, as I have suggested, a fundamental theme in Beng society is the oscillation between what I term identity and difference, the kapok becomes a symbol of that dual theme: it encapsulates the oscillation between the connections, on one hand, and the disjunctions, on the other, that together define the relationship between human-occupied village and spirit-occupied forest. In so doing, the kapok tree embodies the richness that is a mark of the most powerful symbols: ambivalence (Fernandez 1974, Sapir 1977a).

This situation constitutes an intellectual paradox that is very much at the structural heart of Beng society. For much of Beng society is based on a conceptual opposition between the two models of society that I have termed identity and difference, and in many cases these two opposed principles combine in unexpected ways. Their combination in the kapok tree is one of several such that we will be exploring through the remaining chapters.

Before continuing on to these other realms, however, I want to ponder briefly an issue that emerges for me when I consider the relevance of all the foregoing at the level of individual consciousness. In keeping with the current set of issues now being actively discussed in anthropology concerning the role of the individual actor in producing and interpreting culture, I am moved to ask: In what sense do the Beng "believe in" the Earth? Is there space for skepticism? I found an answer to this question in an unexpected place. I was talking one day with a Master of the Earth about children. He had told me that red-haired people were bestowed on parents by spirits of a particular Earth. I was eager to find out the sociology of this phenomenon and asked him questions about who could be the recipient of such a special gift. He responded that in this case the Earth is not particular: it gives red-haired infants to anyone, whether or not one is a member of the matriclan associated with that Earth. But I was not sure that I had exhausted the bounds of the Earth's generosity, so I asked my interlocutor teasingly, "But what about me? Could I give birth to a red-haired child too?" To my surprise, he answered: "Of course; if you believed in the Earth, its spirits might give you a red-haired baby."

This was quite an extraordinary statement. It revealed a profound reflexiveness on the part of the priest, a level of understanding of his culture that we have come to expect of anthropologists, not their informants. In effect he was saying, "My religion is powerful, it is real, but it is we who create it. Without our faith it does not exist. Our gods are our invention."[32] In the West, we credit such philosophical insights to a modern, post-Enlightenment world; even before Nietzsche, such a statement would scarcely be thinkable. Africa in contrast is often seen in the West as the heart of rampant belief to the point of "superstition," a pejorative term that inevitably implies utter gullibility coupled with a total lack of self-consciousness. Even Needham's otherwise sophisticated work on the notion of "belief" (1972) questions the very applicability of the concept to many non-Western settings. He argues that firm, sure knowledge is far more present, with the skepticism inherent in the category of "belief" simply absent in many non-Western cultures. Yet here among the Beng, we have an exceptionally sophisticated understanding of the role of individual mind in giving force to cultural symbols, and conversely an acknowledgment of the existence of doubt and its role in excluding the skeptic from the charmed circle of the believer's religion and its powers. The priest's insight was worthy of a Cassirer (1944, 1955) or a Geertz (1973c).

CHAPTER THREE

Double Descent as a System
of Thought

The old witch Sopi died—feared, widowed, and childless. She had only one living relative: a grandson, Konakala, who had been raised by her. At the funeral, Konakala called out to the assembled crowd of mourners, "One sheep from her son! One length of cloth from her son!" as he offered his required funeral donations. But there were no sisters or brothers, no nieces or nephews, to offer the rest of the obligatory offerings of cloth, chickens, and sheep. Resentful as people were of Sopi, they couldn't let her funeral proceed in disgrace, with no clanspeople to lighten the atmosphere with their publicly offered gifts of sacrificial animals. So as the villagers proceeded in single file to the funeral gathering, they dropped small coins on the ground facing the public plaza, and as they did so they gaily called out, "One sheep from her brother! One chicken from her niece!" This double charade made the funeral look right.

In this chapter I look at that hoary anthropological topic, descent, as a locus of rich meanings that order the lives of the Beng people. In the past two decades, there has been much soul searching on the part of anthropologists grappling with issues emerging from a consideration of social structure in general and descent in particular. There are those who feel the urge to discard as much as possible of previous models, now seen as outdated at best (Eickelman 1976, Kuper 1982a, Rosen 1979); those who defend vigorously the need to retain the classic frameworks, viewed as still viable (Gellner 1969); and those who take a mediating position, modifying or rejecting some portions of our intellectual legacy but still retaining some key components of it (Dresch 1986, Şaul 1991, Shapiro 1988). My own position is closer to the latter. In this chapter, I will be looking at descent from a perspective that makes use of certain aspects of the classic sociological framework, but I combine that with a heavy reliance on current, more culturally oriented perspectives.

First, unlike some recent writers, I accept the notion of descent itself as both useful and relevant in comparative anthropological discourse in general and in the Beng context in particular. Moreover, I will be using the English terms *clan* and *lineage* as acceptable translations of Beng words.

This does not mean that I accept all the theoretical baggage that has accompanied these terms over their years of anthropological usage. Certainly the classic British social anthropological emphasis on corporation is no longer taken seriously as an adequate model for understanding descent groups. Radcliffe-Brown's (1952) early focus on the legal aspects of descent groups (creating an incessant invocation of "rights and duties" as the most interesting point for discussion) is hardly compelling today. Nor has Jack Goody's (1961) later shift in emphasis to the transmission of economically valuable property proven viable as the single most crucial dimension to descent groups. Both these models are now seen as far too restrictive to be embraced without major refinement (for a recent cogent, ethnographically based critique of the jural model and an argument that it is still extremely influential despite the many critiques offered over the years, see John Comaroff 1980a).

For one thing, a welcome injection of the issue of strategy and tactics into anthropology in the late 1960s and the 1970s (Bourdieu 1977) seriously questioned the homogeneous and static model of society that was inherent in both the earlier jural and economic emphases. Pioneered by Turner (1957) in his development of the notion of social drama, this general processual approach to social life was then developed in different directions by Barth and Bailey in such a way as to permit a consideration of individuals manipulating kinship structures, and in several other directions chronicled by Ortner in her overview of the influence of practice theory in anthropology (1984). The approach has been used to good effect by several Africanists, including Karp (1978) and others.

The possibility of individual strategizing also raises the issue of change in kinship structures at a more structural level. Recent work among Africanists has done much in specific ethnographic areas to explore important changes that have occurred in some areas even in relatively short periods. For example, in East Africa, Karp (1978) has traced out with admirable precision how, over the past two centuries, local raiding and a new source of arms from Arab traders combined with British colonial forces to produce major changes in the way the Iteso of Kenya view and act toward their kin. In particular, Karp has shown how kinship has to some extent become dissociated from politics as the agnatic group has loosened its attachment to a strongly localized place. Current population pressure, combined with the introduction of individual holdings in land, have further modified earlier kinship patterns (1978:114–117).

Also in East Africa, Moore (1986) likewise charts some major changes in descent norms from the colonial period, here among the Chagga of Tanzania. Like Karp, she notes the reduced political role of the lineages. In addition, she discusses how a shortage of land has combined with an increase in population to in effect "freeze" the lineages to their current locations (225–226).

Much as I admire these and a growing list of related works, my own discussion of Beng clans and lineages cannot likewise focus on historical transformations. By no means do I deny change in Beng society. In the section on slaves, for instance, I bring up the possibility of changing contours of the clan and lineage structures as a result of areal disruptions caused by a local Muslim empire builder; and chapter 6 focuses explicitly on new influences from the West. Nevertheless, what I have been able to discern from both archival work (in Côte d'Ivoire and France) and, more, from oral histories I collected while living among the Beng, suggests a fair degree of continuity in the basic contours of Beng social organization, at least since the inception of the French colonial period in the 1890s. However, I cannot state this position with certainty, as the written historical records to confirm or disprove this impression have so far not been uncovered: as an obscure minority group, the Beng are rarely mentioned in the archival records I have been able to consult, leaving me simply unable at present to construct a comprehensive model of nineteenth-century (or earlier) Beng society with any great confidence. While I hope that further research will be able to expand the historical depth of my analysis to situate it in a longer temporal span, my analysis of descent in this work is based on the system as it exists today. I do, however, make extensive use of case histories in this chapter (as well as the next one) to give voice to individual agency in the construction of experience as it relates to structural expectations. In so doing, I hope to avoid at least somewhat the pitfalls of "committing the group noun ('The Nuer do this, the Nuer do that')," as Rosaldo (1990) has phrased our pernicious anthropological habit.

On a broader level, the approach I take here will join other recent efforts in approaching kinship from a vantage point that in effect significantly loosens the traditional boundaries of how we have defined *kinship*, to include considerations beyond the strictly legal or economic factors that dominated kinship theory in earlier eras. Rather than assuming a priori what the fundamental linchpin of a given kinship system is—be it a legal system of rights and duties, an economic system of property ownership, or some other single posited factor—the cultural perspective begins inductively by inquiring into the specific meanings that kinship relations hold for the participants in the system. In this way, it takes seriously the statements of the actors in the system, although it may certainly go beyond them in recognizing the potential difficulties inherent in this strategy: especially, the variability from informant to informant concerning the meaning or meanings of given practices and the inability to see beyond one's own system to a wider perspective.

In trying to find a middle ground between taking seriously my informants' own statements and views, on one hand, and stepping back from these to provide my own analysis grounded in anthropological theory, on the other, I have in good part been inspired by David Schneider's approach to kinship as an "idiom in terms of which the system is phrased" (1984:57), which led Schneider to analyze American kinship as a set of symbolic propositions that impart meaning to people's lives (1968). Later, Schneider (1984) used the same approach in reinterpreting from a cultural perspective his own earlier field data from Yap, which he had first analyzed in terms of a classic legalistic model of rights and duties. His restudy offers a rich analysis that allows the reader to understand Yap views of the world as they define family ties at a far more penetrating level than Schneider had done previously.

Schneider's approach has had a major impact on kinship studies, especially in American anthropology. For example, Schloss has stated by way of introducing his own cultural study of kinship among the Ehing of Senegal: "Symbolic anthropology can deal with problems in social structure in a manner that goes beyond the range of the classic approaches in African ethnography that are governed by a more narrowly social or legalistic perspective" (1988:11). Brenda Clay (1977) has also used a Schneiderian approach in examining the specific contours taken by the indigenous notions of "nurture" and "substance" through which the Mandak people of New Ireland define and understand family relations. In a similar vein, Witherspoon (1977:84–112) offers a symbolically informed analysis of what kin relations "mean" to individual Navajo. Barth has used a similar approach in analyzing the Baktaman of New Guinea, where, he writes, the notions of "descent" and "property" are irrelevant as isolated categories (1975:251). Instead, Barth tries to situate his analysis of family issues in wider contexts, including pig and wealth exchange, notions of sexuality and pollution, agricultural fertility, and notions of health (ibid.:252). His approach is especially welcome as it takes seriously the views of the participants in the system, who may not group the segments of their social life into the same conceptual categories with which Western anthropologists have long felt comfortable.

In the sections that follow, I will endeavor to treat Beng descent as an intellectual means of organizing the world. I will begin by inquiring how Beng view their own descent groups, stressing the symbolically important qualities that Beng themselves find most relevant in their clans. In effect my use of symbolic anthropology here will lead me to look at Beng thought and discussion about their own clans and lineages as constituting an indigenous theory of descent. Specifically, I will argue that the existence of two clan types—matriclans and patriclans—forms the basis of a philosophical system that allows Beng to experience two fundamentally different ways of understanding the world and constructing social life. At first glance, these two intellectual models appear mutually exclusive, if complementary, but a more penetrating look reveals that there is a complex overlap between them. In considering such issues from the perspective of my own brand of symbolic anthropology, it is my hope that the study of kinship can be reclaimed as the locus of culture, properly speaking (Schneider 1984).

BENG CLANS

The terms *identity* and *difference* that I have been using in this work are, as I mentioned in chapter 1, translations of phrases that Beng use in daily discourse: à sé do, which I have glossed as "identity," means literally "we are all one"; ā tɔtɔ, which I have glossed as "difference," means more exactly "we are different." Both phrases are heard frequently in Beng courtyards when the topic of conversation is descent. In my own conversations with Beng about their clans, à sé do was a phrase that they used when I asked them about the nature of membership in matriclans, while ā tɔtɔ was invoked in describing patriclans to me, in particular in referring to the differences between given patriclans. As this would imply, in Beng society the two types of clan, uterine and agnatic, are based on fundamentally different ideologies and play quite different roles. However, at certain critical points these associations become reversed, lending processual complexity to the configuration. In the remainder of this chapter, I will explore the richly embedded meanings of both these clan types.[1]

MATRICLANS

The Beng word that I have translated as "matriclan" is *wla*. Derived from the Baule language *(awlɔ)*, it means literally "house" in both languages. In fact, it is common for Africans throughout the continent to speak of "house" in referring to what anthropologists have commonly termed "clans" (Kuper 1988). In the Beng case, what can we learn from this metaphor?

"House" obviously stresses a physical referent, but it also alludes to those who inhabit it. Considering this, it is surprising that "house" should refer to matriclans in the Beng case, for the formal Beng residence rule is in fact for married couples to live patrilocally or at least virilocally. Such a rule should act to obviate the creation of a united uterine family. However, an ideal of matriclan endogamy, which we will explore more fully in the following chapter, serves de facto in many cases to create a matrilineally constituted household. While a bride indeed moves in with her husband, her new in-laws are often her uterine kin (in particular, her mother-in-law is often her mother's matrilateral parallel cousin—a woman the bride would address as "little [or senior] mother"). In practice, then, the household may have a very uterine feel to it despite the formal rule of patrilocality. I suggest that the Beng use of "house" to refer to the matriclan is a comment on such an ideal residential creation along matrilateral lines. More generally, "house" as a descriptor of matriclans evokes the feelings of warmth and security—and, conversely, frustration and even aggression—that emerge within a household. In this sense, "house" is an apt term for the matriclan indeed.[2]

The matriclan defines one's social and emotional identity to the point that fellow matriclan members in many senses are seen as mutually interchangeable. The focus is decidedly on shared identity within the matriclan. A given matriclan is structurally not much different from another. Primarily all the matriclans share the same basic attributes and privileges. These attributes testify to an inward focus that has the effect of creating a feeling of oneness between clan members.

To Radcliffe-Brown or Fortes, such a feeling of oneness should be apparent at the jural and behavioral levels, and indeed in the Beng case this is so. There are strict obligations circumscribing the behavior of matriclanmates in innumerable circumstances. Younger clan members owe older clan members absolute respect; this means, for example, that junior clan members must visit closely related matrikin when they are ill or otherwise in need of help, even if such visits are troublesome and financially onerous.

The Nephew and His Pregnant Aunt

In late September 1980, Kouadio's aunt, Au—the younger sister of his mother—was eight months pregnant. For reasons of her own, she decided to give birth in a hospital in Abidjan—235 miles and two long and expensive bus rides away—rather than in the village. Once she arrived in Abidjan, her lodging would be assured: she would stay with another sister who lived there. But reaching her sister's place might be difficult because she didn't know a word of French, and the ways of the city can be quite perplexing to such a villager.

Therefore, her nephew Kouadio, who did know French and was generally more accomplished in city ways, accompanied her, taking the two buses down to Abidjan with her and then escorting her to her sister's house. Then he returned to the village.

About a month later he heard the news that Au had given birth to twins, but that one of them had died. Kouadio wanted to go back to Abidjan immediately to pay his condolences to his aunt about the twin who had died, but he was short of cash for the expensive bus trips. He told me he would wait a few weeks until he sold his cocoa crop, which was ripening, and then use the money he earned from the sale as bus fare to Abidjan to go see his aunt. This is indeed what he did.

Not only do younger clan members go to visit their elders when the latter are in need, but juniors can be dispatched on endless errands by their clan elders and have no right even to complain, let alone refuse. Furthermore, when elders travel locally, they often demand that junior matriclan members accompany them. This is especially true of funerals in other villages, which have their own intense kinship demands attached to them, as the following case shows.

The Reluctant Mourner

One day in 1980, a man named Komena died in another village. The deceased had been Kwame's matrilateral parallel-cousin. Kwame, a man perhaps in his late fifties, went to the funeral along with his sister and one of his own daughters. But Kouassi, his sister's eldest son, didn't go along with them. A young man in his late twenties, Kouassi was ordinarily employed at the sugar factory some thirty miles up the road where he and his Beng wife were living. They had returned for a short period to the village during a layoff, and Kouassi had no intention of spending his time doing anything but sleeping late and carousing with his village buddies. Biking five miles to attend the funeral of an old man he barely knew was not part of his social agenda.

When Kwame returned from the funeral, he immediately came over to my husband's and my house, where I was sitting chatting with Kouassi. Kwame started insulting Kouassi for not having gone to the funeral.

"You're my sister's son," he said angrily, "and it's you who will inherit from me when I die."

Stretched out comfortably in a palm-rib lounge chair, Kouassi straightened up to listen attentively.

Kwame continued, "You should have gone to the funeral. . . . I'm the sub-chief of Denjuwla [their matriclan], and you're my heir. When Late Kona [the current chief of Denjuwla] dies, I'll inherit the chiefship. If I die, you'll be the chief."

Kouassi took the harangue with grace and said gravely, "I'm sorry, uncle. Please forgive me, I'm sorry." Even if he had no intention of attending the next funeral of a distant relative, he was clearly touched by the gist of the conversation.

Here, Kwame is invoking the entire span of matriclan obligations, all the way to inheritance of the chiefship, in order to impress on his nephew his clan duties. What makes the case even more interesting is that Kwame, in fact, is a rather obnoxious drunk whom no one respects; moreover, he doesn't live in the village in which his matriclan is localized. Considering both these factors, it is inconceivable that he would ever inherit his clan's chiefship, no matter how appropriate his genealogical situation might be (but even this latter is doubtful). Yet he perseveres in his own personal fantasy of clan glory in order to make his point to his maternal nephew concerning matriclan duties.

Another sign of matriclan exchangeability-as-solidarity is found in a related sort of visiting pattern. Not only do matriclan elders demand that younger clan members accompany them on their trips out of the village, but there are innumerable occasions on which one matrikinsperson may substitute for another. For example, if an elder is too tired or ill to attend a funeral of a clanmate in another village, he or she may send, say, a matrilaterally related niece, nephew, sibling, or younger cousin to stand in as a mourner. When I asked why this should be, Beng said simply of matriclan members, "We're the same" (ǎ sé do).[3]

Another funeral obligation may bring a different sort of matriclan substitution. When a parent dies, the oldest surviving son and daughter must contribute certain funeral gifts. But the direct lineal descendants are not necessarily singled out: whoever among their generation is oldest within the matriclan will actually provide the offerings. Again, one member effectively stands in for another by virtue of shared identity.

This principle is taken much further in fostering arrangements. Among the Beng, as among many African groups (e.g., M. Etienne 1979, E. Goody 1982), fosterage and adoption are frequently practiced. In the Beng case, it is most often within the matriclan that one finds foster arrangements, mostly between women and girls. Indeed, any woman has the right to raise any girl in her matriclan; and theoretically the mother does not have the right to refuse if approached. Here we see the fund of shared identity taken into the arena of deep and enduring personal ties, potentially restructuring the resident household, and the Beng version of the nuclear family.

The principle of identity is responsible for what might seem a curious fact: matrikin are rarely, if ever, friends (gwe). Beng told me repeatedly that it is impossible to be friends with those who are members of one's matriclan. I suggest that this is so because to be friends, there must be a bridging of a structural gap (Suttles 1970:97). But with matrikin, there is no gap, hence there can be no opening for friendship. As Warren Shapiro writes unequivocally in a general discussion of social ties: "[B]oth (total) estrangement and (total) identity are forms of non-relationship" (1988:291). Working on such a principle, Beng instead find their friends among members of their patriclans (for reasons we will soon explore), or they may become friends with people who are not members of either of their clans.

The internal focus of the matriclans is echoed in another, more literal sphere. Beng matriclans are quite unusual when compared with matriclans elsewhere in that they are ideally endogamous. As a result, the matriclans are de facto quite often localized, even though there is a formal postmarital residence rule of patrilocality. Indeed, Beng villages are divided into neighborhoods (tuwa) that are organized by reference to matriclans: they take their name from the matriclan that is dominant. While we will analyze the marriage system in the following chapter, suffice it to say here that the ideal of matriclan endogamy helps greatly to heighten the sense of identity that permeates matriclan relations.

Beng matriclans also conform to the jural model's definition of corporation insofar as the clans are internally organized, with both a male and female clan chief. The relationship of the members to the clan chief, in particular the male chief, involves absolute respect, as signaled by certain ritual requirements. For example, when male hunters kill large game—especially the larger varieties of duiker and antelope—they must always give one leg to the male matriclan chief. Moreover, fitting a further classic criterion of corporation, all the clan's adult members, even those emigrés living in towns and cities throughout Côte d'Ivoire, do endeavor to meet on the occasions of each other's weddings and funerals. In these ways, we can say, Beng matriclans meet the standards for corporation developed by Radcliffe-Brown and Fortes, and they exhibit the sorts of jural and behavioral norms we would expect of them.

Along the same lines, Beng matriclans also conform to Jack Goody's primary interest in descent structures: to Goody, the most obvious source of clan unity should certainly be at the economic level. In the Beng case, each matriclan indeed owns communal property: not land, however, but a clan treasure consisting of gold nuggets, ancient French coins, and a stool. The male or female chief is the custodian but not the owner of the treasures.

So far the sorts of considerations I have focused on have emphasized a jural level of analysis combined with behavioral repercussions, in keeping with the classic social anthropological model. But I now want to explore some further dimensions to descent as the Beng themselves perceive it—dimensions that take us beyond the purely legal and economic to more cultural considerations, properly speaking.

For example, in considering the matriclan's treasure just mentioned, we must acknowledge that the manner in which these resources are defined is far more than merely economic. Goody's work can be a starting point for analysis, but more can be ascertained about the local understandings of clanship if the subject is pursued at deeper levels. Thus in the Beng case there are deep moral underpinnings even to what appears to be the most purely monetary component of the clan property—the gold—revealing a feeling of symbolic "substance" as well as finances as shared by clan members (for a similar argument as regards New Guinean clans, see Harrison 1989).[4]

The large sum of gold that is kept as part of the clan's treasure (*koye*) is stowed in a secret hiding place by a clan elder. This elder does not have the right to sell the gold for private use, though in unusual circumstances, all the elders of the clan—male and female—might gather and decide as a group to sell a portion of the gold for some collective endeavor (such as paying off the debt of a matriclan member who died; most often, this would be a debt of animals owed to the Earth for a promised sacrifice). Any decision to sell even the tiniest portion of the treasure must be made in a meeting of all the clan's male and female elders during which full consensus must be reached. In this way, ownership of gold serves as a symbol of moral commitment to the matriclan.

The seriousness with which this commitment is taken is revealed when we investigate the consequences of violating the rule of collective ownership:

The Case of the Sold Gold

A few years ago Amwe, the female chief of her matriclan, was feeling pressed for cash. A year-long drought in the region had totally depleted her financial resources. In what must have been a moment of desperation, Amwe decided to sell for her own profit some of her clan's gold, which she was guarding. She took some nuggets to a neighboring village, where she sold them to a trader who happened to be an affinal relative of hers. A member of another ethnic group, this man had no suspicion that the gold he was buying was being sold illicitly.

Early the next day, people came to say good morning to Amwe, and they found her dead. A diviner interpreted the death as just punishment for Amwe's sin. The villagers all agreed.

As this case illustrates, putting one's own needs above those of the clan may in some circumstances result in instant death.

If some of the clan gold should be stolen by an outsider or by a clan member, it is said that some members of the matriclan would die as well. Here we see further the principle of mutual exchangeability at work: any one member of the clan can serve as an apt representative of the entire group; all are considered equally responsible for the safekeeping of the shared property. In other words, there is not only a jural norm operating that proscribes selling off of the matriclan's property but also a deep acceptance that the moral underpinnings to that norm are universally and equally shared by all matriclan members.

In another case, this exchangeability of matrikin as based on shared moral responsibility took a particularly tragic turn.

The Case of the Stolen Gold

King Bonde Como also happened to be the guardian of his matriclan's gold. On his recent death it was discovered that one gold nugget was missing from the clan's treasury. The diviner who was consulted about the death declared that the gold had been stolen, and that it was this that had killed the king. In other words, the treasure's guardian, even more than the other clan members, was held especially responsible for the safekeeping of the gold. As it happened, the thief, who was also a clan member, fell sick and confessed to the deed. Thus criminal and victim, both clan members, were punished in this case.

The discussion now shades from shared morality to shared substance as envisioned in ways that Western anthropologists would probably term mystical but that the Beng find quite empirical. For the identity that Beng feel unites them to matriclan members is visualized in other ways that they see as penetrating to the very constitution of their personhood.

All Beng have a "soul" (neneŋ). Present at conception, the soul is said to be transmitted matrilineally; at death, it goes to some unknown spot. In early anthropological works on kinship, such a fact would hardly have been interpreted as a sign of corporation, as mystical "properties" such as souls would have been seen as far too slippery to be considered a legitimate indicator of social groups. Perhaps Jack Goody might have relegated them to a residual category, as he did with "complementary filiation" (1959). But following the Beng, I take the emphasis on such shared souls quite seriously. For the soul is said to be essential to the maintenance of life. If it is stolen through witchcraft (see Gottlieb 1989), the victim will soon die at least a mental if not a bodily death, for a sane or physically healthy life is literally impossible without a spiritual foundation, as the case of Komena shows.

The Liana and the Soul

One day, Yao and his friend Komena were walking on a path through the forest to go work in their fields. Komena was walking ahead of Yao. Suddenly he stopped; the way was barred. Across his path was a liana, tied to two trees on either side of the path. Recognizing this as a significant sign—of something—the two young men returned anxiously to the village and went to consult a diviner about the incident. The diviner confirmed their worst fear: the liana had been put there by a witch. Into the knotted liana she had tied up Komena's soul, which she had stolen.

Yao, who recounted this story to me, told me that soon after hearing the diviner's proclamation, Komena went mad. He left the village and began living in the bush, roaming from place to place. That was years ago. Today he is considered by everyone to be a madman, and has remained a wanderer in the forest.

The drastic consequences of the soul's alienation reveal its centrality to a socially intact life. That the soul emerges from the matriclan is a powerful indicator of the mystical "substance" shared by clan members.

While the soul might be an abstract entity for Westerners, another source of shared identity as posited by the Beng is more tangible: breast milk. Here, what is mystical for the Western observer is not the object itself, which is empirical enough, but the way it is perceived. While Westerners conceive of breast milk as a substance that is shared privately by two people—nursing mother and baby—the Beng see it quite differently: as a fluid whose ramifications extend far beyond the mother-child tie, to encompass the entire membership of a given matriclan. Indeed, the bodily substance is spoken of as if it were literally shared by all matriclan members. We might say that the image of shared nursing becomes a metaphor for shared mystical substance, though the Beng, of course, would put it quite differently. For them, the image of shared breast milk is experienced in a way that may be intellectually comprehensible for the Westerner but poses a challenge to understand at a more intuitive level—that level of experience that translates an abstract proposition to an experienced sense of biological reality. Here, for instance, is an example of how the image was evoked in a discussion we have already encountered between a maternal uncle and his delinquent nephew.

The Reluctant Mourner, Revisited

In the middle of his harangue to his nephew about having boycotted his cousin's funeral, Kwame explained to Kouassi why the latter's failure to attend the funeral hurt him so much. Kwame said, "Komena [the relative who had just died] and I, we nursed the same milk, and this was an important person whose funeral just had to be attended."

Here we see Kwame adding a symbolic component to the argument, which was otherwise purely jural. While Kwame's phrasing might be said to be an idiom for discussing sociological identity, his mode of expression must be taken seriously. Recall that Kwame was, as anthropologists would put it, the dead man's matrilateral parallel-cousin. Yet by stating that they "nursed the same milk," defining the relationship quite differently from the dry kinship terminology I have just hauled out, Kwame is revealing the intimate level of personhood at which he is defining his relationship to a fellow matriclan member. Considering that the two men's mothers were sisters who presumably did (in the Western view) "nurse the same milk," Kwame may be making a statement of connection back to their shared maternal grandmother, in a fashion similar to the way Luapula people, in discussing clan history, recount the deeds of their distant ancestors in the first person singular (Cunnison 1956). What is a quaint metaphor for us is taken for granted as reality for the Luapula, as it is for Kwame. The maternal connection Kwame emphasized via breast milk is supported in another Beng locution: relatives who are members of one's matriclan are referred to as *da lɛŋ*, which translates as "children of [one] mother."

My argument is that the Beng understanding of biological relatedness needs to be taken seriously if we are to comprehend how the Beng themselves define kinship. As Evens (1989) has suggested for the Nuer, the boundaries of where consanguinity ends and other categories, such as affinity, begin may be astonishingly variable. In the Beng case, breast milk is a means—both biological and richly symbolic—of indicating just where and how such ties are defined and given credence.

There are further methods defying Western models of genetics that are meaningful to the Beng in defining kinship relations. A seemingly more trivial instance of a bodily property that is said to be shared by matriclan members is body odor. Not all people have body odor, but those who do are said almost always to have inherited it matrilaterally.[5] Considering the intimate nature of body odor, its apparent triviality belies a deeper sense of shared identity, an identity that gives yet another sensory cast to the body of the individual as defined by the social group.

In considering the two shared substances of breast milk and body odor, what strikes me is the penetrating manner in which one's personal bodily experience is being defined by the group. Of late, much anthropological work has been done on a variety of topics concerning the body, all pointing in the direction of the social definition of bodily substances and experiences such as pregnancy, childbirth, menstruation, blood loss, semen production, and others (e.g., Buckley and Gott-lieb, eds. 1988, Feher et al., eds. 1989, Laqueur 1986, Martin 1987). The positing of shared breast milk and shared body odor constitutes two further means through which the body can be thoroughly socially constituted in a particular direction: via matrikin. It is significant, then, that among the Beng, there are no analogues of such bodily substances being shared by patrikin.

A final bodily component that the Beng say people of a matriclan share is blood. Here their meaning may approximate that of Western notions of "blood" as an idiom denoting deep moral ties (Schneider 1968). But whereas "blood ties" in the West are cognatic, for the Beng such ties are exclusively matrilineal.

Ironically, there may be tragic consequences of the sense of shared identity that exists within the matriclan. If one has committed a sin against the Earth—which, as we have seen in the previous chapter, is the focus of Beng worship and the locus of its major deities—the Earth may punish either the wrongdoer, *or any of his or her matriclan*. This is so with other offenses not related to the Earth as well. For instance, if a newborn is born with teeth or if an infant cuts his or her upper teeth first, the baby should be killed. If it is not, then someone in the child's matriclan will die. Crimes are punished in the same manner. Thus a Beng proverb states, "A thief doesn't die, his matrikin die" *(krãnli, a gàɛ, a dī nã gaɛ̀)*. My field notebooks are replete with examples of such matrilineal substitutions. They attest not only to the jural level of mutual obligation and responsibility, but also to the level of personal involvement and experienced reality of shared morality felt by matrikin.

Slaves and Clans
The relative stress on personal identity created by the two clan types is underscored when we consider slavery. All Beng clans have at least two lineages: one whose female members were all "free" *(wla nŏ:* "belly of the matriclan"), and one or more lineages that were founded by a female slave ancestor *(wla gbadiŋ:* "off to the side of the matriclan"). It is unclear to me how long slaves have been integrated into Beng society. One Beng consulted could not imagine a time when slaves were absent, but I was unable to confirm this with others, as the topic was simply too touchy. What is clear is that about a century ago, there was a large influx of slaves into the Beng territory from two aggressors, one African, the other European.

Judging from oral testimony offered to me, the African aggressor, Samori, was probably responsible for a greater proportion of the influx of slaves into Bengland. The slaves were all members of a neighboring ethnic group, the Jimini (a subgroup of the Senufo). These people were refugees from raids on their villages perpetrated by soldiers loyal to the Guinean Muslim empire builder, Samori (Binger 1895a, 1895b; Marchand 1894; Monteil 1895; Nebout 1895a, 1895b; Person 1975: 1588).

The other cause for the relatively recent influx of slaves was the onset of French colonialism. For the Beng, as for many African groups, one of the most onerous duties imposed on them by the colonial French regime was the obligation to pay taxes to support the colonial system. As this could only be paid in French francs, and as francs could only be obtained by rural villagers through selling crops designated by the French as cash crops, all adults became dependent on a decent harvest in order to have a saleable crop. A bad year—from drought, insects, illness, and so on—might force some to drastic measures, and this is indeed what happened: some farmers sold their junior relatives—children, nieces, nephews—as slaves to neighboring groups that were faring better, for cash with which to pay the family's tax. In other cases, individuals sold themselves as slaves to others, so that the new slave owner would be responsible for paying the tax on them. In either case, the Beng profited from these acts of desperation, buying some Jimini as slaves and even some Beng who sold themselves (or their junior kin) as slaves to other Beng. Both Beng men and women might be slave owners (cf. Robertson and Klein 1983).

As with slaves elsewhere, the life of a Beng slave was, predictably, difficult. Every day, slaves worked in the fields for their owners. The dullest or most demanding jobs were invariably assigned to them. For instance, it was their responsibility to survey the crops (especially the yams) that had begun to grow or were already ripe, to protect them against crop predators. Acting in effect as human insecticides, they spent ten-hour days for weeks on end chasing marauding insects (as well as birds and small animals); for this they were called "yam field protectors" (sɔ́ŋ lo dwāli). In general, a wealthy slaveowner—wealth here being measured in the number of slaves owned—did not have much work to do. He or she simply sent the slaves and their children into the fields to work; occasionally the owner came by and yelled at the slaves if they were not working hard enough.

The following case reveals how the traditional field travails of a slave were combined with further burdens with the onset of colonial rule.

A Former Slave's Memories

Kouassi was one of the oldest men in Bengland, and I was eager to hear his reports about earlier Beng cultural practices from him. But to my great disappointment, he said that he didn't know the answers to many of my questions because when he was young, instead of listening to the elders talk, he was obliged to go to the fields to chase the red monkeys who came to eat the yams. So he was never really given the time to sit and learn esoteric Beng customs and history. At the time, I wasn't aware that Kouassi had been bought as a Jimini slave, and he didn't offer me the information. Only later, when someone else whispered his background to me, did his odd story become comprehensible.

Kouassi told me that he was born before the French had come to Bengland [in the 1880s]. Because of the French colonial presence, Kouassi spent six of his early married years out of the village in colonial towns: two years in Dabakala, three years in M'Bahiakro, and one year in Dabou. While living in Dabakala, which was the sous-préfecture of the region, Kouassi was a messenger to the Beng area. He was chosen by his villagers for this role precisely because he was a slave: when the French demanded someone for this position, the Beng considered a slave an obvious choice for what they saw as a demeaning and exhausting position. Indeed, the job demanded tremendous physical stamina. Whenever the French colonial officers in Dabakala wanted food (tribute?) from the Beng area, they sent Kouassi, who walked the ninety miles to Bengland to fetch it, then walked back to Dabakala, carrying the heavy load.

Kouassi recalled that he had completed each portion of the trip in a mere two days. Assuming a fifteen-minute mile and only an hour and three-quarters to eat and rest, this would put him walking about thirteen hours a day on the trip to Bengland. Further assuming a very heavy load on the way back—perhaps up to a hundred pounds—and assuming this might slow him down to a twenty-minute mile (and granting him two hours of resting and eating time), this would have him walking seventeen hours a day back to Dabakala to make it there in two days. Even if Kouassi's memory has slipped and he took three days to complete at least the return trip, it was clearly a physically—and no doubt emotionally—grueling assignment.

Not only did slaves do a far greater proportion of labor, but they were also prohibited from holding political offices: anyone with a female matrilineal slave ancestor could not become a full village or clan chief or the regional king or queen.

Considering these economic burdens and political exclusions that distinguished slaves from other Beng, it is all the more striking that in other ways, slaves were deeply integrated into Beng social life, and especially into their adoptive matriclans. Indeed, the Jimini slaves were in many ways almost fully adopted into the matriclan, although they founded separate lineages for their descendants.

A clear sign of this emerges at marriage. There is no taboo against marriage between slaves and other Beng. Indeed, Beng told me that in the last decade of the nineteenth century, when slaves were taken in by the Beng in great quantity, most slaves were given nonslave spouses from their adoptive matriclan, in the same way that nonslaves are often married endogamously (see chapter 4). Of course the gift of a spouse is the most valuable gift that one can bestow in virtually any African society, so this act in the case of slaveowners demonstrates the extent to which the slaves were structurally integrated into their matriclans.

Furthermore, slaves are said to share "blood" with their matriclanmates. When I asked a Beng woman how this could be, since a slave lineage would have been founded by a female slave and "blood" is said to be transmitted matrilaterally, she was not at all perturbed by the seeming discrepancy. In trying to find an answer suitable to my own system of logic, encased as it was in a Western model of genetics, she speculated that the "blood" would have started out in the nonslave lineage of the matriclan and was somehow transferred to the slave lineage. On another occasion, she said that all the "blood" in the matriclan originates from the "free" lineage because "the money to buy the slaves with came from the clan." Thus even if two slaves, or their uterine descendants, were to marry one another, their children would inherit blood from the free lineage. Whatever the purported mechanism for the transfer of blood from one lineage to another, it is clear that the deeply shared mystical substance that constitutes "blood" is crucial as a locally meaningful symbol through which matriclan identity can be defined.

A further instance of slaves sharing in matriclan identity concerns the sorts of substitutions I discussed earlier. As I mentioned, if one has committed a sin against the Earth, the Earth often punishes someone else in the transgressor's matriclan. But here I note that in such a case, the victim would not have to be in the sinner's lineage: a slave clanmate might be punished for a nonslave's sin or vice versa. Here again we see the extent to which slaves, while put in their own lineages, nevertheless participate deeply in matriclan identity.

Finally, by the third generation, slave ancestry is in one sense effectively dissolved. At this stage, other matriclan members may no longer oblige the slave descendants to work for them.

In contrast to all this, a slave was barely integrated into the owner's patriclan.

For example, slaves (and their agnatic descendants) do not observe their masters' patriclan food taboos. Moreover, at their funerals, Jimini dances are danced as a sign of their Jimini origins. This is a powerful symbolic statement differentiating the slaves from their owners' patriclans—for, as we shall see, the patriclan would normally dominate the funeral with its own symbols, such as cadaver-washing leaves.

In considering all these factors, the centrality of matriclans in defining one's identity is highlighted. To be a lone individual in the Beng world without identity with matriclan members is unthinkable. On the other hand, patriclan membership is certainly important, but it is ultimately secondary. While rare, it is possible to define oneself as a Beng and yet have no patriclan. For the Beng, such is not true of the matriclan.

Witchcraft
So far I have focused on the sense of identity that pervades matriclan relations. Yet while identity is an explicit focus of the matriclan, it is not the exclusive one. For part and parcel with the sense of identity is a good deal of internal competition, a competition born of identity. Such competition is generally played out not in the economic but in the religious realm.[6] As we saw in the preceding chapter, if the Beng are known at all in Côte d'Ivoire, it is generally for their religious activities, which have given them a somewhat formidable reputation. But this is due not only to their powerful Earths but also to their reputed skills at witchcraft. Here, for instance, are the impressions that a hotel owner in the distant city of Bouake (about seventy miles from Bengland) offered me concerning my village hosts:

> They can burn down another village purely by witchcraft. They can overturn a car purely by witchcraft. Once, a Jula man driving a car passed by a man who was hitchhiking. About two miles ahead, the car overturned, though the driver wasn't hurt. The car was bewitched by the angry hitchhiker, who was Beng.

In effect this story is part of the repertoire of urban folklore that classifies members of the sixty-odd ethnic groups in Côte d'Ivoire according to assorted stereotypes. In the Beng case, the stereotypes all tend in the direction of occult powers. My husband and I were treated with some awe by this particular storyteller, as he assumed that we ourselves must be powerful witches to withstand the attempted acts of witchcraft that he assumed must be directed our way regularly in the Beng villages.

Beng themselves usually deny such stories because they claim that their powers cannot operate outside the ethnic group, and within that are even more confined: to one's matriclan.[7] This is because all the witches of a given matriclan are said to be "in harmony" with one another over their work—another, more malevolent, form of identity. As such, they are said to "own" the right to bewitch their fellow matrikin.[8] When they successfully bewitch someone the witches of a matriclan are said to share the "meat" of the victim, in a sinister variation of the custom of hunters sharing their game with certain matriclan members (especially the clan chief, as we have seen). Should a witch harbor designs against someone from another matriclan, she or he would need to secure the permission of that clan's witches to kill the designated victim. But this is unlikely because, given the sense of identity that holds sway among witches of each matriclan, the witches are reluctant to share their "meat" with an outsider at their collective feasts. Should an outsider witch try to buck the system and endeavor to bewitch someone in another matriclan, the witches of the would-be victim's clan would use their mystical powers to protect the intended victim.

As for the exact relationship between witch and victim, a favorite line of inquiry in the classic anthropological accounts, this is quite irrelevant in the Beng context. It does not matter exactly how the witch and his or her victim are related, with regard to gender or exact genealogical relationship. What is crucial in Beng eyes is merely that the witch and his or her victim belong to the same matriclan. Beyond that, common clan identity is sufficient to define the scope of witchcraft activity.[9]

For women, a common, particularly tragic occasion for being bewitched is during childbirth.

The Tragic Case of Ajuakro

Ajuakro had a difficult labor during her first childbirth. She was taken to the dispensary in Prikro, about twenty-five miles away, where she had a cesarean delivery. Then she and the baby were taken down to M'Bahiakro. But as soon as she returned to the village, the baby died. It was surmised that all this might have been the result of witchcraft aimed at her by her elder sister, Ajuakala.

For her second delivery, there was no doubt in anyone's mind that Ajuakala had bewitched her. The day Ajuakro left the village to go down to M'Bahiakro to deliver the baby in the dispensary, her maternal grandmother wept. Ajuakala told her not to cry, but in comforting her, she said something bizarre: "If Ajuakro dies in M'Bahiakro, I'll return to announce her funeral." And indeed, this is what came to pass.

The delivery was a little difficult, and Ajuakro's father, a Master of the Earth who had come along, prayed to the Earth for his daughter. Then the doctor performed a cesarean operation and the baby, a girl, was born. But Ajuakro herself was unconscious, and the baby had to be nursed by Ajuakro's cousin, who was also there.

Ajuakro came to, and over the next five days, she and the baby seemed to be in perfect health. But they planned to stay in the hospital a while longer, so Ajuakro's father went up to the village to bring down some yams for them to cook over the next week or so. That evening, Ajuakro suddenly developed diarrhea, and in a little while she died.

Normally, when a Beng person dies in the M'Bahiakro hospital, the Beng nurse who works there tells the *sous-préfet* of the town about the death, then he sends the nurse (or another Beng government official) up to the village of the dead person to announce the funeral. But in this case, as soon as Ajuakala found out about her sister's death, she herself went up to her village to announce the news. This was considered highly inappropriate, and was taken as further proof that it was she who had bewitched her younger sister.

Another of Ajuakro's sisters adopted the surviving baby and is now raising her as her own.

The ability to conduct witchcraft may occasionally be purchased, but it is more likely to be inherited. In the latter case, it is transmitted exclusively through the matriline. However, the commonest method for acquiring witchcraft skills is from a teacher, who is always a close uterine relative, generally one's mother (or sometimes one's maternal grandmother). Hence the circle completes itself: witchcraft is created, operates, and kills within the confines of the matriclan.

In a sense the matriclan is a microcosm. It contains the ultimate sense of closeness, including the possibility of hostility and aggression, which derive from that very closeness. It is a self-enclosed system. While the explicit focus of the matriclan is identity, that very identity creates the ultimate form of difference—annihilation (by witchcraft) of the Other, an Other who, ironically, is defined in this case as the Self.

PATRICLANS

Compared to matriclans, Beng patriclans are far less a source for the emotional definition of the individual. Instead, when one considers the patriclans in their totality, one is struck mostly by how different the clans are in relation to each other. While Beng describe matriclans by referring to the members of a single matriclan and commenting about it, à sé do ("we're all one"), they describe patriclans by referring to the ensemble of clans and commenting, à tɔtɔ ("we're different"). Thus they themselves shift the level of discourse in changing orientations.

The very term used to identify patriclans reveals a stress on the distinctions between patriclans to which the phrase à tɔtɔ alludes. The Beng word I have translated as "patriclan" is síá. This word, borrowed from Jula, means in both languages "type" or "kind"; in other contexts it refers to "species."[10] All these meanings emphasize difference, the theme that will guide my initial discussion of patriclans.

The differences between patriclans are apparent in arenas that once might have been considered relatively insignificant but that, following the Beng lead, I view as critical to an understanding of the patriclans. I have in mind several forms of what might be termed mystical property, inasmuch as they have no direct economic value. Indeed, the only sorts of property that patriclans transmit are mystical or invisible items: ritual goods and shared personal characteristics that serve to distinguish each patriclan and its members from the next in symbolically interesting fashion.[11] The latter include food taboos, the right to use particular herbs with which to wash deceased clan members' cadavers, a place to bury the clan's corpses, and either an "innate" predisposition for a particular body of knowledge or an "innate" tendency toward a certain type of personality.

When asked what members inherit from their patriclans, the first answer that generally came to an informant's mind was "food taboos" (só pɔ). Throughout my field research I tried to obtain "deep"—i.e., totemic—reasons for these food taboos, but often I met with no success. Instead, there seems to be one reason why specific foods are generally said to be taboo to patriclan members: the clan's founder ate the food, got a stomach ache, realized it did not agree with him, and told his children that henceforth they and their agnatic descendants should never eat that food because it would not agree with them either; should they eat the taboo food, they would die. This is the sort of answer that demonstrates pointedly how culturally defined is the presumption of "practical reason" (Sahlins 1976)—for example, Westerners who find that they get stomach upsets from eating certain foods do not instruct their agnatic relatives to refrain forever from eating those foods. Indeed, the Western anthropological response to the Beng invoked explanation for clan food taboos would likely be to dismiss it as irrelevant in favor of an assertion that the patriclan food taboos are simply arbitrary.[12]

It is possible that one day I will uncover other meaningful relations between taboos and clan history for the remaining patriclans. But illuminating though they might be, I suspect such associations would not be crucial for understanding Beng patriclans. It seems that what is crucial is the simple fact that Beng differentiate themselves on the basis of patriclans and particularly the food taboos that go with those clans.[13] Thus although technically not all the Beng patriclans could be called totemic, the logic behind them is very much in keeping with the Lévi-Straussian model, which sees totems as a forceful way of metaphorically differentiating clans, much as animals are segmented into species (Lévi-Strauss 1963e).

Alongside the food taboos are rules concerning what to do if the taboos are broken. Each patriclan has rights to a particular type of medicine with which to treat a taboo violator. The following story illustrates the way that clan food taboos are internalized even by a villager who lives in a wholly non-Beng setting in the city.

Akissi and the Snails

Several years ago, Akissi was being educated as a student by some French teachers in a large city in Côte d'Ivoire. She lived in a dorm with other Ivoirian students where they ate food prepared for them by the school chefs. Often the students didn't have much idea of exactly what they were eating.

One day Akissi found herself violently ill. She was taken by her teachers to some doctors in the city, but the impressive range of pills and shots they gave her had no effect. Finally her teachers counseled her to return to her village to be treated by a local healer.

Akissi returned to her village, where a diviner revealed that she had eaten snails, the taboo food of her patriclan. The only thing that would cure her, he said, would be for her to consult the chief of her patriclan. Only he could administer the herbal remedy and conduct the necessary ritual that is required of her clan's members when, knowingly or not, they eat their taboo food. Akissi did so, and she recovered in a few days.

This case has several interesting features. First, at the time of her illness in the city, Akissi had not ascribed a link between her recent diet and the violation of her patriclan food taboos. Indeed, she told me that before she had returned to Bengland for treatment she had not realized she had eaten snails and would not have knowingly done so. In the future, she said, she became more careful about the stews served to her at school. With the failure of Western medicines, it was reasonable for Akissi to return to her natal village, where she could hopefully be correctly diagnosed and treated by those who were familiar with the sorts of disease to which she, as a Beng, might be especially vulnerable. By returning to the village, she was making a statement about the culturally constructed nature of disease, and about the relevance of faith in doctors of one's own cultural tradition to deal with bodily afflictions. The diviner's pronouncement, among other things, served as an assertion that though Akissi might be living far away—in a large city surrounded and being schooled by white people—her body was still subject to diseases whose contours are defined by her home culture. Distance does not attenuate the strong claims that the patriclan makes on its members' bodies. And in telling me the story, Akissi averred—to me and to herself—the reality of the taboos and their automatic action on the violating clan member's body, whether or not the violation is willful.

In Akissi's case, the diviner she consulted was not able to prescribe or administer the proper herbal remedies for a particular reason: he was not a member of Akissi's patriclan; the medicines for counteracting broken food taboos are considered clan secrets, never to be divulged to nonclan members. I was able to find out the medicines of only two patriclans; members of other patriclans feared that I might tell the names of the secret medicines to nonclan members and thus dissolve one major means of differentiating patriclans from each other. As with many other West African societies, Mande (e.g., McNaughton 1982) and otherwise (e.g., Bellman 1984), knowledge is viewed as a form of power, and this helps account for the secrecy surrounding the patriclan medicines (Gottlieb 1990b). Moreover, this obligatory secrecy helps to differentiate the patriclans from one another by ensuring a discrete corpus of knowledge and insisting on a certain mental discipline in all members—and faith that they will do so—to maintain that discrete body of knowledge.

Another aspect of the food taboos concerns their scope. Because of patrilocal postmarital residence, the individual household is constituted patrilaterally. In the old days the Beng lived in large round houses (figure 2; for a photo, see Loucou 1984:74) and it was an extended patrilocal family that inhabited the dwelling. Nowadays, for reasons we will consider in chapter 6, this group tends to live in separate houses grouped around a common courtyard. The unity of the household is emphasized symbolically by a shared food taboo. For not only do the male residents—by definition, members of the same patriclan—share their clan's taboos, but all their in-married, premenopausal wives must also observe their husbands' patriclan taboos. The reason given is that as nursing mothers, their babies must not ingest their fathers' taboo foods through the breast milk. Beng say that should a nursing mother eat her husband's taboo food, the baby will develop cuts, sores, or pimples in the mouth. Considering in-married wives' adherence to their husbands' taboos, then, almost all the residents under one roof observe the same taboos.[14] This certainly reinforces the solidarity of the coresidential group, but it also serves to differentiate it qualitatively from its neighbors, who observe different food taboos. The extent to which this symbolic differentiation of houses permeates individual consciousness is evident in speech: in referring to a particular house or household, Beng say, "This is a Kri house" or "That is a Bola house," where "Kri"

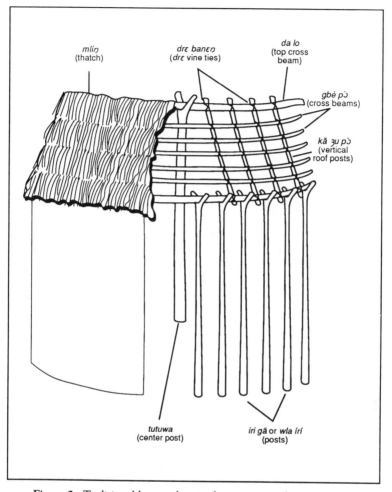

mlíŋ
(thatch)

drɛ banɛŋ
(*drɛ* vine ties)

da lo
(top cross
beam)

gbé pɔ
(cross beams)

kā ʒu pɔ
(vertical
roof posts)

tutuwa
(center post)

iri gā or *wla írí*
(posts)

Figure 2. Traditional house, showing basic aspects of construction.

and "Bola" are the names of particular patriclans. In this way, each house is "named" by reference to its predominant patriclan.

Another type of secret knowledge exclusive to the patriclans is a monopoly on specific leaves used for washing cadavers. When anyone dies, his or her patrikin take over the immediate burdens of preparing the cadaver. Beng stressed that if after death one is not washed with one's own patriclan leaves, then one's spirit (*wrú*) will not be able to proceed to the afterlife. Inasmuch as the identity of these funeral plants is kept strictly secret, knowledge of clan corpse-washing leaves constitutes a further basis for distinguishing patriclans from one another. As Simmel has aptly observed, "The secret contains a tension that is dissolved in the moment of its revelation" (1950:333).

Not only is the treatment of the corpse effected by patrikin, but the patriclan also determines the final placing of the cadaver: the location of the tomb varies according to patriclan membership.[15] The burial spots themselves are varied: some are in the village, some in the forest, some along the village-forest boundary. Again, this spatial variation points up fundamental distinctions that are created and upheld by the patriclans.

Furthermore, each patriclan owns the right to certain items that are viewed as crucial to the funerals of clan members. These range from the cloth in which the cadaver will be buried to the color of the chicken that will be sacrificed. The fact that the ritual objects used in funerals vary in these ways from patriclan to patriclan additionally helps to distinguish the clans by creating richly developed public symbols of paradigmatic differences between them.

A more sociological source of difference between patriclans concerns marriage patterns. Unlike the matriclans, Beng patriclans are exogamous. While this rule is now occasionally being violated, elders assert that it was enforced rigorously until recently. With exogamy comes the requirement to ally with another clan. Such an alliance can exist only to the extent that a substantive difference is acknowledged to first exist between the allied clans. Exogamy further reinforces an external focus, in contrast to the matriclans, whose endogamous ideal creates an internal focus.

Any potential emphasis on feelings of clan unity is further undercut by the dispersal of patriclan members, many of whom rarely see one another or may not even recognize other distant clan members as such. For despite a residence rule of postmarital patrilocality, the patriclans are not systematically localized. This is so for two reasons. First, when an extended family begins to outgrow its house, one or more married sons will move out to build their own house. If there are no schisms within the household, the new house may be located adjacent to the older one, or at least in the same *quartier*. But a number of factors may act to pull the married sons away from the father and to another *quartier* in the village (or occasionally even to another village). This might happen if a son had a serious dispute with someone in the household; if he generally felt closer to his maternal relatives in another *quartier*; if he had recently inherited a distant plantation—of coffee trees, palm wine trees, or, in the old days, kola trees—from a maternal uncle (or other matrilineal relative) and wished to move closer to that piece of land; or because of a combination of these factors. The above factors, when combined with the preferred practice of matriclan endogamy (which we will explore in the following chapter), mean de facto that it is matriclan rather than patriclan members who more often reside in the same quarter (cf. Şaul 1989:62). As a result of all these factors, members of a given patriclan tend to find themselves scattered throughout the Beng region in a more thoroughgoing manner than do members of a given matriclan. Such dispersal drastically undermines any potential feelings of solidarity among patriclan members.

The symbolic sources of difference that distinguish patriclans from each other are responsible for another social relationship: one's friends are generally one's patrikin (or they might be nonrelated people). This is so, I have suggested, because to be friends there must be a social distance that is then bridged by the friendship. Such social "bridging" is impossible within matriclans, as we have seen, but by contrast it is eminently possible within patriclans.

Furthermore, certain pairs of patriclans are linked as ritual joking partners.[16] Members of these clans may insult one another with impunity any time they happen to meet. I suggest that such joking is a sign of distance in much the same way as friendship is: both joking and friendship create bonds between people who are first separated by culture.

I view a related role of the patriclans along the same lines. Members of patriclans may serve as mediators in disputes in which a fellow clan member is involved. Again as with friendship, the clan member is engaged in bridging a structural gap: in this case, a veritable social rupture. I suggest that it is appropriate for patriclans to be assigned both these roles, as the nature of patriclans is to highlight difference. Matriclans ignore difference, and so it would be inappropriate for them to be involved in patching up particular differences (whether through humor or dispute mediation).

Finally, membership in a patriclan is contingent while membership in a matriclan is a given. One's genetrix always determines the identity of one's matriclan. By contrast, one's genitor usually does determine one's patriclan affiliation, but this is not inevitable. The genitor in effect must earn the right to pass on membership in his patriclan by helping to support and rear his children. In case of divorce by a couple with young children, if the mother remarries a man who fully raises and feeds his stepchildren, then the children become members of their stepfather's patriclan and will adopt that clan's food taboos. In considering this, we see how membership in the patriclan, with its switchable nature, is a shallower affair than is matriclan membership, which is defined as immutable.

The psychological ramifications of the natures of the two clan types as I have considered them so far might be summed up by the following statement by a Beng elder concerning how individuals experience clan relationships:

> People are insulted easily by their matrikin but not by their patrikin. . . . Relationships among patriclan members are sweeter than those among matriclan members [*de lɛŋ e nene da lɛŋ ni mà*]. It has always been like this!

But I do not want to draw too stark a sketch of the patriclans by overly focusing on the binary system that I have so far implied, which associates identity exclusively with the matriclans and difference with the patriclans. Just as we saw hints of difference contained within the matriclans—in the practice of witchcraft—so too there are several important respects in which a potentially significant feeling of unity should be created among members of a given patriclan, despite the substantive, symbolically resonant differences between patriclans that Beng themselves tend to focus on when they consider patriclans. While interclan difference is indeed the most pronounced mode of defining Beng patriclans, nevertheless there are rays of intraclan identity that shine through and cannot be neglected.

For instance, all patrikin are said to be born with an inherited predisposition for a certain talent or personality type. The members of one clan, for example, are said to be cowardly (see note 12). Two additional clans have special privileges and ritual roles not available to other clans. Members of these two clans are also aligned as each other's joking partners. One of these clans, Bolalɛŋ, tends to produce healers.[17] Their members also have a monopoly on a certain medicine that is said to make them fearless and so they are responsible for cutting down hanged suicides found anywhere in the Beng region. Members of another clan, Krilɛŋ, are said to be the royalty of the Beng and as such have several privileges and responsibilities. Although neither kings and queens nor village chiefs (male and female) need be members of this clan, the king does choose the female leader of the patriclan Krilɛŋ when its reigning leader dies. If the clan goes without its female leader the situation may cause a drought for all Bengland. This is because of the special relationship that Krilɛŋ holds to the Sky, from which this clan's members are said to be descended, and which is of course responsible for rain. This relationship accounts for the fact that the leaders of Krilɛŋ are the rainmakers for all Bengland and as such are called on to produce rain regularly every year and in times of drought. Members of this clan have another important ritual prerogative: they may serve as mediators in serious disputes that break out between any Beng. In addition, when young Kri women are married they must undergo a certain ritual, complete with sacrifices and prayers offered to the Sky, as a complicated and protracted extension of the wedding ritual that other women undergo (Gottlieb 1983:133–137).

The sorts of talents, proclivities, and privileges that mark the patriclans do indeed contribute to a certain feeling of unity among clan members. In this respect, they complement the shared sets of knowledge that each clan possesses. In effect, the very bundles of secret knowledge that distinguish patriclans from one another also create a sense of unity among clan members simply by the fact of secrecy.

A feeling of unity among patriclan members is maintained in what is perhaps an even more important arena. I noted above that patriclans control the washing of corpses. Washing a corpse with its patriclan's secret leaves is said to enable the ghost (*wrú*) of the deceased, which is created at death, to travel the path to "ghost-town" (*wrugbe*). Here it rejoins those members of its patrilocally constituted household who are already dead. Hence washing the cadaver with its patriclan's leaves helps to recreate the agnatic group in death that (for at least the greater part of its members' lives) resided together in life. In essence, if the general (though not exclusive) focus of patriclans in life is difference, that emphasis reverses itself at death, when the general focus becomes identity.

Not only do the ghosts of each patriclan live together in *wrugbe*, but traditionally the ghosts traveled to the Beng villages every evening to rejoin their living patriclanmates. At dusk the ghosts were said to enter the compounds of the large round houses, where food was left on the ground in bowls for them. At night, the door to the house was locked, and the patriclan ghosts took their places inside, where they slept alongside their living clanmates. In the early morning, the first person to arise opened the house door and let the ghosts out; then they traveled back to ghost-town (which Beng say is located in the major cities of West Africa), where they spent the day, to return to the village again in the evening. And so if, as a result of matriclan endogamy and other factors, most members of the patriclan live dispersed by day, the situation changes somewhat at night, for then, at least traditionally, a portion of the patriclan is reunited by food and sleep. This ghostly reunion with the living patriclan members no longer obtains, however, as changes in house design in the 1960s and 1970s no longer accommodate the notion of a charmed closed circle encompassing an extended family, as we will see in chapter 6.

Still, for the traditional system, we may conclude roughly that by day and in life, identity more or less holds sway for matriclans and difference for patriclans, while at night and in death, patriclans also emphasize identity. Once again, as with the relationship between the village and the forest that we explored in the preceding chapter, the dichotomy that appears so neat in fact dissolves at another level.

From a general grounding in Morgan's emphasis on consanguineal ties, kinship has long been thought by anthropologists to be fundamentally about "blood," which was taken as a biological given. But as Schneider has shown so convincingly (1968, 1984), "blood" is itself a cultural construct that may or may not be relevant in a given society. For the Beng, I suggest that the way kinship is made relevant is through two idioms: identity, which includes matrilineal "blood" and "soul" and patrilineal ghostly reunion, and difference, which includes the potential ultimate difference of matrilineal witchcraft as well as food taboos and other symbolically significant features that distinguish patriclans from each other by day.

By the combination of the two types of clans, the Beng have access to two of the fundamental ways of organizing a society that are normally dominant only singly: one based primarily on competitive identity, the other on allied difference. Put another way, we could say that at least by day, the matriclans provide a syntagmatic model while the patriclans provide a paradigmatic model (Wagner 1975); by night and at death, a syntagmatic set of links also defines the patriclans.

Elsewhere in Africa, anthropologists have recently observed that there may be more than one principle operating at the ideological level. For instance, Bloch writes that the very principles of identity and difference that I have identified for the Beng are present among the Merina of Madagascar in the spheres of descent and affinity, respectively (1985:638). The Beng contribution to this discussion is to focus both these principles within the sphere of descent itself. In this way, the system of double descent provides the Beng with a complete, multilayered set of intellectual statements that offer two means by which to interpret the world.

The discussion of this chapter has emphasized the enduring and meaningful ties created between Beng people by virtue of their membership in clans, especially matriclans but also patriclans. The funeral scene I depicted at the opening of this chapter attests to the utterly crucial role played by clan members in one's life. As the scene shows, one cannot even die a properly social death without the active participation of clan members—or, in their rare absence, the fiction of such participation.

But I would mislead the reader if my portrait of this chapter were to have the effect of painting a picture of a society so "lineage-based" that descent provided the only medium of relationship for people. Jackson (1977b) has shown with wonderful clarity how descent itself, so emphasized by previous generations of Africanists, is but one of several modes of organizing society. In particular he has demonstrated how residence may intersect with descent to form a more complex system full of multiple possibilities for the participants. Among the Kuranko, who might have been classed as a "lineage-based society" in an earlier generation and left at that, the pattern of sacrifice reflects this, as most ritual offerings are made not to the discrete household, lineage, or clan but to wider groupings that are defined in relation to contiguity (1977c:134 et passim). This and related work has the effect of counteracting the potentially reductive effects that the earlier jural and economic frameworks sometimes produced, with their frequently exclusive focus on descent.

In fact, among the Beng, as we have seen, most villages (though not all) contain at least two matriclans, as well as several patriclans, and villagers find ways other than descent by which to relate to one another. Simple propinquity creates another level of social ties; Beng often forge friendships out of neighborliness. Other cognatic ties also provide means for forging social relationships. For instance, while fostering of children is most often arranged between matrikin, this is not a necessity; occasionally Beng adults who are not related at all will foster their children to one another simply because they like one another and think they have something to offer the children; or they may feel that they have a debt to repay. This is even more the case with fostering of domestic animals, which are raised mostly for sacrificial purposes and may be fostered out to another person for more effective raising.

In women's lives, a further daily means for forging extrakinship ties is in food exchanges: every night, almost all women cook far more food than their families can consume for the express purpose of sending over dishes of the extra food to other households. Most women have several exchange partners with whom they conduct such nightly food exchanges (in some cases the exchanges are one-way). Food exchanging partners include matrikin and patrikin, but also affines and unrelated friends—the networks are fairly particularistic. In short, descent, while a major focus of Beng life, is certainly not the only means for defining significant social relationships.

Finally, and along the same lines, in having focused on descent in this chapter, I do not mean to revive and take sides in the old descent-alliance debate of the 1950s by implying that descent forms an ur-text or master template for the rest of Beng society. Indeed, in the following chapter we will see how central the alliance system is to Beng society. And in the work overall I mean to show the mutual interdependence of kinship and other realms of social life in general, as equally embodying deep patterns in Beng thought. So I apply the opposed phrases that I have translated as "identity" and "difference" in other chapters, where they are not necessarily invoked regularly by Beng themselves, but where, I suggest, they are equally relevant. In so doing, I am not suggesting that these terms are rooted irrevocably in descent and can only be awkwardly "extended" outward to other arenas by stretching their meanings. Rather, I suggest that the meanings are relevant in these other arenas, if more explicitly in one than in the others.

My argument approximates the situation with kin terms. In the 1960s, a core group of kinship analysts, centered around Harold Scheffler and other ethno-science-oriented anthropologists, insisted on a biological underpinning to kinship in arguing that kin terms have the "nuclear family" (whatever they meant by that) as their root locus, and that the terms are "extended outward," increasingly attenuating their power, with corresponding loss of biological closeness. The critique of this position from symbolic anthropology offered an alternative explanation: that kin terms are a superb means of classifying individuals according to consistent cultural criteria that are not strictly oriented to biological relatedness (which itself is in any case defined quite differently in different cultures) and instead focus on intellectual principles (e.g., Schneider 1984; Wagner 1972a, 1972b, 1974).

I am making a similar argument with regard to the terms *identity* and *difference*: they have their most explicit roots in descent structures, but they are equally at home in other spheres of Beng thought. And so in the next chapter we turn to Beng alliance patterns, which define the principles of identity and difference in other ways.

CHAPTER FOUR

The Marriages of Cousins

> Two couples announce their children's engagement in the village. Then they tell
> the children themselves. The daughter ritually wails what may or may not be a
> genuine grief, while the son agrees stoically to the match and puts on a grateful
> face. He, too, may be ecstatic or miserable. Their feelings are discounted. Soon
> their families gear up for a year's worth of meetings, thanking rituals, and
> preparations. Representatives are sent to other villages to inform the bride's and
> groom's kin of the match. Then the representatives of the groom's kin thank the
> bride's kin for agreeing to the match, decide on a suitable date for the wedding,
> and decide which villages in which to formally announce the wedding. Finally
> the wedding is held; it lasts six days.

The great quantity and elaborate quality of the rituals surrounding engagement and
marriage reflect a strong preoccupation with alliance on a structural level. Perhaps
too, on the psychological level, the rituals serve to divert or absorb the attention of
the bride and groom themselves, one or both of whom may be miserable with the
selection of marriage partner. For the traditional marriage system of the Beng is
predicated on a system of arranged marriage in which the prospective bride and
groom both have little to say. Technically illegal now in Côte d'Ivoire under the
Civil Code of 1964 (Levasseur 1971), arranged marriage is nevertheless still practiced by the Beng, though undoubtedly not as regularly as it was in precolonial
times.[1] Although it was not possible for me to measure accurately the percentage of
arranged as against nonarranged marriages, one estimate that a Beng consultant
offered me is revealing; he speculated that traditionally, as many as 90 percent of all
women's first marriages would have been arranged, while the figure might now be
down to 80 percent. If this informant's guess was too high—and it was probably not
so by very much— it does indicate the importance of arranged as against nonarranged marriage perceived by Beng themselves.[2]

The arranged marriage system of the Beng is in fact an extensive structure that
catches the vast majority of individuals in its net. It includes what might appear to
be the basis for an "elementary" system (Lévi-Strauss 1969a), as it encourages three
types of cousin marriage: so-called matrilateral parallel-cousin marriage (see note 5)
and both types of cross-cousin marriage. All three forms of cousin marriage are
"preferred" in the sense of being positively valued and sought after. But none of
these forms, though practiced often, is required, or "prescriptive," for a given
individual.[3] Moreover, a set of rules barring marriage between certain affines serves
to restrict the impact of the preference for cousin marriage. There is, however,
another significant component of the alliance system that creates a certain "pull"

toward cousin marriage, though not for all individuals. This is the addition of birth order as a factor to be considered in deciding on a match. In short, Beng alliance is a complex system that in effect includes several models. They combine to form a multilayered system that cannot be reduced to any of its individual component models.

It has hardly gone unnoticed in the anthropological literature that a given society may have two or more varieties of marriage. Vellenga (1983), for example, has outlined a rather extreme case—twenty-one forms of traditional marriage that the Asante practice—and she details the problems that a contemporary Ghanaian family may encounter in trying to establish for legal purposes which of them is the "real" form of marriage. (For other examples of multiple marriage forms in a single society, see Comaroff 1986; Evans-Pritchard 1950; Fardon 1984). There has, however, been no systematic analysis of the existence of multiple marriage models from the perspective of alliance theory. In this chapter I will attempt such an analysis, while also looking into the ways in which some individual actors in the system have coped with—reproduced, approximated, or rebelled against—the system.

First I will explore the preference for the three types of permitted cousin marriage from the perspective of the Beng themselves. Next I will discuss the wide-ranging set of prohibitions against repeated alliances—a set of rules that works against the preference for cousin marriage. In the last section I will show how the use of birth order intersects with the preferred cousin marriage forms, on one hand, and the prohibitions against repeated alliances, on the other, to create an interesting mosaic. In its totality the system lies somewhere between Lévi-Strauss's categories of "elementary" and "complex" (1969a). Indeed, for reasons we will explore, it fits in nicely with the category of "semi-complex" discussed by Lévi-Strauss (1966a) and Héritier (1981).

At a general level, I hope in this chapter to show how the Beng system of alliance, with its multiplex foundations, reveals a profound oscillation between the principles of identity and difference, here seen at the structural level of marriage arrangements. In this setting, the oscillation between identity and difference takes place specifically with respect to the matriclan. That is, the decision to marry is essentially one that involves either choosing or rejecting a matriclanmate as a spouse. Still, a potential matrikinsperson-as-spouse should be close but not too close: identity is a good thing for marriage, but not absolute identity. Here the incest taboo (as defined by the Beng) is a moderating force on the principle of identity, subdividing it in ways we have not seen in the previous chapter in our discussion of matriclans.

MATRILATERAL PARALLEL-COUSIN MARRIAGE

Let us begin with matrilateral parallel-cousin marriage, a rare form of marriage (Van Baal 1975:95; for another West African example, see, Şaul 1991:33 on the Bobo of

Burkina Faso). In the Beng world, this is in fact the most highly valued marriage form. There is one reason that most Beng advance for arranging a matriclan-endogamous marriage (whether or not it is within the matrilineage).[4] If the young couple argues, it is said their matriclan members will be distressed and will hold a formal trial to save the marriage. In contrast, it is said that if spouses belong to different matriclans, their matriclan members will be indifferent to their disputes and will not take the trouble to hold a trial, making divorce far likelier. In fact, my statistics (Gottlieb 1983, appendix 5) suggest that the divorce rate is indeed somewhat—though not overwhelmingly—lower among couples who are in the same matriclan than it is among spouses who are not clanmates; in one village, where the matriclan affiliation of both spouses was known to me, 43 percent of all divorces were of couples who were matriclanmates, while 57 percent of such divorces were of spouses from different matriclans.

This indigenous justification for matriclan endogamy in terms of greater clan involvement during marital conflict reflects a wider theme that we pursued in the previous chapter: the general principle of identity that characterizes matriclan relationships. As we have seen, matrikin are viewed as exceptionally close and caring. Overall, in terms of the level of affect involved, we might term matrikinship a "positive" relationship (while patrikinship is more a "negative" relationship) (cf. Lévi-Strauss 1963d:40–49).

Apart from talking about matriclans by referring to identity, Beng describe matriclan relations in a related way that is, however, more relevant to marriage: concerning matrikin, Beng say "their affairs are intertwined" (ŋo zà jéjé). This is of course an outcome of the identity that matriclan members share. But it refers to the active side of social life more than to the philosophical principle underlying it. As such, it helps to explain at the indigenous level why it is good for matriclanmates to marry. To put it succinctly, there is a kind of potential emotional intensity beneath uterine relationships that does not normally exist with agnatic ones. For this reason, Beng feel comfortable situating marriage, which may certainly be an emotionally intense relationship by itself—and in this system usually intensifies even further by drawing in the spouses' families—within the framework of the matriclan.

Another advantage to matriclan endogamy—this one for women only—was suggested to me by a male elder. If a woman who marries outside her matriclan is widowed, she inherits nothing from her husband. However, a dying man may allocate one or two cash-crop fields (especially coffee) to a wife who is a clans-woman. Still, this is a modern innovation, as inheritance of cash-crop fields (especially kola plantations) was impartible traditionally (see Gottlieb 1983, chap. 3).

Significantly, the first-degree matrilateral parallel-cousin is *not* approved as a spouse, while the second- and third-degree matrilateral parallel-cousins *are* approved. Should first cousins in the uterine line marry, they must ritually split a goat; in any case, it is said the marriage will be barren.

The Taboo Marriage of Lande and Aukala

Lande was considered ugly, and no woman wanted to marry him. Finally, Aukala was given to him in an arranged marriage. But she was his mother's sister's daughter, and the marriage proved sterile. As Aukala had no children of her own, one of her sisters felt sympathy for her and gave her one of her daughters, Mona, to foster-raise.

It was when I asked about the possibility of this sort of marriage that I was immediately offered this story and others like it. Clearly they build up in people's minds as a repertoire of appropriate cases that serve to discourage this marriage form. I will have occasion in the concluding section to discuss further the rule against first-degree matrilateral parallel-cousin marriage, which, considering the overarching identity shared by all matriclan members and the rule encouraging second-degree matrilateral parallel-cousin marriage, certainly seems paradoxical.

When one marries into one's own matriclan, the spouse may or may not be a member of one's matrilineage. In discussing matriclan endogamy, Beng did not emphasize to me any difference between marrying within or outside one's own matrilineage. Yet from a structural perspective, there is indeed a difference between matrilineages within a single clan; as we have seen in the previous chapter, one lineage within each clan is composed of "free" Beng (on the uterine side), the other (or others) of descendants of a female slave. Marriage between two lineages within a clan, then, would entail uniting two groups between whom there are no "real" uterine ties, as Western discourse would perceive it, while marriage within a matrilineage would unite those with uterine ties the West would perceive as "real." From the Lévi-Straussian perspective, the difference between these two kinds of marriage should be crucial (see the concluding section), all the more so because the distinction between inter- and intralineage marriage also involves a consideration of slave versus free status. As yet, the intricacies of the relationship of slavery to alliance theory have not been fully explored; as Mona Etienne has remarked (personal communication), future work in Africa on this topic may prove quite illuminating (also see note 12).

In the present case, what remains intriguing is the explicit Beng emphasis on denying the difference between inter- and intralineage marriages within the matriclan. This is in keeping with what we have observed in the previous chapter, that the Beng assert no substantive differences between the slave and free members of a given matriclan. While there are indeed consequential differences in access to economic resources and political office that distinguish slaves from nonslaves, nevertheless these differences are not defined by Beng themselves as permanent, nor as biologically based. It may be this ideology that permits Beng not only to construct marriages uniting slaves and free Beng but also to assert that this type of marriage is fundamentally no different from a marriage between two free Beng, or one between two slaves' descendants. Linguistic usage reinforces this emphasis. In both cases—intra- or inter-lineage marriage—marriage within the matriclan is referred to by the same phrases: *wla leŋ plaŋ* ("two children of the matriclan"), or *a zyã (na) a wlaleŋ lo* ("her [his] husband [wife] is a child of the matriclan").

CROSS-CUSTIN MARRIAGE

But the scope of Beng marital alliances is by no means restricted to the matriclan. As I mentioned at the opening of this chapter, the Beng also practice cross-cousin marriage, in fact both kinds: the matrilateral and patrilateral varieties.[5] Informants explained that once a cross-cousin match of either form is effected between two families, a reciprocal match should be completed at a later date, thereby creating an exchange in classical Lévi-Straussian fashion. I will interpret this form of marriage below.

In Beng eyes, the best possible marriage would be to combine the advantages of each of the two alliance types so far outlined by marrying someone who is both a cross-cousin *and* a member of one's matriclan.[6] As we have seen, matriclan-endogamous marriage has the advantage of marrying two people whose uterine relatives, being the same, presumably care about them equally and are concerned that the marriage last. In contrast, cross-cousin marriage of either variety has the advantage of initiating or completing an exchange between two "families" (see below). Combining these two marriage forms would mean initiating or completing a formal exchange between two families within a single matriclan—families that should have an emotional stake in seeing the marriage endure. Such a combination marriage could be accomplished if the parents of one's cross-cousin were themselves members of the same matriclan. As an example (figure 3), Kwame married his father's sister's daughter, Akissi, who happened to be a clan member (and a classificatory "sister"), since his father, Yao, had himself married a matriclans-woman.

Despite the reasons adduced by the Beng for preferring one or the other form of cross-cousin marriage, as well as matrilateral parallel-cousin marriage, neither of these three forms is practiced with any regularity by a given family. Thus one does not achieve a true extended form of either "restricted" or "generalized" exchange for a group of interconnected lineages. This is because it is forbidden for people to marry many of those who are counted as affines. We come now to a second model of Beng marriage, which I view as partaking of a "complex" model.

PROHIBITIONS AGAINST REPEATED
ALLIANCES

In Lévi-Strauss's terms (1969a), what defines a "complex" system is that the choice of spouse is governed by a set of negative rules (prohibitions) but not by positive rules (preferences or prescriptions). As we have seen, the Beng do have positive rules dictating marital alliances, but the system also includes a far-ranging set of negative rules that effectively undermine the potential effect of the positive rules.

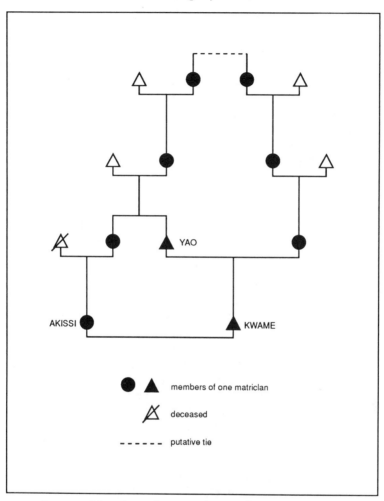

Figure 3. Matriclan-endogamous marriage between cross-cousins.

In this sense, the Beng alliance system hovers between an "elementary" and "complex" categorization, as it hovers between subsuming identity within the marital tie and repudiating it. As such, it fits nicely into the "semi-complex" category.

The Beng marriage system has four negative rules. The first forbids the usual set of close consanguines (parents, siblings, etc.) (see Gottlieb 1983:196–198). The second is a simple rule of patriclan exogamy. If this latter is violated, it is said the marriage will be childless. (Nowadays the rule against patriclan endogamy is not followed rigorously, and one encounters an occasional patriclan-endogamous marriage.) Third, it is forbidden for all Beng to have sexual relations with, much less marry, people of certain ethnic backgrounds or craft specializations (Gottlieb 1983:204–206). None of these three rules is exceptional: the first two are compatible with an "elementary" system, while the third lies outside its scope.

There is a fourth rule, however, that directly contradicts the logic of an elementary system. This rule concerns affines and is fairly wide-ranging: once two people have married, a large proportion of their same-sex relatives may not marry others from their own and future generations. If such a repeat alliance occurs, the result is disastrous: the individuals fall ill, and unless they seek a diviner and healer for extensive medico-ritual treatment of the disease, they die.

The Beng rules concerning which affines may not marry (figure 4) may be stated as follows:

1. Neither a married man nor any of the living or future male members of his matrilineage may marry any of the living or future female members of that man's wife's matrilineage, unless the potential couples in question are themselves cross-cousins;

2. Neither a married man nor any of the living or future male members of his matrilineage may marry any of the female cross-cousins, or daughters of any cross-cousins, of that man's wife;

3. The male cross-cousins of a married man may not marry any of the female cross-cousins, or daughters of any cross-cousins, of that man's wife.

It will be noticed that the first rule effectively precludes the levirate and the sororate, as well as sororal polygyny.

For all three of these rules, informants were divided as to how far laterally the prohibitions should extend; in other words, whether just first cousins or second and third cousins of the married male ego are prohibited from contracting the stated affinal alliances. This uncertainty may reflect a recognition that second and third cousins, though structurally identical to first cousins in relation to oneself, are in personal terms less "close" to one, the more so as the intervening links are forgotten. The issue revolves around the question "How close is close?" which is a pertinent one to most Beng, and which has no single, universally accepted answer for them, as we will explore in the concluding part of this chapter.

A marriage between any of the prohibited affines is called *dalɛ cɛŋ mà* (literally, "to reach each other"). This term also applies to the above-mentioned affines having nonconjugal sexual relations as well. Indeed, a man should never even sleep with a prostitute (who would invariably be non-Beng) with whom a "real" or classificatory brother, father, or son has slept. Transgression of any of these rules is said to be fatal.

A certain ritual may be performed to save the guilty parties—in particular, two sisters who have had sexual relations with the same man (generally, one of their husbands).[7] To conduct the ritual, the two sisters must go to the king's village, taking with them a chicken or preferably a goat. They kill the animal and split it in half. Each sister takes a half and runs around the village holding her half of the

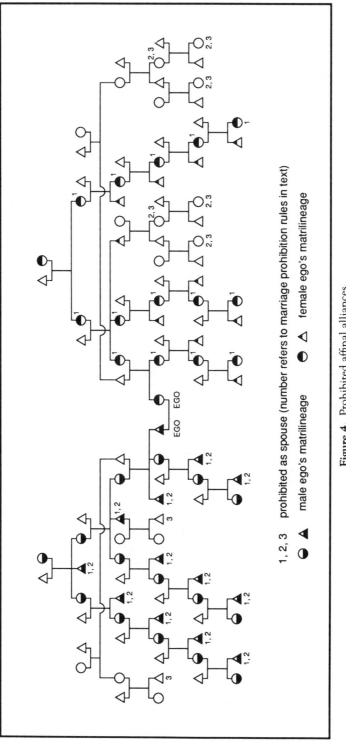

Figure 4. Prohibited affinal alliances.

1, 2, 3   prohibited as spouse (number refers to marriage prohibition rules in text)

● ◁   male ego's matrilineage   ◐ △   female ego's matrilineage

animal carcass, until the two sisters meet: then they begin hitting each other with
the two carcass halves. This done, other women of the village come to cook the
animal, and all present come to eat some of the cooked meat. The sisters have now
been symbolically separated and, as with all ritual actions, such symbolic separation
is seen as having practical efficacy. Assuming they do not repeat their earlier
offense, they can go on to live their lives in a normal manner.

The rules that prohibit repeated marriages between certain affines result in the
casting of a wide net of alliances. Any real sort of elementary system, in which the
same set of kin repeatedly and categorically marry each other from a finite number
of groups, is precluded. The potential impact of the first marriage model, then, in
which three kinds of cross- and parallel-cousins are seen as ideal spouses, is
effectively blunted by this second model of marriage.

Indeed, one might well inquire how any form of cousin marriage might take
place at all, given the above rules prohibiting repeated alliances between affines.
The answer is that the Beng prohibit such repeated alliances *only so long as the
relationship connecting them is remembered by the living*.[8] Once the connection has
been forgotten, such marriages would be permitted, as they would no longer, in
effect, be forbidden. Significantly, the typical and collective Beng genealogical
memory is only three to five generations long. After three or four generations,
distantly related affines are no longer recognized as such, and so they might then be
allowed to marry. As Lehman writes (1983:380) on the general format of semi-
complex regimes of marriage: "An alliance, once formed, may not be renewed for an
amount of time, generally specifiable in numbers of generations" (see also Kittel
1975).

Those familiar with the longstanding Crow-Omaha debate might have already
suspected that the Beng employ Crow-Omaha type kin terms, since this system of
kin terms has been associated with the semi-complex form of marital alliance (Lévi-
Strauss 1966a, Héritier 1981), and as we have seen, the Beng alliance system as I
have described it might well be classified as semi-complex. In fact, the Beng kinship
terminology system is a peculiar hybrid form that does not fit neatly into a single
classical typology, instead combining aspects of Iroquois-Dravidian, Hawaiian-
generational, and Crow-Omaha. The Beng system of kin terms does, however,
accord with the general principle that a prescriptive alliance rule is not associated
with separate affinal terms, and vice versa (Needham 1961:243).

It is now understandable how the Beng may in theory forbid repeated alliances
that are structurally similar, yet conduct "exchange" marriages such as I mentioned
above. The stated goal of a cross-cousin marriage is often to pay off an alliance debt
(*ŋ'a peŋ do*, "they paid"). That is, at some time in the past (often in a previous
generation), a male relative in a man's matrilateral cross-cousin's "family" married a
woman in his own "family," and it is now time to "even the score." Thus his
marriage to his matrilateral cross-cousin would be a loose form of what we might
term a one-time brother-sister exchange (though it might be delayed for up to
several generations). On the other hand, a marriage of a man to his matrilateral
cross-cousin might be viewed as the first between the two "families" (if it is the first

in several generations) and would serve to initiate a later match. Once again, according to one level of Beng alliance theory, such a brother-sister exchange should be one-time only, for a repetition would violate the rules stated earlier proscribing structurally identical alliances for same-sex kin. As we have seen, in effect the Beng keep conducting such cousin marriages (be they with parallel- or cross-cousins) by attenuating their genealogical memory to an average span of three or four generations.

Despite this, the Beng do recognize a marriage form that approximates an "elementary" system. The initiation of such an alliance is termed *lamoyā popolɛ*, "to beseech friendship," and should in theory institute a perpetual exchange between two matriclans. Yet a true elementary structure, which is implied in this form, is precluded by the extensive set of rules prohibiting affinal alliance. Thus the reciprocation of exchange in two alliance-linked matriclans must either wait several generations to take place or must link at least third—or more likely fourth—cousins; that is, it should be between affines who can no longer trace the route of their affinal connection. The Beng system in this way manages in effect to retain the structure of an elementary model without admitting to it.

As an example, let us consider the following case, which is illustrated in figure 5.

Matriclan Exchange

In the case of P and Q matriclans, we see that there appears to be a regular exchange of spouses between the two clans. P matriclan has given two wives to men of Q matriclan, while Q matriclan has given four wives to men of P matriclan. The two women of P matriclan (and the four women of Q matriclan) would be so distantly related, however, that the links connecting them are no longer traceable, though common clan membership is acknowledged.

In fact, in this case, my informant—Kouadio, himself a member of Q matriclan—complained that the set of marriages he described to me was in fact not a true case of "exchange" because the two marriages involving women of P matriclan had not been arranged marriages but rather love marriages decided on by the couples themselves. Because of this, they in effect did not "count" insofar as the technical system of formal exchange is concerned.

Still, the formal principle that should in theory define these repeated marriages between two clans remains relevant, as Kouadio himself revealed in bringing up the case to me.

Examples such as this reveal that the Beng system can creatively accommodate the paradox of an alliance between two clans that, while conducted repeatedly, is at another level denied.

Another way of stating this is that the system hinges on an oscillation between marrying close and marrying far: in this case, marrying an affine and marrying a stranger. An affine is good, but only so long as she or he is so distantly related that the connection is forgotten! Applying the terms more loosely than we have thus far, we might say that there is yet again an oscillation between identity and difference, here defined with respect to affinity rather than (as in the previous chapter) descent. Perhaps in this respect Beng alliance surprises us, as the classic Lévi-

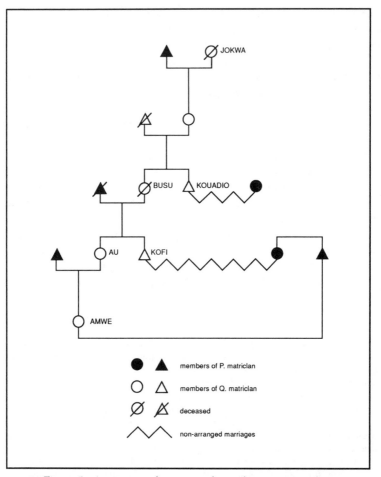

Figure 5. Asymmetrical spouse exchange between matriclans.

Straussian understanding of alliance certainly stresses difference. But the Beng practice of matriclan endogamy introduces identity into the realm of affinity, an unexpected insertion whose implications I will explore further in the concluding section of the chapter.

BIRTH ORDER

The above-described patterns of arranged marriage are crosscut by yet another parameter: birth order. Having presented the basic structure of the Beng preferences for cousin marriage, let us now see how this system is further circumscribed by the factor of birth order. In looking at how these systems interweave, we will explore how a structure is created that is quite thorough in the extent to which it arranges marriages for any given woman. And we will see how it further refines the way identity and difference are played with in the Beng system of marital alliance.

Almost thirty years ago, Needham noted (1961:250), "It is one of the commonest features of descent terminologies that brothers and sisters are distinguished by relative age. . . ." It is puzzling, then, that relative age has not been systematically analyzed since then in the literature on kinship and alliance systems. In a recent collection of essays on age and anthropological theory (Kertzer and Keith 1984), for example, no mention is made of this potentially significant association. Needham himself addressed the issue of birth order in his article reanalyzing Wikmunkan (Australian) marriage. He pointed out that a Wikmunkan man may only marry a woman who is the daughter of his parent's younger, never older, sibling (1961:230–231), thereby dividing a sibling group in two (older and younger) for the purpose of assigning spouses. Needham then turned his attention to other more relevant features, however, while admitting that the issue of relative age remains a "great puzzle" in the Wikmunkan system (1961:250).[9]

The Beng system is more thoroughgoing than the Wikmunkan system in that it assigns each and every daughter in a sibling group a unique place for the purpose of alliance. In this section I will explore the birth-order system as it defines the choices for a marriage.

The Beng birth-order rule is simple in principle, though it is often difficult to carry out: a couple's odd-numbered daughters "belong to" (pɔɛ) their father to betroth as he deems fit, and the even-numbered daughters "belong to" their mother to be married as she deems fit (see figure 6 for a sample family of four daughters).[10]

A girl's place in the birth-order system of alliance is determined at puberty; the effect of this is that the system takes into account only daughters who reach marriageable age. If, for example, a second daughter dies in childhood, the third daughter would now be considered the second and would accordingly belong to her mother. Of note, too, is that in a polygynous household the daughters of each co-wife are counted separately in determining their birth order. Likewise, a divorced or widowed woman or man would begin counting anew for each group of daughters she or he had with each spouse.

Generally, the parent who "owns" the daugher marries that child into his or her "side." The complex way that these "sides" are defined is one of the features that makes the Beng marriage system of interest. For this single rubric contains a cognatic dimension, admitting both cross- and parallel-cousins who may or may not belong to the relevant parent's own matriclan. As we have seen, there are three possible cousin types who are marriageable: the matrilateral parallel-cousin and two forms of cross-cousin. We will now see how these three possible forms of cousin marriage intersect with the birth-order system to create a complex set of alliance possibilities.

Let us suppose it is time for the first daughter to marry. Since she belongs to her father, he will normally marry her into his side of the family. Traditionally, she would not have married her patrilateral parallel-cousin of any degree, in keeping

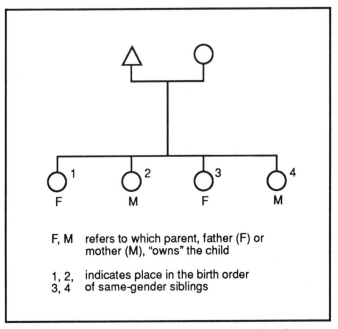

Figure 6. Birth order and parental "ownership" of daughters.

with the rule of patriclan exogamy. Thus if she married into her father's side, she would likely marry her patrilateral cross-cousin of any degree.

A second daughter, who is "owned by" her mother, has two obvious alternatives. Her mother will marry her either to a man in their matriclan (generally to the daughter's matrilateral parallel-cousin of at least the second degree, occasionally to such a cousin's son or even daughter's son) or to her own "brother's son" (that is, to the daughter's matrilateral cross-cousin) of any degree. In the second case, the fiancé may or may not be a member of the young woman's own matriclan, depending on whether his parents themselves had married matriclan-endogamously. Thus when a woman marries into her mother's side of the family, she may well be marrying into her own matriclan, but that is not inevitable. For the moment, let us suppose that the second daughter marries a mother's brother's son who is *not* a matriclan brother.

When we come to the third daughter, the choices will have narrowed owing to the rule against repeated alliances as I outlined it in the previous section, a third daughter may not make a match that would be structurally similar to that of her odd-numbered predecessor, who married a father's sister's son. Thus the third daughter might also marry a patrilateral cross-cousin only if he were distantly related to the first daughter's husband. Such would be the case if the two men were members of different matrilineages within the same matriclan or if, despite being lineagemates, they were only remotely related, the exact genealogical connection between them having been forgotten.

The fourth daughter, who belongs to her mother, will have more choices than did the third. If the second daughter married a mother's brother's son, then the fourth daughter might marry a matrilateral parallel-cousin (usually of the second or third degree).

With the fifth daughter, the system as such for odd-numbered daughters has probably exhausted itself. Both her odd-numbered predecessors (daughters one and three) have married father's sister's sons who are only distantly related to each other, and it is unlikely that a third father's sister's son of the right age could be found who would be in a different matrilineage from the previous two or would be only distantly related to them while a member of the same matrilineage. The father of a fifth daughter might therefore decide to marry her into a matriclan with which his own matriclan has previously had no alliances. In initiating such an alliance, he would expect a "return marriage" to be effected at a later date. Or if possible demographically, he might marry the fifth daughter into a matriclan with which his own matriclan already has a relationship or perpetual alliance, as explained above.

A similar situation would prevail for a sixth daughter as for a third daughter. Her even-numbered predecessors (daughters two and four) have already married a mother's brother's son and a classificatory mother's sister's son, respectively, so the sixth daughter might now marry another mother's brother's son or mother's sister's son only if he were in a different matrilineage from his brothers-in-law or if the link connecting the two men, though lineagemates, were now forgotten.

Should there be a seventh daughter, her father would have few if any structurally defined choices open, and he would most likely leave the daughter to find her own husband. Assuming she already had a boyfriend, the seventh daughter would probably be delighted. A ninth and eleventh daughters' situations would be parallel.

With the eighth daughter, we still have one possibility left: if the sixth daughter had married a mother's brother's son only distantly related to the second daughter's husband (who was also a mother's brother's son), then the eighth daughter might marry a classificatory mother's sister's son only distantly related to the fourth daughter's husband (who was also a mother's sister's son) or one from a different lineage but within the same matriclan.

A tenth daughter would be in a structurally similar position to that of a fifth daughter. That is, it is unlikely that any cousin marriages would be open to her without duplicating the marriages of her even-numbered predecessors. Consequently, she might be married to someone in an unrelated matriclan to initiate a later exchange marriage, or she might be given as a "return" match to a matriclan with which there had already been an exchange.

A twelfth daughter's situation would be like that of a seventh daughter, and she would probably be left to choose her own husband.

Of course it is quite unlikely that a given couple will produce twelve or more daughters who all live to marriageable age. If a typical couple has two to four adult daughters, the arranged marriage system should be able to accommodate them all amply.

Even so, the vagaries of demography might well throw a wrench into the above-described system. Indeed, given the relatively small population involved in this system (approximately 10,000), it is in fact fairly common that there is *no one* available of both the correct kinship category and the right age. For it is expected that wives be of the same age as, or younger than, their husbands. Hence finding a man not only of the right genealogical category but also of the correct age might well be impossible in a given family. In such a case, a daughter would be left to find her own spouse, no matter what her place in the birth-order system. Alternatively, in a large family the parents might realize that, say, a second daughter has no chance of finding a marriageable father's sister's son who is older than she, but there may be a fourth daughter and a young male cousin waiting in the wings; the parents can then plan to marry this girl, when she comes of age, to the cousin in question and in the meanwhile leave the second daughter to find her own husband.

So far my main concern has been to underline the extensiveness of the birth-order system as a model seeking to accommodate virtually all a couple's daughters. The obvious question that presents itself in considering such a system must now be dealt with: when faced with decisions about how to marry off their children, how do individuals actually manage to continually reinvent this complicated and demanding alliance system? We will now explore two cases I recorded to see how personality interacted with demographics and other structural forces to cope with the system. Here we will see that a certain amount of flexibility is allowed for by the system to make way for unavoidable situations that prevent the exact reduplication of the alliance rules in each case, thereby permitting its approximate reproduction in the long run.

The argument I am making approaches somewhat the argument that Gough suggested (1971) in her restudy of the Nuer. In discovering extensive use of matrilateral and affinal ties in a system made famous by Evans-Pritchard for its supposedly thoroughgoing patrilineality, Gough suggested that the Nuer were able to maintain their ideological stress on patriliny only insofar as they made extensive use of cognatic ties (and interethnic ties, with the neighboring Dinka), then "converted" them to patrilineal Nuer ones. In other words, and to generalize from this example, the more rigid the technical requirements of a system, the more there must be a means to accommodate the unavoidable anomalies. Keeping this in mind, we can now turn to how the Beng system allows people to cope with its own inevitable anomalies by following the sagas of how two large families married off their daughters.

In the first case, Kouakou has two wives, so we will follow the marriages of each wife's children separately, as this is how the Beng manage polygynous families' alliances (figures 7 and 8).

Marriages of a First Wife's Children

With his wife Afwe, Kouakou has three daughters. The first daughter, Sunu, "belonging to" her father, was given her father's sister's son, Maurice, to marry. But Maurice proved impotent, and after a year he and Sunu divorced. Some time later, an unrelated boy in the village asked to marry Sunu, and she and her father agreed.

Because the first marriage of Sunu to her father's sister's son had not worked out, Kouakou found another of his sister's sons, Kwame, to marry his second daughter, Amwe. However, oddly enough, Kwame also proved impotent, and the last that I heard was that the young couple had gone off to the Guro area seeking medicines for him. If he was not cured soon, I was told, they too would divorce.[11]

The third daughter, Ndri, was not yet married at the time that I interviewed Kouakou, and Kouakou wouldn't commit himself about any future fiancé, probably because he was waiting to see the outcome of Amwe's marriage; if it were to break up, he might well seek yet another sister's son for the next daughter, Ndri.

With his second wife, Buru, who is not a member of his matriclan, Kouakou has six daughters.

Second Wife's Six Daughters' Marriages

The first daughter, Aia, is married to Ajei. As she "belonged to" her father, she married into his "side," not into his matriclan but to reimburse a marital debt that needed to be repaid. A woman from Ajei's matriclan—in fact, his mother—had been given in marriage to a man in Kouakou's matriclan, perhaps a first- or second-degree matrilateral parallel-cousin, and it was time to give them back a woman from the next generation. Though Aia herself is not in her father's matriclan, she "belongs to" her father, who has the right to choose her husband. For this reason, the marriage is said to "count the same" in repaying the debt as if she had been in his matriclan.

The second daughter, Ajua, married into her mother's side, following the rules without any fudging: she married Abutu, her mother's (matrilateral-half) sister's son. However, this marriage was in fact so prescriptive that it overstepped the incest rules, as it was too close, and should have been preceded by a sheep sacrifice.

The third daughter, Akwe, "belonging to" her father, nevertheless married into her mother's side (though not her matriclan); she married Andama, a man who was almost a classificatory mother's brother's son (genealogically, her mother's mother's sister's son's son). Possibly she married into her mother's rather than father's side because of a shortage of eligible men on her father's side.

The fourth daughter, Au, "belonging to" her mother, also married into her mother's side, but this time the marriage was actually to a matriclanmate. However, like her elder sister Ajua's marriage, this marriage was also considered affinally incestuous. Akple, her husband, is also her sister's husband's classificatory father (her sister's husband's father's patrilateral half-brother). The result is that this marriage violates the rule that two sisters (Au and Akwe) must not marry two close agnates (Andama and Akple). It is possible that Au and Akple have obtained ritual medicines from a healer for this affinally incestuous marriage, since without such medicines, some if not all of the four spouses involved in this *ménage à quatre* should have died.

The fifth and sixth daughters in this family are not yet married.

In these cases we have seen that the parents for the most part attempted to carry out the alliances as they should be conducted, according to the rules. Yet they were thwarted by such unpredictable and extraordinary circumstances as the impotence of two sons-in-law and possibly by a shortage of eligible young men in the village, which may have been what led them to arrange two (affinally) incestuous unions.

In other cases, families may be unable to re-create the alliance system for another reason: the would-be participants balk. Indeed, one can imagine that the

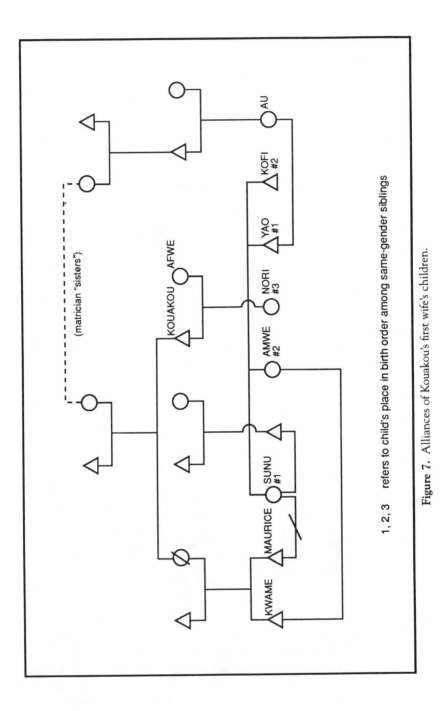

(matrician "sisters")

KOUAKOU AFWE

KWAME

MAURICE

SUNU
#1

AMWE
#2

NORI
#3

YAO
#1

KOFI
#2

AU

1, 2, 3   refers to child's place in birth order among same-gender siblings

Figure 7. Alliances of Kouakou's first wife's children.

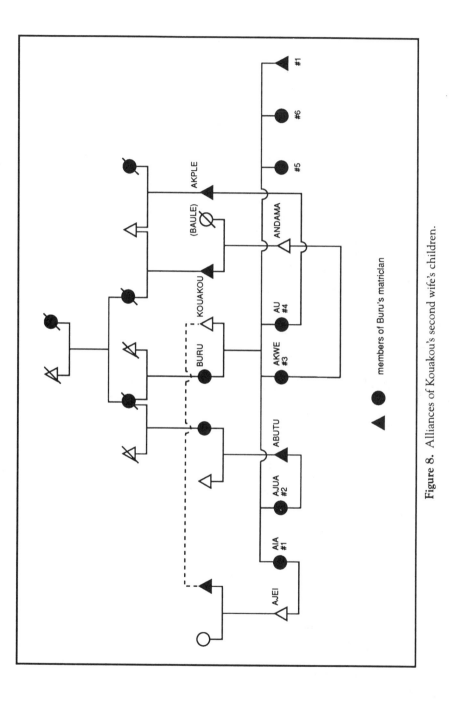

Figure 8. Alliances of Kouakou's second wife's children.

members of Buru's matriclan

individuals who are subject to this system may feel hopelessly trapped by the marital web being spun around them. It should not be surprising that rebellions against it are not unheard of. Still, refusal to participate is certainly not encouraged. In theory, a man may refuse a woman offered to him as an arranged-marriage bride, but great pressure is put on him by his family—nightly meetings for days on end—to accept their decision. In contrast, a woman is technically not permitted to refuse a man offered to her as an arranged-marriage groom. Yet in practice women put up more fuss than men do—sometimes successfully, as the following case shows (see figure 9).

A Family of Three Daughters

Amwe is the eldest daughter and thus "belongs to" her father. However, her father, Busu, was angry with his own matriclan over a long-standing dispute. As a child, Busu had no sisters, and so he did much of the daily work for his mother that a daughter would ordinarily do: he pounded corn to make meal for *foutou*; he carried water on his head from the forest; he chopped wood in the forest to burn as firewood; he dried manioc to make manioc *foutou*. In performing all this heavy labor ordinarily required of a daughter by her mother, Busu virtually changed his gender out of filial duty; but for reasons that were never made clear to me, when it came time for him to marry, his matriclan declined to give him a wife from the clan, and he was obliged to find a wife on his own.

Bitter over what he considered a virtual betrayal on the part of his matriclan elders, Busu in effect took revenge on his clan in the next generation. When the time came for his eldest daughter, Amwe, to marry, Busu refused to give her in marriage to a boy of his matriclan, since he had not been given a wife who would occasion "reimbursement." He thus let Amwe choose her own mate.

First Amwe had a child by a lover. Then she married another man in the village who was not related to her. But she considered her mate a poor father and husband because "he never gave me or our children so much as one franc." One day she had an argument with him during which he accused her of performing more work in her father's fields than in his own fields. She mentioned this to her father, who became quite angry over his son-in-law's remark, proceeded to insult his son-in-law, and asked Amwe to divorce him. Happy to be rid of her stingy husband, she agreed. Moreover, she was disgusted with Beng men in general, whom she characterized as a group as stingy. It is possible that Amwe was convinced that no Beng man was good enough for her—that is, as good as her father, whom, she told me repeatedly, she had loved intensely and whose favorite child she had been.

Nevertheless, Amwe soon married a man of another ethnic group who happened to be living in her village. While this too turned out to be a rather stormy marriage, with her new husband periodically leaving the village with no explanation for months at a time, he eventually did return each time, and the marriage has essentially endured, producing three children.

The second daughter of this family, Amla, "belonged to" her mother and thus should have married into her mother's "side," preferably either a matriclan "brother" or a matrilateral cross-cousin. The first man she was offered by her maternal uncles was Kouakou, who was not quite a classificatory mother's brother's son (actually, her mother's mother's brother's son's son, who is in another matriclan). But she did not care much for Kouakou, and she asked her elder sister, Amwe, to support her in her refusal to marry him. Amwe agreed. As the eldest of her sibling set, Amwe wielded a certain amount of authority, and because of her support of her younger sister, their uncles agreed not to force Amla to marry Kouakou.

As a second choice, the uncles then selected Etienne, who was in the same classificatory relationship to Amla as Kouakou had been (another mother's mother's brother's son's son). But personality mismatch was clearly a problem here. Amla was a pleasant, somewhat serious, and very responsible young woman, and she refused to marry this second choice—a rather obnoxious and smug young man who would, within a few years, commit affinal-incestuous adultery with a woman who became his wife's mother's sister (and also happened to be his own father's brother's daughter), thus violating two incest rules: the ones prohibiting sexual relations with a patrilateral parallel-cousin and with someone in one's spouse's matrilineage. Because Amla was turned off by this newly proposed man, whose character she clearly discerned, she again enlisted Amwe's aid to intervene for her. Again Amwe argued with her family against their choice. But this time a large dispute developed, for the whole family was for this marriage, including not only the two uncles but also a classificatory uncle (mother's mother's sister's son), the two girls' mother, and their brother. Amwe was alone in the family in supporting Amla. When the dispute flared up one day, Amwe went into the forest, where her father was working in the fields, to tell him about it, and the two returned to the village together.

Amla had declared that she would only agree to marry her boyfriend, Yao. Perhaps because he had been entreated by Amwe, his oldest and favorite child, or perhaps for other reasons we will never know, Busu decided to support his daughter, and he announced that Amla must marry Yao alone; he would not give his consent for her to marry anyone else. Because of her father's veto, Amla was permitted to marry Yao. Perhaps the uncles agreed because Yao also happened to be an "honorary" member of Amla's matriclan; since his mother was Baule and he had little to do with her family, he considered himself as virtually belonging to his father's matriclan, which also happened to be Amla's matriclan (as his father's parents' marriage had been a matriclan-endogamous one). And though he was structurally two generations above Amla, the couple were more or less agemates.

The third daughter of this family was Jabi, who "belonged to" her father and thus should have married into his "side." By this time, Busu had died, and so Jabi's two father's brothers took his place and made arrangements for her marriage. They offered her Kumwe, her classificatory female patrilateral cross-cousin's son (genealogically, he was possibly her father's mother's sister's daughter's daughter's son), who was a member of her father's matriclan. But Jabi refused Kumwe, citing as her reason that Kumwe lived in another village in the forest region, and she did not want to leave her village in the savanna region to marry.

Her father's brothers then offered Jabi a second choice, Duwe, who was Kumwe's mother's sister's son, hence also a member of Jabi's father's matriclan. But for reasons that are less clear to me, she refused him too. At this, her father's brothers gave up—possibly because they were nice enough not to insist on Jabi's marrying a man of their choice whom she seemed inevitably to dislike or because they had run out of energy for the enterprise or had run out of genealogically suitable candidates. In any case, they let Jabi find her own husband. She married Gaosu, a man in her own village who seems not to have been a member of her own or her father's matriclan.

What is interesting about this case is that for all three of the sisters, the marriages were not made according to the preferred rules. In Amwe's case, this was because of the history of the parents' marriage, which itself was not arranged; in the other two

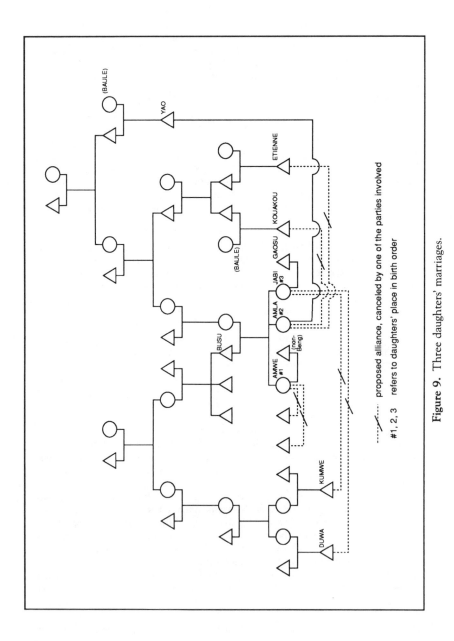

------ proposed alliance, canceled by one of the parties involved

#1, 2, 3   refers to daughters' place in birth order

Figure 9. Three daughters' marriages.

daughter's cases, it was because the daughters themselves refused the choices offered them by their father or their uncles. This is significant in light of the fact that in principle, girls have no say about who is given to them in marriage. While this holds true in theory, this case shows us how a sympathetic father or uncle may bend the rules or ignore them completely to accord with his daughter's or niece's wishes—remembering, though, that he is not required to do so.

During my first long stay among the Beng, I witnessed two alliance sagas playing themselves out, both initiated by reluctant brides. Both brides kept running away from their grooms, only to be caught—in the forest, in their father's homes, in a favorite aunt's home—and brought back to their equally unhappy grooms. The stories had vastly different outcomes. In one case, which was said to involve spirit possession, the bride, Ajua, was so bent on leaving her husband that he himself begged his father to be liberated from the marriage. But neither set of parents would agree to a divorce, and finally, after a ritual exorcism of the possessing spirit, Ajua agreed to return to her husband. Despite the tragic deaths of two babies subsequently born to the couple, the marriage has endured (see Gottlieb and Graham n.d.). The other reluctant bride, Afwe, also steadfastly refused to be married to her groom, a second-degree matrilateral parallel-cousin, who, she said, had a "rotten face." Finally she left the Beng region altogether and took a job on the coast, some four hundred miles to the southwest.

Another case that I recorded had an even more tragic outcome than did these (see figure 10).

The Jealous Cousin

Afwe Ba was an even-numbered daughter and the youngest daughter in her family. As is often the case with the last daughter, she wasn't given an arranged marriage husband; the youngest daughter often stays with her mother to help her out, and some potential husbands find the prospect of matrilocality (or duolocality) a reasonable option.

When Afwe Ba's mother died, her mother's older sister, Apise, in effect became her mother. It was Apise who would be responsible for arranging her marriage.

Now, Afwe Ba had a lover, but she had her eyes on someone else to marry: Bande. However, because of Beng alliance rules, Bande was judged ineligible for her, as his brother was married to a matrilineal relative of Afwe Ba's. In fact, this relative was Amwekala, a cousin of hers—the daughter of Apise, precisely that aunt who was responsible for her marriage; moreover, it was that very aunt who had arranged her cousin's marriage. Thus Afwe Ba held Apise responsible for her misery, and she further blamed her cousin Amwekala for thwarting her own marriage.

Some years later, her cousin, Amwekala, was pregnant with her first child. She had a difficult labor, and her father went to consult a diviner to discover the cause of the painful contractions. The diviner told her father to go ask Afwe Ba about the problem, implying that Afwe Ba was bewitching Amwekala. However, Amwekala's father, being a Master of the Earth, instead offered an egg to the Earth with the prayer that whoever was bewitching his daughter should die that very day.

About that time, Afwe Ba had asked her aunt Apise if Amwekala was in

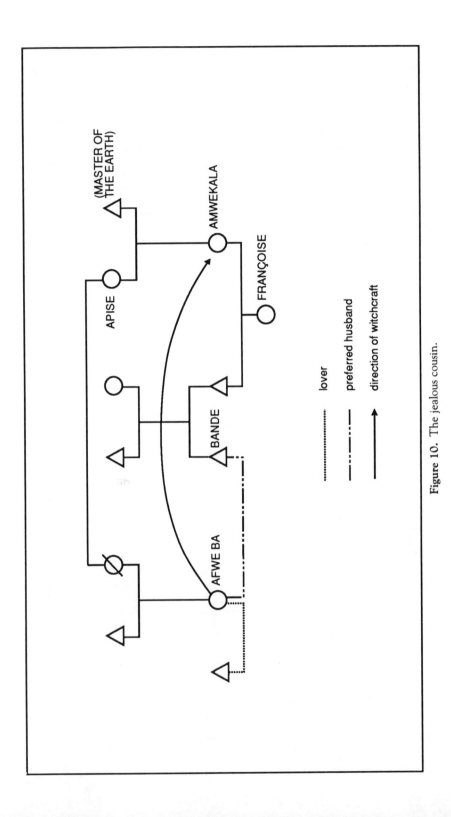

Figure 10. The jealous cousin.

labor. Then she went into the forest to chop down a tree for firewood. But the tree she was chopping down fell on her head and her tongue fell out. The companion who was with her ran back to the village to announce the news; when some villagers reached the forest to rescue Afwe Ba, they found her dead. In a short while, Amwekala delivered her baby, Françoise.

The general opinion was that the Earth had killed Afwe Ba for bewitching Amwekala. As soon as Afwe Ba died, her spell over Amwekala was lifted, and the childbirth proceeded normally.

This case shows how personal rebellions against the system can take on drastic proportions, involving witchcraft and attempts at disruption of the reproductive cycle in women. What I find equally interesting is the attitude of my Beng friend who told me this story: her sympathy lay entirely with Amwekala, and she had nothing but contempt for Afwe Ba—who, because of the affinal alliance taboo, was not able to marry the man with whom she was in love and remained unable to accept her fate of marrying someone else.

Still, despite rebellions such as these, for the most part the Beng alliance system that I have described in this chapter does "work," insofar as it achieves a very high level of compliance even in the face of both demographic constraints and individual protests. It is a construction that is logically elegant and attempts to be all-encompassing.

The Beng means of choosing spouses is a complicated amalgam of rules. Here I sum up their significance both for a general theory of alliance and for our understanding of Beng notions of identity and difference.

Looking at the system of cousin marriage alone, undoubtedly the most surprising component of the Beng marriage system is the practice of matrilateral parallel-cousin marriage. From the perspective of alliance theory, marrying within the clan, and even more so within the matrilineage, is, as John Comaroff has remarked (1980a: 164, 1980b: 28–29), a flagrant violation of the Lévi-Straussian premise that the purpose of marriage is to unite two distinct groups, even perhaps two enemy groups. Like father's brother's daughter marriage as practiced in much of the Muslim world, mother's sister's daughter marriage among the Beng plays the opposite role from that advanced in the Lévi-Straussian model: it unites people who are already united and between whom there is, in a structural sense, no sociological difference. Indeed, in the Beng case it unites people who are seen as sharing in a fundamental conception of identity in the many ways we have seen. Orthodox alliance theory might well put this kind of union into the category of incest. For if the goal of mother's sister's daughter marriage is to marry "close," what prevents Beng from marrying their true siblings? Terminologically, in fact, there is no difference between full siblings and any degree of matrilateral parallel-cousins, including those who become spouses: all females of both those categories are called "older sister" (dre leŋ) or "younger sister" (zu leŋ), and all males are called "elder brother" (drɔ gɔŋ) or "younger brother" (zu gɔŋ). In marrying a mother's sister's child, then, one would be wedding someone whom we might gloss as "sister" or "brother"; Beng who speak French indeed refer to such spouses as soeurs or frères.

In this regard, I have stated that the Beng system of alliance lies somewhere between Lévi-Strauss's categories of elementary and complex. That remark must now be explained in view of the foregoing. Seen in its totality, the Beng alliance structure reveals a noticeable oscillation between marrying close and marrying far.[12] This is seen with the very preference for matrilateral parallel-cousin marriage. For although this is stated as a decided preference, nevertheless the Beng distinguish forcefully between degrees of matrilateral parallel-cousin: a first degree mother's sister's child is forbidden as a spouse, while a second- (or higher) degree mother's sister's child is preferred as a spouse. Structurally, these sets of people are identical: both are referred to by the same set of sibling terms just mentioned; both may be members of a single matrilineage; and surely second-degree mother's sister's children, like first degree mother's sister's children, are seen as close, being members of one's matrilineage, with all the shared identity that that entails. Yet, as Radcliffe-Brown observed, that difference may be quite important (1950:9). In the Beng case, the system has indeed bifurcated the two degrees of cousin to the extreme degree, making one of them a preferred spouse while the other is prohibited. This bifurcation embodies the Beng view of alliance as a whole, here writ small: the predilection for marrying close, but not too close, for collapsing identity (in this case, matrilineal descent) and difference (in this case, affinity), but not completely.

The preference for cross-cousin marriage also embodies in its own ways this ambivalence about marrying close, yet not too close. Here we see the ideal for marrying close applied in a manner that would seem suitable for producing an orthodox elementary system of regular marital exchanges between two groups. And indeed, in a sense the Beng strive for such an exchange, in initiating a *lamoyā popolɛ* match that should result in future exchange matches between two matriclans. Yet at the same time they deny the possibility of a regular exchange by forbidding repeated alliances between certain sets of affines whose links are still remembered. It is as if they are simultaneously striving for alliance with "foreigners" and avoiding such alliance.

As we saw in the previous chapter, the Beng descent system contains the complementary models of identity and difference that are partially embodied, respectively, in matriclans and patriclans. In the alliance system we see again both principles at work, but divided up in an even more complex fashion. On a superficial reading, one might associate cross-cousin marriage with difference and matrilateral parallel-cousin marriage with identity. But as we have seen, matrilateral parallel-cousin marriage itself contains an ambivalence about identity, as viewed in the injunction against first-cousin marriage, combined with a preference for second- or third-degree parallel-cousin marriage. And as a whole the alliance system contains a tension within it, as it alternatively embraces both sociological distance and proximity as ideal principles to guide alliance choices and both emotional identity and difference as models for individual's marriages.

In short, we see a complex play between the principles of identity and difference at work here. In the alliance system, identity and difference interweave in unexpected fashion, contravening what we have come to expect from a certain close reading of alliance theory, yet still flirting with the main tenets of alliance theory for all that.

The ambivalence that we have seen concerning identity and difference at the level of marriage structures appears in aesthetic arenas as well. As we will see in the following chapter, in myths and rituals Beng engage in a variety of ways—ranging from playfully to respectfully to fearfully—with this set of themes.

CHAPTER FIVE

Hunting Dogs and Laughing Hyenas

... every animal is a moral waiting to be identified. Watch any
animal: before long it will let you know something about mankind.
John Ciardi, An Alphabestiary

In the previous chapter I traced out structural tensions in several forms of marriage
practiced by the Beng. We saw how the alliance system hovers at the edges of
identity and difference, never making a firm, exclusive commitment to either
principle. In this chapter we will explore variations on this theme in another
domain: the realm of myth. I have chosen two common protagonists in Beng myths
that exemplify the conjoined themes of identity and difference in complex ways
that allow us to continue our discussion of these principles.

I use the term *myth* where some might prefer *folktale*. Many folklorists posit that
myths must concern ultimate truths and issues of explicitly cosmological significance, as Dundes (1972:93) put it, embodying "a sacred oral narrative explaining
how the earth or men came to be in their present form," and so by this definition
myths are said to concern deities and their actions (Bascom 1965). By these
standards, Ruth Finnegan (1970:362) has effectively eliminated myths from Africa
altogether. I would contend, however, that forms of seeming entertainment such as
the Hyena stories recounted here do indeed offer serious moral lessons about the
world, albeit in a fashion that allows for amusement on the part of the listeners.
Moreover, the same Beng stories may have as their protagonists both animals and
"deities" (forest spirits and the Sky), thus confounding the folklorists' distinction of
story type on this basis (see Bascom 1965). For these reasons I resist demoting Beng
stories about Dog and Hyena to the category of folktale, perceived commonly as
both less influential in social life and less weighty in philosophical speculation. [1]

In Beng myths, Dog acts now as ally, now as traitor to the human cause,
wavering between maintaining identity with humans and asserting critical difference from them. The Hyena is in some ways an even more complex subject. In
myths Hyena plays the role of buffoon who is laughed at by his Beng audiences
because of his immoral deeds, but in life hyenas are treated seriously; indeed, they
are the object of intense rituals aimed at curtailing or counteracting the animals'
anomalous behavior. The moral of the two incarnations of the hyena is thus dual:

the adversary who is laughable in one context can be fatal in another; difference can be now amusing, now dangerous.

THE DOG

Dog Myths

Two myths that Beng tell about Dog as a mythical creature reveal his paradoxical position vis-à-vis humans. An understanding of these two myths will be central to our comprehension of dogs' place in both Beng cosmology and society.

First, the Beng blame Dog for having bestowed death on humanity.[2]

The Origin of Death

There was Death. So everyone had a meeting to tell Sky that they wanted reincarnation for themselves, but that the grass that is used for thatch, once having been burned, would never grow back. They sent Dog and Cat as messengers to tell this to Sky.

When they set off, Dog found some bones and ate them on the path. So Cat went on ahead of him. But Cat hadn't understood the message well and told the Sky the opposite of what he should have: that when burned, the grass for thatch would grow back quickly, but that humans would not be revivified. And that's how it is that humans die today.

Throughout Africa, myths of this type, termed by Abrahamsson (1977:4) "the message that failed," are told as an explanation for the origin of death. However, there are significant variations throughout the continent; a variety of other animals are used elsewhere as the two protagonists (ibid.:4–34). For instance, among the KhoiKhoi of southern Africa, Insect is the one who should have told the proper message, but instead, Hare took on this role (Bleek 1864:69–70); among the Asante of Ghana, these two roles are played by Goat and Sheep, respectively (Feldmann 1963:109); significantly, among the Yaka, it is Dog who brought the news rather than Goat (Abrahamsson 1977:13); and so on. In view of the comparative variation in characters, it is appropriate to inquire why Dog plays the role he does in the Beng version.[3]

I suggest that in the Beng story it is Dog who is ultimately responsible for creating the confusion and is consequently responsible for the inevitable death that all humans now face. Although on the surface it is Cat who causes the mix-up by delivering the incorrect message to Sky, in fact it is Dog's prior behavior that causes Cat to bear the incorrect message. The implication is that had Dog, who is more intelligent, reached Sky first, he would have given Sky the correct message. In his case, it is greed—a craving for bones—that proved problematic, while with Cat it was limited intelligence.[4] Because of Dog's petty greed, humans now suffer the worst calamity that could befall them: death.

Dog's greed is confirmed in another Beng myth that can be summarized briefly. The Beng say that once upon a time, Dog was very rich, having pilfered one of everything and put these items in his hunting bag (like a veritable Noah's Ark, although of objects rather than animals). But in his great greed, Dog spent all his wealth, and that is why he is so poor, mangy, and lazy today. Dog's greed, then, is a trait that is mentioned elsewhere in the Beng corpus.

The other important myth in which Dog figures as a major protagonist presents a radically different portrait of Dog. Here he emerges as a hero, at least where humans are concerned.[5]

The Dispersal of All the Animals

It used to be that all the animals of all the different species worked together building yam mounds [i.e., farming]. One day, Dog found someone's egg, and he yelped. He was asked, "What did you see?" He responded, "Nothing."

Dog took the Egg to the village and put it inside a round gate [a common means of protecting important items, including ritually powerful objects]. In time, the Egg hatched and a Man and Woman popped out. The couple grew up. The Man got a gun to go hunting. He caught some game and went to eat the meat; Dog ate the bones. Hyena said to the other animals, "That gate will ruin the village! Let's destroy it tomorrow." All this he said while eating. He was angry because the Man, with his gun, had killed some of the animals, and they had begun to diminish as a population.

But Dog snitched and told Man about the plan. The Man said, "Okay, let them destroy the gate." The Man put some cartridges in his gun to load it. The animals came to break up the gate: Elephant, Lion, etc., all the animals except for Dog. The Man shot the gun into the group and all the animals fled in different directions. Hyena said, "I knew about it; I knew the Man and Dog's gate would ruin us; I told you so!"

And that's why all the animals are now dispersed and the different species no longer live together.

This myth contains quite a different view of Dog from the one contained in the first myth. Rather than giving in to his selfish desires and thereby destroying or betraying Humans, in this myth Dog acts generously to Humans while betraying his fellow animals.[6] Moreover, there is some indication that the couple portrayed in this myth are the first humans to be created. If this is so—the point is ambiguous—it would support the argument even further: not only did Dog save the lives of this man and woman, but because of their possible status in the creation, he might also be seen as having safeguarded the very creation of Humanity. In any case, Dog did in effect serve to "hatch" the two humans from their Egg within the gate enclosure, in essence giving symbolic birth to them.

Considering the two myths together—"The Origin of Death" and "The Dispersal of All the Animals"—Dog can be seen as responsible for both the destruction and the protection (and perhaps even the creation) of humans. Taking these two very contradictory roles into account, I suggest that Dog may be seen in these myths as an alter ego for humans. Here I am taking *alter ego* to mean another character who embodies both the hidden hopes and the hidden frustrations of the main character.[7] In this sense, in the two myths Dog represents both positive and negative aspects of being human, and both positive and negative ways of relating to humans. Put differently, mythical Dogs act at times as if they were human to the point of identifying with humans; they protect humans against the revenge of other animals. At other times they differentiate themselves from humans to the point of helping to create the ultimate disaster for them: death.

Dogs in Ritual and Daily Life

In some ways dogs are taken care of much as humans are by the Beng, while in other ways they are treated nonchalantly, even callously.[8] What may seem like inconsistency in the way Beng treat their dogs is, I suggest, related to the ambiguous role that we have seen dogs play in Beng mythology cum cosmology.

We begin by looking at the fundamental question of how Beng address their dogs. As in Western culture, Beng owners name their dogs. But unlike Western dog owners, they choose names reserved specifically for dogs. Now, the fact and style of naming animals is always a clue to their conception in the wider scheme of things, as Lévi-Strauss has shown so insightfully (1966b:191–216). That Beng name dogs yet bestow on them nonhuman names signifies a certain ambiguity in their nature when seen in relation to humans. Highlighting this ambiguity is the further fact that Beng dog names are either in African languages other than Beng or, in one case that I noted, may be nonsense words (in this case, made up by a two-year-old child of the dog's owner). Nowadays, dog names may also be in French, often selected by owners who know very little French. Unlike human names, dog names are more often proverbs or expressions than single words.

Let us consider some of these names:

Kotɛ Mɔ Nyré (in Jula): "Problems don't seek people, people seek problems"
Yrelɔ (in Jula): "Know yourself; stand by yourself"—i.e., one should not get into disputes
Kófla (in Jula): "Two things"—i.e., if someone is sick, it is as if she or he were on two roads; maybe she or he will live, maybe she or he will die, but no one knows
È tɔé (in Baule): "We're always swimming"—i.e., if several people are swimming, no one knows who will float and who will sink
Bekanti (in Baule): "If one speaks, I hear"—i.e., if someone speaks ill of me, I will hear about it, but I must not take it too much to heart
Quelle Année? (in French): "Which year?"—i.e., which year shall I be rich?
Sabu: A nonsense word made up by a two-year-old boy

Through the exegeses offered to me of these dog proverb-names, it is readily apparent that many of them express rather negative, even fatalistic, views about life. A pervasive theme is that one can have little control over one's destiny; worse, many malevolent people and actions await one in the world.

That the Beng choose their pet dogs as the medium through which to express such statements is indicative, I suggest, of the ambivalent view they have of these animals. That is, people in a sense humanize their dogs by the simple act of naming them (unlike other animals, which they do not name). But the names they choose—in foreign languages, and expressing quite negative views of the world—seem to express the most problematic aspects of being human.[9]

In keeping with this dual view, dogs are never petted or shown overtly any other forms of affection. When my husband, a dog lover, tried to pet a Beng dog, both the dog and its owner looked at him in surprise—it had clearly never occurred to anyone, canine or human, that such a thing should or even could be done. Furthermore, humans never feed adult dogs from their own stores of food. The Beng were appalled once again when on one occasion my husband and I were seen throwing a dog a part of our dinner. Dogs live on scraps (including bones) that they pick up in the village and are rather mangy-looking by Western standards.

But Beng treatment of their dogs is by no means brutal. When their dogs are sick or injured, for instance, owners make concerted efforts to nurse them back to health by using traditional herbal medicines. When one village dog cut itself badly, its owner asked me for some antibiotic cream, and he dabbed it regularly on the wound until it healed.

Furthermore, a male owner of a puppy might feed the dog another form of traditional "medicines" (la) in order to make the animal into a good hunting companion. Such medicines, probably composed of leaves, roots, or barks of certain plants or trees, are seen to have a mystical influence on the animal, in the manner of other medicines administered to humans to gain similar effects (for instance, to give courage to a man who must cut down the corpse of a hanged suicide). Puppies are also fed an additional kind of medicine to make them grow. In this case, the ingredients (kaolin mixed with water, or the soft [rotten] bark of the kapok tree) are identical to the ingredients of a medicine given to most human infants for the same purpose.

Now it is striking that with one exception, which we will explore below, it is forbidden for the Beng to sacrifice dogs. I suggest this is because of its intimate and ambivalent relationship to humans. In choosing an animal for sacrifice, one generally wants to select a victim that is enough like oneself to serve as a substitute but enough unlike that it is clear that it is in fact a substitution—that is, there must usually be some conceptual distance between sacrifier[10] and victim for the substitution to be meaningful. Between Dog and Human there does not seem to be enough of this conceptual distance, whereas between themselves and the other livestock that Beng raise—chickens, sheep, goats—there is the right mix of conceptual difference and identity for the one to serve as a sacrificial substitute for the other (see note 11).

Moreover, unlike some other groups in Africa (e.g., the Kabiye of Togo; Charles Piot, personal communication), Beng do not eat dogs in nonsacrificial contexts. An early work by Leach (1964) may be relevant here; he points out that dogs are not considered edible in Britain because they are too close to the category of "human" or "self." Only those animals that are more conceptually removed than dogs are from the human sphere—but not too far removed, like wild animals—are eaten by the British. My analysis of the Beng material owes much to Leach's approach, and my findings on Beng culture are not unrelated to his for British culture. But they are not exactly parallel. Leach has postulated that the English view dogs almost as replicas of humans in the positive sense of sympathetic identification; out of sympathy for them, and out of extension of the rule against eating other humans (called, contemptuously, "cannibalism"), they abstain from eating dogs. The interpretation I present of the Beng's relationship to dogs in general and their reason for abstaining from eating them in particular is related but not analogous.

I suggest that Beng do not eat dogs precisely because dogs are conceptually ambiguous, like and yet unlike humans. Of all the animals, dogs are the most loyal to humans. In myth, Dog saved Humans mythically from the rampage of the other animals. Yet, if Dog betrayed his fellow animals, who is to say Dog might not betray Humans in turn? This seems to be the message of the other major Dog myth, in which Dog introduced death to Humans. As what I am terming loosely an alter ego, Dog can play a complex role in the lives of humans, at times identified as an ally, at other times differentiated as a traitor.

In accordance with Dog's mythical allegiance to humans and betrayal of his fellow animals as revealed in the second myth I presented, Beng men take their dogs on hunting expeditions in the forest, where the animals help their owners to track down forest game. In fact, Beng say that forest animals are all stupid and should be easily killed by hunters. They evade detection only because they are protected by forest spirits. But these forest spirits are afraid of dogs, and it is partly for this reason that Beng men bring along dogs on the hunt: to bark at spirits, scaring them away and hence dissolving the game's cover. Thus in daily life, as in the creation myth, dogs act against the interests of the other animals and in support of humans. Furthermore, dogs are also separated radically from the forest animals in terms of how the bush spirits act toward each of them.

A related contemporary use for dogs is as field surveyors. Dogs survey fields quite effectively. On their own, they kill any animals that come to eat the crops, even larger animals such as monkeys or the smaller varieties of duiker. If no person is available to tend a particular field, the farmer may send the dog to that field. There the dog remains all day and kills any animals that come to eat the crops; at dusk the dog returns on his own to the village. Once arrived, he walks around in circles to attract the attention of his master. Then he leads the owner to the field and points out the animals he killed.

Finally, a dog can be used by a woman to watch over her baby while she works in the fields. After recovering from childbirth, most women slowly resume their farm work. By the time the baby is a few months old, most mothers are back working full time in the fields. If a mother has another child who is too young to be of much use in farm labor but old enough to look after the infant, she uses this child as a babysitter in the fields. But in the absence of another child of the right age, a mother of an infant might use a dog as the babysitter. Once arrived in the fields, she puts the baby on a mat on the ground and instructs the dog to lie down next to the infant. There the dog stays to chase away any insects or animals that come to bother or injure the baby.

All these practices reveal the role of the dog as an ally of humans, protecting them against other animal species. In this way, dogs replicate in daily life their mythical betrayal of the other animals for the sake of protecting humans.

But insofar as Dog mythically introduced death to humanity, he is also a traitor—even if inadvertently—to humans. Because of this, dogs must at another level be despised as well. As I mentioned, dogs are not deliberately fed and indeed are allowed to grow thin and mangy. Moreover, unlike the Kujamaat Diola of Senegal, whose dogs bark at witches to chase them (Sapir 1981:534), all dogs are themselves viewed by the Beng as witches, though with beneficial as well as destructive capabilities. They can kill people, as human witches can, but in contrast to ordinary human witches, they also have clairvoyant powers. If someone in a compound is about to die, the dog of the compound knows ahead of time and absents himself from the compound until the death occurs. The dual capabilities of dogs as witches, with both destructive and benign capacities, contrast starkly to the other animals that the Beng say are witches—domesticated goats and sheep. These latter the Beng consider as only evil, with no clairvoyant powers. But the ambivalent powers of dogs as witches also bring them into contrast with human witches, who are considered either good or bad witches, but rarely both combined.

There are, however, two categories of human witch that are said to possess both malevolent and benevolent powers. The first is the twin, who, it is said, is born with such dual powers. Moreover, like dogs, twins are said to be clairvoyant, particularly about imminent deaths in the compound. In a sense, this parallel between mythic Dog and human twin may not be gratuitous. For the dog himself may be seen as a metaphorical twin to humanity, in some ways a part of us, partaking of our identity, yet also differentiated as another being.

The second category of person who combines benevolent and malevolent uses of witchcraft is the political officeholder. Both male and female village chiefs as well as the two kings and queens who rule the two regions of Bengland are required to be witches. For the most part they use their occult powers to protect their citizens. But as they are said to "own" everything in the kingdom, they are ultimately in control as well of destructive witchcraft, which, as we saw in chapter 3, is viewed as having been reluctantly preauthorized by the local king (see Gottlieb 1989).

Are dogs like kings? In some ways, yes. Dogs too have both benevolent and malevolent mystical powers. They certainly do not "rule" the Beng in the ways that kings (and queens and chiefs) do. Yet the striking similarity in the ambiguous powers of witchcraft held by both kings and dogs suggests that dogs resemble humans in the ultimate sense: as the most powerful people of all. Thus Dog not only caused death to humans in mythic times; he can still kill people now, not only through witchcraft but also by inflicting a potentially fatal disease on people. The disease, called either Corpse (*galε*) or Dog (*jεŋ*), reveals by its name that the very essence of the canine form can be fatal to humans in a particular circumstance: at death.

The symptoms of the illness caused by dogs are obvious: the sufferer becomes weak, loses all appetite for food, gets stiff—in a word, becomes corpselike. Now it is notable that Beng are vulnerable to Corpse after having close contact with a human corpse as well. That dog corpses, like human corpses, also sicken people once again reveals the power over humans that dogs, like kings, hold.

There are two contexts in which people can find themselves made ill by dog corpses. The first concerns sick dogs. If a dog is so ill that it should be killed (as with a rabid dog), the deed is done in the forest and the cadaver thrown deep into the bushes, where no human will venture. Should a woman have close contact with the cadaver (or should its odor waft into the village) the ghost *(wru)* of the dead dog would "catch" the woman and give the disease, Corpse (sometimes called, in this instance, Dog), to her future progeny. Any children coming near such a dog corpse would themselves be afflicted with the disease.[11]

Traditionally only a very old man (generally a widower), who would never again sire children, would have performed the task of killing a sick dog. If a younger man (or a woman) had done so, his or her future children would have been afflicted with Corpse. Nowadays younger men (but not women) may administer certain ritual medicines to themselves to keep from catching this disease, and they may kill sick dogs. Significantly, the medicine consists of washing with a decoction made with leaves of the lemon or lime tree (or cleaning one's teeth with the branches of these trees), the same medicine that people use when they have had close contact with a human corpse and wish to avoid getting Corpse as a result.

The second way to catch Corpse from a dog is related to the first: if a person beats a healthy dog to death for no legitimate reason, it is said that the dog's spirit will also inevitably "catch" its killer. Not only will the killer become corpselike but, though the individual may be treated successfully with herbal remedies, if he or she does not apologize ritually to the dog's spirit by means of a sacrifice, the next child that this person bears or sires will die when reaching the age that the dog reached when it was beaten to death. This will be repeated with all successive children until the dog's killer ritually apologizes to the dog's spirit and offers it a sacrifice.

Alternatively, the dog's owner may himself be so angry over the animal's death that he curses the killer. To do so, the owner wraps the cadaver in a *pagne* (a length of fabric used for clothing), as is done for human corpses, and then buries the dog. If he wishes to make the curse less drastic, he may bury the cadaver without first wrapping it in a *pagne*. Wrapping the dog corpse in human clothes (and, to a lesser extent, burying it) serve to humanize the animal, and it is the act of humanization that brings the curse into effect.[12]

Thus the Beng realize that levels of humanization of dogs are possible. Both the illegitimate killing of a healthy dog and the deliberate killing of a sick dog reveal a profound identification of human with dog, yet both entail decidedly negative consequences for humans. In both cases, humans are, in effect, punished or even killed by the ghost of the dog. Indeed, the human deaths that a dog is seen as capable of causing might be seen as a sacrifice to the dog's ghost. In this case, the normal master-servant relationship between human and dog is reversed, and the dog decisively gains the upper hand, acting more as traitor than as ally.

Another instance of negative reciprocity between human and dog involves what could be seen as an indirect sacrifice of a person on behalf of a dog. The Beng say that a newborn puppy's eyes remain closed until it hears of a human who has just died. Thus as soon as the owner of new puppies hears a funeral announced—be it in a Beng village, or anywhere else—she or he must tell the puppies of the litter, "X died, open your eyes" *(X e ga, ka ka yɔwle pú)*. Though Western veterinary science tells us that all healthy puppies open their eyes within about four days of birth, the Beng maintain that only after they are told this news will puppies be able to open their eyes and develop into adult dogs. And only then will their owner be able to sell them, if some of them are being kept for sale. We see here the idea of an exchange: one human life for (at least) one dog life (depending on how many puppies are in the litter). Though there is no notion that a particular puppy killed the person in question, the exchange, far from being even, is ultimately weighed heavily in favor of the animals: a dog can grow up only if a human dies. In other words, each new dog life (or set of sibling lives) requires the reduction by one of human life. On a broad level, again, one might see this as a kind of sacrifice of humans to dogs.

But the Beng on rare occasions also perform the reverse kind of ritual, killing a dog as a sacrifice to appease the spirit of a human. This is performed after a woman has died while pregnant or during childbirth. In this case, a certain ritual specialist operates to remove and bury the fetus, and he later sacrifices and eats a dog. The dog is clearly meant as a close substitute for the human fetus and, as such, an offering of forgiveness to the dead woman's ghost. To my knowledge, this is the only occasion in the Beng ritual repertoire that calls for a dog sacrifice.[13]

THE DOG IN BENG THOUGHT

This set of activities and ideologies surrounding dogs and death reveals a profound dualism in the relationship of human to canine. On one hand, dogs are so closely identified with humans that puppies are given the same ritual growth medicines as are human infants. Moreover, a dog is sacrificed to appease the ghost of a woman who died while pregnant or in labor, and as symbolic compensation for the loss of the baby. But as I noted earlier, in order for the substitution to be meaningful, an animal to be sacrificed must first acknowledge difference from the species on whose behalf it is being sacrificed. So difference is introduced into the relationship between dog and human even in this intimate act. Likewise, dogs' role as ally of humans itself reveals a hint of wavering between identity and difference, for as with a friend, one may be an ally only inasmuch as there is some gap to be bridged.[14] So perhaps it is not surprising to encounter dogs in the opposite role as well: as traitors to the human cause. Thus in keeping with their role of mythical traitors, dogs may bewitch humans and can kill children if mistreated.[15]

We can detect here an interesting pattern in the way time is dealt with in the sets of ritual and mythical connections between dog and human. In the Origin of Death myth, Dog introduces a legacy of death that will afflict all future generations of humans. In the myth explaining the animal species' dispersal, Dog is responsible for creating a human couple—possibly the original Humans—and in so doing, he disperses the other animals, again for all future generations to come. In the ritual treatment of a woman who dies while pregnant or in labor, a dog is sacrificed as a substitute and symbolic equivalent to the dead human fetus, who would have embodied the next generation. And in the case of a human beating a dog to death, the next generation of offspring of the guilty human is in effect doomed, cursed, until the dog's killer ritually atones for the sin. In each of these four cases, dogs and humans produce results that have dire consequences on each other's offspring (or the offspring of other species). Dog and human are engaged in a kind of permanent duel that can prove fatal not only to one or the other parties but also to their offspring, given transgression of certain codes.

Perhaps the ambivalence with which the Beng view dogs is best revealed in the relationship of dogs to food. On one hand, as already mentioned, dogs are fed little and live primarily on scraps. But the Beng do say that the dog is the only animal that does not eat raw food, only cooked food, precisely because it eats scrounged leftover scraps from human meals. Viewing cooking as a symbol of culture (Lévi-Strauss 1969b), we can see the significance attached to this dual statement: dogs share with humans the craving for cooked food, but they do not deliberately get fed, for all that. In short, the Beng attitude toward dogs comprises a continuum of ambivalence, a distorted mirror that sometimes reflects more accurately than a normal one the flaws as well as graces of human existence.

The alter-ego role that I see Dog playing for humans may be comparable to the role that the "double" sometimes plays in Western literature (for examples, see Rank 1971:8–33). As in Edgar Allan Poe's story "William Wilson" (1894), another being serves as critical commentary on one's actions (cf. Hoffman 1972:213–218), and it is not clear whether that being is fully differentiated from oneself; at best, the relationship is problematic.

What makes Dog resonate so strongly for the Beng, I suggest, is that in myth as well as in daily life, dogs act both as Self and as Other to humans. As Jackson stated of the Kuranko, "The abstract or moral principles of kinship and reciprocity enable Kuranko to think of the Other, both as a potential ally or neighbor and as a potential foe or stranger" (1974:414). In this formulation, the Other contains both identity and difference within it. As I see the role of the dog in Beng thought, it also incorporates the essence of identity and difference within it, but in such a way as to embody both the Other and the Self. As such, reflecting what humans both seek and dread in one another—the faith in an ally, the terror in a traitor—the dog can journey back and forth between the two realms of mythic time and social time as he travels back and forth between animal and human.

THE HYENA

If dogs are ambiguous in both myth and life, hyenas occupy an even more complex space in the Beng world. In this section we will explore from a similar vantage point the role of the hyena in Beng thought. Here we will encounter a further level of complexity in analyzing the relationship between the hyena's assigned role in myth and in daily life. As we will see, in one realm the hyena's foibles are amusing while in the other they are dangerous indeed.

In the oral literature of Africa, the hyena is probably the best-known animal; prowling at night, scavenging on other animals' prey, howling in an eerie way, this creature has suggested all that is immoral to humans, symbolizing a range of negative character traits from avarice to malice to stupidity. Hyena often presents a clear-cut morality tale, a tale of inversion of all that is admirable, and it is easy to look down upon him when he appears in myths and folktales throughout Africa, including among the Beng.

Jackson (1982:112), for example, describes the role of the mythical Hyena among the Kuranko in terms that could easily apply to the Beng corpus:

> [Hyena] acts blindly, selfishly, and instinctively. . . . The Hyena can never integrate his intentions with the consequences of his actions; he lives in a world of emotion and impulse, a world pervaded by his own subjectivity.

Similar views of the mythical Hyena emerge elsewhere in Africa, from the Kaguru of Tanzania (Beidelman 1961, 1963, 1975) to the Dogon, Bamana, Bozo, and Fulani of the Western Sudan (Calame-Griaule and Ligers 1961) and the Kujamaat Diola of Senegal (Sapir 1981:532–33). Yet given varying social contexts, similar myths take on vastly different burdens of meaning.

The moral bankruptcy of the mythical Hyena and the ways in which hyenas are treated in everyday life reveal much about the specific contours of Beng culture and its varying views on social conformity and rebellion. In Beng myths, Hyena indeed appears to represent a clear-cut morality tale: he always displays greed coupled with stupidity, and his stupidity prevents him from indulging his greed to his full satisfaction. But rather than playing a villain, Hyena is seen by the Beng as a foolish creature, and the telling of Hyena tales is always accompanied by much laughter from the audience. In contrast, the actual hyenas that Beng might encounter are dealt with quite seriously; indeed, their perceived defects are highlighted in the ritual treatments of hyenas. Thus we can see that myths and rituals concerning hyenas do not reflect but rather distort each other. Specifically, in myth Hyena's difference from human values is accepted as amusing, while in daily life this is seen as threatening to the point of requiring drastic ritual action.

HYENA MYTHS

Let us begin by considering a typical Hyena narrative from the Beng repertoire.[16]

Hyena and the Fish

Here's one of my stories. They say there was a river that had fish in it. The river dried up and the fish said they'd better move and go into another river. It's then that Hare, who was passing by, saw them. He said, "Where are you going?" They said, "We were in the big river over there but it dried up, so we're going to another river. Choose two of us to take for yourself: one to sacrifice, the other to eat." So Hare went off to sacrifice and eat his two fish.

As for Hyena, when he went and saw the fish . . . the dummy started dancing, enjoying himself sweetly. Then he said, "I'm not going to take only two, I'm going to get a basket and cart and I'll come back and gather you all up." All the while he was dancing, dancing, following the fish.

Then he left them to go get his wives, the basket, and the cart. He returned with his wives, but the fish were already on the river bank. He shot out a paw to grab some of them, plem! But he was too late; the fish had already gone into the water. He grabbed one to give to his children, but it slipped out of his hand and went to the bottom of the river. And that's how Hyena is stupid.

In this myth, as in others about Hyena, the moral lesson is stated clearly: "And that's how Hyena is stupid." Hyena's inability to foresee the consequences of his actions prevents the full exercise of his avarice. The implication is that in the end, greed, which is incompatible with wisdom, will always be thwarted. The temptation to satisfy unreasonable desires at the expense of others is doomed to defeat. Certainly Hyena's continual failures would seem to present this message to those, including children, who sit around the courtyard fire late at night listening to the storytelling sessions. Yet listeners, both child and adult, take pleasure—perhaps guilty pleasure—in hearing of Hyena's attempts at indulging his selfish whims. It may be that Hyena's motives, while condemned, are secretly admired by many, as a seductive challenge to what is considered acceptable social behavior. (Hyena's greed here contrasts with the greed exhibited by Dog in the myth that I presented in the previous section. There Dog's greed was by no means amusing but thoroughly condemnable, with drastic consequences, as we saw.)

In other myths Hyena is represented not only as stupid, greedy, or generally opposed to human interests; he may also be portrayed as a Muslim (cf. Calame-Griaule and Ligers 1961:95). As such he is radically differentiated from the moral universe that traditional Beng recognize as giving meaning to their lives. In one myth, for example, Hyena's status as a Muslim is used to show how he can undermine the basis of Beng magical practices.[17]

The King, the Hyena, and the Bird

There was a little Bird whose feathers were sought by the old people of the village. They needed the feathers to give to the king.[18] Three (Snake, Hyena, and Lion) were chosen by the king to go look for the Bird. They went into the forest and Snake went into Bird's nest where the eggs were. Lion was hidden where there was a very thick stand of thatch. Hyena hid behind the kapok tree. All the while, the Bird was watching them. The birds were flying back to the nest, *kplí kplí kplí.* . . . The *bɔŋɔ* Bird sang [in Dyula]:

> Here I am, I see you,
> The Snake is sitting on my eggs in the nest,
> The Lion is hiding in a thicket,
> The Hyena is hiding behind the kapok tree.

Hyena stayed behind the kapok tree, but he wasn't very well hidden, and he laughed, "*Hu hu hu,* I hid behind the kapok tree, but Bird's seen me!" The birds flew off, *kplí kplí kplí* [knowing there was trouble here].

The three returned to the king and recounted their story. . . . The king told them to go back again and have another try. The king advised Hyena not to laugh this time. The three returned to the spot, and the birds flew back too, but . . . Hyena started laughing again. The three returned to the king again and told him. . . . The king said, "This time . . . Hyena will take Lion's place in the thatch and Lion will take Hyena's place behind the kapok tree." [They did so with the same results.] . . .

So the three went back to the king. . . . The king said, "This time, Hyena won't go; just Snake and Lion will go together."

Lion went and hid in the thicket, and Snake hid in the bird's nest with the eggs. The bɔŋɔ Bird started singing: "This time the Hyena is gone." The birds all flew off, kplí kplí kplí, into their nests, and Snake caught the bɔŋɔ Bird and brought it back to the king.

Everyone in the region went and met in the king's village . . . to hear the news. That same day, they sent Hyena off to another village [to keep him away from the king's meeting] to announce a funeral. When he was returning from announcing the funeral, he found everyone walking down the road, with Bird, to the king's village.

When Hyena reached the village, he went to the house of the village chief. First he went inside, then he went out and walked around the house a few times. He went and got his big bubu [gown; see below].

Snake and Lion were bringing the Bird, but just as they were about to enter the village, Bird started singing:

> Here I am, I see you,
> The Snake is sitting on my eggs in the nest,
> The Lion is hiding in a thicket,
> The Hyena is hiding behind the kapok tree.

At this, Hyena started dancing, and danced all the way from the house to meet the arriving party. By the time he got there, his bubu was all ripped. He walked around the village chief's house, walked around, walked around the house. He even started beating the funeral drums. But that's not what he was sent for. Everyone was supposed to watch out that Hyena didn't approach Bird, since he'd been excluded from the group. But it wasn't the case!

When everyone went to the public meeting place to set things up for the funeral, they forgot about Bird and left him at the chief's house. But Hyena hadn't forgotten. . . . When Hyena went up to Bird, he said, "Eh! Eh! Eh! Eh! You really see people! Eh! When I left my first hiding spot and hid elsewhere, you saw me; when I was hiding behind the kapok tree, was it my name you called out? Sing the song again, I want to hear it." Bird said, "No, I can't sing it here. . . ." Hyena said, "If you sing, it'll make me very happy. Sing it, let me hear." The Bird said, "If you want me to sing it, you have to take off your big bubu in front of me. Move back, take off your big bubu, and untie my feet for me, let me be free. . . ."

Hyena said, "Start singing first. Sing the song once, then I'll untie your feet." So Bird started singing [the same song]. Hyena started laughing, "Uhhu uhhu uhhu, really, you sing it well, sing it again for me." But Bird said, "I don't want to sing, really, but I'm doing it secretly, for you. Now you want me to do it again!" Hyena said, "Yes, sing it again!" Bird said, "First, untie my feet, then I'll sing."

So Hyena untied the feet, and Bird started singing [as before]. Hyena started singing, turning around, and Bird flew off, kprrrr.

Meanwhile, everyone at the public meeting place heard the sounds of Hyena dancing. They saw Bird flying off and started yelling, "Catch him! Catch him!" Some started jumping up to catch hold of him. One barely caught hold but only managed to get some feathers, and Bird flew off. Those who got some feathers were the ones who are now wealthy.

This myth emphasizes Hyena's greediness; his insistence on two songs results ultimately in Bird's escape and the loss of Bird's feathers, considered by the animist Beng to be symbolically efficacious charms (see note 18). Perhaps it is because he is a Muslim that Hyena acts to undermine traditional Beng religion.

Yet in neglecting his *bubu*, Hyena also debases his own religion, Islam. The *bubu*, an ankle-length, long-sleeved gown, is worn by Muslim men on special occasions such as weddings and funerals. As such, it is taken by the Beng as a specific visual marker: a sign of adherence to Islam. Hyena rips his *bubu* in dancing for Bird, then happily takes it off at Bird's request. Hyena not only challenges Beng animism; he is in effect not even a good Muslim. How can such a religious lightweight be given respect? Indeed, at strategic points in the story, Hyena himself cannot keep from guffawing, giving away his hiding place and foiling the group's plans. It seems that even Hyena cannot take himself seriously.

In another myth, Hyena is depicted as utterly opposed not only to the interests of humans but also to their very existence. In "The Dispersal of All the Animals," which we have already explored from Dog's perspective, we see Hyena scheming to evict people from the animal's midst. Hyena endeavors to persuade all the other animals to destroy the human couple, who may be the primal representatives of their species. (As we saw, it was thanks to Dog, who informed the man and woman, that the plan failed and the couple survived.) Here the attitude to Hyena takes on a more serious tone. Acting selfishly in the other myths, Hyena readily provokes laughter in his audience, but in this myth his selfishness has become dangerous to the interests of humans. We are approaching the more wary attitude that Beng have toward the actual hyenas with which they may have come in contact.

LIVING HYENAS

If Beng are for the most part amused by the mythical Hyena with his antisocial character flaws, they hold a different attitude toward living hyenas, which represent a profoundly disturbing potential for causing mayhem to human society and are thus seen not as amusing but as terrifying. I look first at how Beng view the anatomy and behavior of hyenas, which are considered disturbing enough, then consider how Beng deal with them through their own rather intriguing ritual actions.

Hyena Anatomy and Habits

Beng praise the hyenas' great running speed, remarking that the spotted hyena (*Crocuta crocuta*) can outrun a dog.[19] But that may be the only hyena trait they admire. Beyond that, the Beng condemn as monstrous and anomalous a group of features that set hyenas apart (cf. Douglas 1966; also Bulmer 1967, Leach 1964, Tambiah 1969).

When asked to describe a hyena, Beng remark on its fur, which they describe as *frika* or *fri fraye* ("variegated-striped" or "mottled"). Beng do not admire mottled appearances, preferring an even, monochromatic look or, barring that, crisp stripes or other clearly delineated patterns. For this reason, they think the hyena is simply ugly (for a similar Kaguru view, see Beidelman 1986:186). They account for its ungainly coat in a myth ("Hyena, Lion, the Worker, and Forced Labor"), which I summarize briefly.[20] Hyena took advantage of Lion's absence by trying to sell an animal that was hired by Lion to work in his fields. When Lion discovered this, he grabbed at Hyena, trying to catch him, but he only managed to snatch him with his claws, producing the variegated-striped pattern the hyena has today. Thus the fur on living hyenas is seen as the result of an immoral deed that Hyena once committed in myth.

Hyenas not only look ugly to the Beng; they also move about at inappropriate times. They have a habit of traveling at night, particularly to hunt (Grzimek 1975:186). Beng have used this trait in naming the animal; one of their terms for the hyena is *yiruyali*, "night walker." Now the Beng are especially mistrustful of night creatures, for, like many other Africans, they see night as a time for sinful activities, especially witchcraft (cf., e.g., Beidelman 1975; Jackson 1982:54–56; Needham 1978; Winter 1963:292). All night travel is virtually forbidden; those who do leave the village after dark are said to be either foolish or witches. Indeed, as we will explore further in the following chapter, the occasional car that passes by after dusk is said to be the transformed human victim of a witch, who is driving it off somewhere to be eaten later.[21] The Beng name for the hyena, "night walker," thus speaks directly to the Beng's level of mistrust of the animal.

Hyenas also eat inappropriate food. They are perfectly capable of hunting their own meat (Kruuk 1972:106ff.)—a fact the Beng recognize, as they used to tie up sheep and goats inside the courtyard to protect them from the hyenas that were once in the area (cf. Sapir 1981:536 and Walker 1964:1265). But it is hyenas' occasional scavenging that seems to have caught the attention and criticism of most Africans, including the Beng. Kruuk tells us that "the hyena shows some morphological and physiological features which make it the supreme utilizer of every bone or scrap of animal remains," including special bone-crushing third premolars and other shearing teeth (Kruuk 1972:107); thus, unlike other animals, hyenas can eat and fully digest the largest bones of even sizable game, such as the East African wildebeest and zebra (ibid.:108). Perhaps it is because their men are hunters that the Beng find the notion of scavenging so repulsive. In any case, hyena meat is itself taboo to all Beng.[22]

The ossiferous nature of the hyenas' diet produces feces that are starkly white, from the powdery, calcium-rich remains of scavenged bones (Kruuk 1972:107–108). Beng comment on the uniqueness of such white feces in the animal kingdom (indeed, this feature appears as a major plot mover in a Beng myth, "Dog, Hyena, the Mothers, and the Names,"[23] in which Hare tracks down Hyena by tracing the path of this Hyena's white feces), and they emphasize their disgust at the sight.

Not only do hyenas prey on animal carcasses; they also scavenge on human ones. Throughout Africa, hyenas have a nasty habit of coming into villages at night and digging up fresh corpses. This is particularly troublesome to the Beng, for their religion includes a strict taboo against the unearthing of human corpses under any circumstances. The violation of this taboo (for instance, in the case of a police autopsy of a suspicious death) results in pollution of the Earth spirits, requiring a series of atonement sacrifices, usually offered by the village chief, to lift the pollution.

Nowadays there are few hyenas left in Bengland—most have gone north to the savanna regions—but the Beng say that within living memory, the numerous hyenas present in the region were a risk to new burials.[24] Therefore, after a funeral, the corpse would have been buried in the village and a high gate erected around the tomb. For a few weeks after the burial, while the corpse was still decomposing, a light would be kept burning all night inside the gate to frighten off the hyenas. However, if the cause of death was what the Beng classify as a polluting condition— leprosy, elephantiasis, or suicide—the corpse was buried in the forest rather than the village. In this case, the cadaver would be left to its own fate, unprotected against hyenas (cf. Bloch and Parry 1982:15–18, on "bad deaths").

The taboo against unearthing a human corpse derives from a wider premise of Beng religion that a discrete division of space must be maintained for various beings and that specific activities may take place only in certain culturally defined zones. As we saw in chapter 2, sex, menstruation, and childbirth (as signs and agents of human fertility) are restricted to the village, while agricultural activities (as agents of crop fertility) are restricted to the forest. Moreover, visible humans live in the village while invisible spirits live in the forest. Violation of these boundaries brings on retribution (by spirits against humans) or disaster (by animals against humans). The rule that human cadavers must remain underground is thus part of that system, which dictates the proper spatial arrangement for various beings and activities. When hyenas disturb human tombs they threaten a wider set of spatial categories that should remain discrete.[25]

Given the hyenas' desires to raid human burials, there is also the potential that their excretions will contain fully digested human remains. In this case, the human corpse, disturbed in its underground resting place and taken into the forest to be eaten, would be redeposited as feces in the village. Such a cycle would be the perverse triumph of a forest animal processing village humans as food. Alternatively, any human bones in the hyena feces might come from the forest burials of polluted persons (such as lepers) exiled from the village. Their illicit return to the village via hyena feces would be yet another level of perversion, a violation of the banishment to the forest of cadavers deemed outside the scope of human society and unworthy of funerals.

While no Beng ever mentioned this, their descriptions of the white feces of hyenas reminded me of balls of kaolin, the powdery white clay that the Beng utilize on innumerable occasions as ritual body paint to attract protective spirits.[26] If this association is indeed relevant, hyena feces would further appear as a monstrous parody of a primary ingredient (and color) in the Beng religious palette.

So far we have isolated several anatomical and ecological traits of the hyena that the Beng have seized upon as signs of their abnormality. These include mottled fur, nocturnal traveling, scavenging animal and human remains, and white feces.[27] In dwelling critically upon these anomalous features, Beng reveal their discomfort with the living hyena and its habits. This discomfort serves as a backdrop to the dramatic rituals that the Beng enact when confronted with actual hyenas. We will explore two such ritual treatments. Both reveal strikingly how threatening Beng find the flesh-and-blood hyena and its perceived violations of human norms and boundaries.

HYENAS IN RITUAL AND DAILY LIFE

Preoccupied by an anatomical peculiarity in the hyena, the Beng have observed that for a short period after a hyena dies, its rectum moves in and out. A hyena specialist I spoke with, while he has never seen this described action, confirmed for me its likelihood (Alan Schumacher, personal communication, 1988). Hyenas scent-mark by conspicuously everting the rectum about an inch, and Schumacher deemed it likely that a dying hyena might evert the rectum as a death reflex. This action would take place while the animal still technically lay dying and would be terminated before its clinical death, but Schumacher acknowledged that an untrained observer could reasonably conclude that the hyena was already dead.

In describing the situation my Beng informant said that the body part "breathes like a heart"; to illustrate the process he rhythmically curled and uncurled his hand into a fist. In drawing this analogy, I suggest, he was emphasizing the component of life that the heart represents. For a heart, or any other organ, to continue moving (allegedly) after the creature's death is certainly a contradiction, a reversal of a normal causal sequence. In a sense the hyena is insisting on holding on to life even in the face of death. Beng classify this anomaly as symbolically dangerous and have invented a ritual of sorts to deal with the perceived danger.[28]

If someone happens to see a newly dead hyena, Beng say, he or she must immediately find a dried, stripped corncob and use it to plug up and still the hyena's rectum.[29] If this ritually required act is not performed, the observer of the trembling rectum will be seized with a fit of laughter that will continue for the rest of his or her life. "Even if your mother dies," my informant told me, "you won't stop laughing; you'll laugh so long and hard that eventually it will kill you." Where the mythic hyena is mocked by his human audience, the laughter that is directed at the dying hyena rebounds on his human observer. It is as if in death the hyena achieves revenge on his human audience for ridiculing him in his mythic incarnation—a revenge that ironically takes the form of incessant laughter.

If laughter, as Bakhtin says (1984:92), represents "the social consciousness of all the people," then we must inquire: what is the joke? Why is this sight seen as funny to the Beng, and how is it that laughter, if not stopped by ritual, turns lethal?

Laughter is said to be the empirical recognition of anomaly (Douglas 1968; also cf. Apte 1985). In the Beng case of the dying hyena, we start with what is surely an anomalous sight: a body part that refuses to die. I suggest that this anomaly comes to stand for the continual reversal of normal activities for which both the mythical and the actual hyena are noted. The sight thus provokes precisely that behavior in humans that is found detestable in hyenas and is a travesty of daily social relations. The immorality of laughing continuously through one's life was stressed by my informant in two ways. First, it was tied to the death of one's mother.[30] With the existence of matriclans, the idea of laughing at the demise of one's mother is a horrifying negation of the basic affective and jural bonds that lie at the heart of the matriclan. The implication seems to be: if one could guffaw at the death of one's mother, what couldn't one find funny? The answer, of course, is nothing. Thus such uncontrollable laughter was said by my informant to have only one possible outcome: one's own death. This situation embodies the ultimate irony; "caught" by his mythical nemesis, the human observer has been in essence transformed, through his mocking of social ties, into that antisocial creature itself, the hyena.

If the hyena threatens the individual who witnesses his demise, he poses a far greater peril to an entire group of villagers under another set of circumstances. I discovered this perceived threat while talking one day with a male elder who, in telling me the history of his village, explained that the very village in which we were sitting had within memory been located elsewhere. One day, perhaps about a century ago, a hyena had come in from the forest and defecated on the ground, causing the entire village to be *wi*, "broken"; had not the village been evacuated, he assured me, it would soon have been the locus of innumerable deaths. Thus the villagers immediately abandoned the old village and chose the present site. To avert just such drastic upheavals, it is said that any hyena seen near a Beng village should always be killed and its carcass thrown in the surrounding bush.[31]

Although the elder told the story as a historical event, I am unable to determine its historical accuracy; it may be "just a story" that people tell about their village. But stories such as these, and the issues they reveal, have great import for those who tell and listen to them, who follow the rules the stories lay out. In other words, stories can serve as creative means for making sense of the world (Bruner 1986; Carrier 1987; R. Rosaldo 1986; Schwartzman 1984).[32] Indeed, in this ritually obligatory action, the hyena is construed as the most powerful subverter of human society. The differences in their respective interests could not be stated more clearly, for hyena's subversion here takes the form of perceived symbolic destruc- tion. Given this, we are prompted to ask: why are the feces of a hyena conceived— and treated—as so dangerous to the village as to require a collective and permanent exodus?

The hyena is an appropriate vehicle for such a drastic set of meanings because of a constellation of interrelated features perceived as meaningful. This includes the ways that Hyena is perceived in myth as an antisocial character, the anatomy and habits of the living hyena as remarked upon and criticized by the Beng, and the ritual action that Beng have prescribed to deal with the encounter with a newly dead hyena. In other words, several features that are valued negatively in anatomy, myth, and individual ritual combine to make the actual hyena whose droppings pollute the Beng village a potent symbol of the dissolution of that village.[33]

The Hyena in Beng Thought

As we have seen, Beng valuations of the hyena in myth and ritual are dramatically opposed, with their conception of the hyena's anatomy and habits playing a mediating role between these two poles of experience. In the discussion that follows

I focus on the relationship between the contrasting domains of myth and ritual, leaving anatomy as the implicit backdrop to these two.

In both classical and recent anthropological formulations in Anglophone and Francophone traditions, myth and ritual have been seen overwhelmingly as pieces cut from the same cloth (e.g., Malinowski 1948: 138–143; Raglan 1958; Griaule 1965:194; Dieterlen 1973:49–53; de Heusch 1985, chaps. 6 and 7; for a review of this literature, see Okpewho 1983:45–52). Even Lévi-Strauss's elegiac finale to *The Naked Man* (1981) adheres loosely, if creatively, to this framework. Lévi-Strauss proposes that myth operates as the primary medium of thought, and he relegates ritual to a subsidiary, dependent role, embodying nothing more than a "reaction to what thought [i.e., myth] has made of life" (1981:682).[34] Still, in reacting to myth, ritual endeavors—though never successfully—to destroy it (Lévi-Strauss 1981: 675ff.; cf. de Heusch 1985:2). Thus despite the postulated reactive role of ritual, there is a potential tension in Lévi-Strauss's model that I find appealing. Unlike the position taken by functionalists, it leaves space for a disjunction of meaning between myth and ritual.

Myth and ritual may be seen as two kinds of texts or media that, while dealing with the same subject, still exist in mutual contrast. Put another way, I have explored two Beng "voices" that, each in its own way, make statements about the nature of subversion. Both provide, as Hymes has put it, an "imaginative analysis of worlds alternative to the accepted" (1979:xii). In Beng myth, Hyena's foibles are seen as a source of degeneracy but they also provoke much amusement, and the storytelling sessions in which these foibles are recounted are as much times of entertainment as education. In his mythical appearances, Hyena acts much as humans do during periods of play when the ordinary frames of social life are creatively undone, and Hyena, as the protagonist, and humans, as his appreciative audience, are permitted to threaten the social order by ridiculing it (cf. K. Basso 1979; Beidelman 1986:161, 180, 197; Handelman 1977).

If the mythical Hyena permits its Beng audience the luxury of celebrating subversion while at the same time taking heed of it, the actual hyena that a Beng might encounter in the forest or the village represents to the Beng a singleminded and serious perceived danger to the official order. The Beng have construed a set of potentially dangerous acts of immorality that the hyena can commit against humans and that, in dying, he can provoke in humans. As seen in myth and treated through ritual actions, the hyena is an excessive creature. Yet the divergences from human values that seem amusing in myth become potentially catastrophic in daily life.

Beng ritual may challenge the moral of Hyena myths in taking seriously what the myths propose as entertainment; but it is a mutual challenge, for the myths also challenge the seriousness of the ritual treatment. In short, I am proposing that we view myth and ritual as related but semi-autonomous means of contemplating a major intellectual and sociological problem. The contrasting views of hyena in myth and ritual do not engage directly in dialogical fashion. Rather, they exist on two different—and complementary—planes of experience (cf. Handelman 1977:190 on the complementarity of ritual and play). By no means do I suggest that one of these presents the "authentic" or definitive understanding while the other offers an obfuscation, as an earlier model might have proposed. Rather, each presents one possible reading, through its own medium.[35]

Together, the Beng views of the hyena in myth and in ritual constitute a complex set of commentaries on human society. They provide a seductive pleasure based in, as well as a warning about, the nature of escape from society. They offer what Bloch (1985:645) in another context has called a "continuing speculation on problems which are irresolvable."

DOGS AND HYENAS

As Drummond writes (1981:634), myth "is primarily a part of an ongoing process that continuously creates culture by formulating images of human identity." The path between myth and contemporary society must be an open one with a sort of conceptual travel possible in both directions. This path may be traveled particularly by animals, who are, after all, in Lévi-Strauss's famous phrase (1963e:89), "good to think." Animals are creatures that can resonate symbolically in myth and ritual as well as in daily life. As a "moral waiting to be identified," an animal presents a ready sense of Other that humans have often taken as a contrast or counterpart to themselves. Put another way, we have used animals to present to us the negative traits of our own humanity "with an exaggerated license . . . [yet] without jeopardizing any ideals of potentially moral human conduct" (Beidelman 1975:195) by the very fact of projection of disapproved traits onto nonhuman characters.

Not only does Dog serve as an alter ego to Humans, but there is a reverse relationship; as Roy Wagner has pointed out (personal communication), Hyena in effect serves as an alter ego to Dog. Just as Dog sided against the animals and with humans, so Hyena sided with the other animals and against Dog. Another shared trait concerns knowledge of the future. Hyena was clairvoyant about Dog's impending betrayal of the animals and the resultant disaster for the animals, and Dog is likewise clairvoyant about the ultimate disaster that now befalls all humans (which he himself caused, in the first myth cited): death. Hyena and Dog thus play inverse roles in relation to Humans.

Furthermore, both Hyena and Dog have an inverse relationship to the eating of bones. In both myths analyzed earlier, Dog is described as a bone chewer. As is made explicit in the second myth, the bones come from game animals hunted by humans, and today dogs still scrounge the leftover bones from human meals. In contrast, hyenas are known by the Beng, as by people throughout Africa, as graverobbers, gnawing on the bone remains of fresh human corpses. Dogs and hyenas thus play opposite roles: the former eat the bones of other animals provided casually by humans, while the latter eat the bones of humans provided quite unwillingly by themselves.

As we saw earlier, Beng treatment of their dogs is very much in keeping with the place that Dog occupies in Beng myths. In both spheres, the dog is an ambivalent creature, capable of great acts of loyalty and also of betrayal when it comes to human beings. The situation of hyenas is more complex. While Beng myths about Dog may reflect, and in turn be reflected by, rituals and other actions taken by humans in relation to living dogs, such is not the case for hyenas. As we have seen, myth and ritual offer dramatically contrasting statements about the nature, value, and effect of hyenas.

While the mythic Hyena amuses his human audiences, the real-life hyena terrifies his human viewer. Thus by looking at both dogs and hyenas, we see how different modes of relationship between myth and ritual may occur, ranging from the mutually reflective (as with Beng dogs) to the mutually contradictory (as with Beng hyenas). In keeping this in mind, we see how multiple voices and structures can coexist creatively within a single culture. It is a "heteroglot sense of the world" (Bakhtin 1981:331) that the Beng understanding of dogs and hyenas, and of myth and ritual more generally, offers us.

The heteroglossia that is evident in looking at the relationship between myth on one hand and ritual and daily life on the other is evident at another level as well. We have seen how dogs themselves embody aspects of identity with humans and at the same time represent crucial differences from them, and in the second section of this chapter we have seen how hyenas, in their own ways, represent difference from humans, while the nature of that difference is variously interpreted by the Beng as amusing and threatening, depending on the context. Taking Dog and Hyena together as a pair, we can see how they offer their own statements on both the virtues and the dangers of identity and difference. Through their relationship with these two animals, the Beng have no final statement to make concerning identity and difference; rather, they let their ambivalence concerning both animals speak to their continuing meditation on the principles they represent.

In the chapter that follows, I continue the theme of the relations between the Beng and the nonhuman world. While following the general ideological themes of identity and difference that I have been tracing through this work, I investigate the Beng reaction to the multitude of commodities and certain other items that have made their way to the Beng villages from the Western world.

CHAPTER SIX

Commodities

> What is significant about the adoption of alien objects—as of alien
> ideas—is not the fact that they are adopted, but the way they are
> culturally redefined and put to use.
>
> Igor Kopytoff, "The Cultural Biography of Things"

The Beng have not had the sort of long-term and sustained contact with the French
that would lead to a thorough and irreversible transformation of their consciousness, as has happened in other parts of the Third World colonized by
European countries. In India, for example, as a result of some 130 years of
continued and penetrating British colonial rule, the writer Nandy has observed
(1983:76), "The everyday Indian, even when he remains only Indian, is both
Indian and Western." The same could not be said of the Beng; their contact with
the French colonizers, and with their world, has been far more recent, sporadic,
and shallow. They have not become both Beng and French.

But saying this should not imply that the Beng are an isolated enclave, removed
from all knowledge of the wider world and living in a purely subsistence economy.
From my very first hours in a tiny, rural Beng village that had no electricity or
running water, I saw meals served in enamel ware imported from Rumania, bottled
Coca Cola as a special treat, factory-made fabric worn in Westernized styles of
clothing, battery-run radios playing world news in French. Not only that, but the
villagers came excitedly to the local weekly markets to buy the colorful cotton print
towels, white blocks of soap stamped with "Marseilles," plastic beads, and dozens of
other Western commodities that itinerant traders had brought with them from
distant lands.

In the course of fieldwork, as I came to chart the enduring influence of the West
on what I had initially and quite naively envisioned as a rather more remote and
independent group, I unintentionally resorted at first to an old but venerable
framework of interpretation in social anthropology: as Lauriston Sharp had found
among the Yir Yoront of Australia (1952), and many others since then have posited
for other places, I reluctantly began surmising that the visible presence of imported
goods must signal cultural decay. The reasoning went that the importation of
industrial commodities must be a sign, and perhaps an agent as well, of irreversible
damage to the foundations of a local village society, making it essentially no longer
viable.[1] Yet in the months that followed, Beng culture, if under pressure from the

modern world, certainly appeared vibrant; I observed regular dances, divinations, weddings, funerals, and trials, all attesting to the continued vitality of at least ritual and other collective events. The welcome influx of Western trade goods had by no means wrought devastation on traditional Beng society.

And so I came to question whether rapid or even gradual disintegration of a seemingly autonomous culture is the necessary result of "culture contact." Indeed, along with James Clifford (1986b:113), I now "question the assumption that with rapid change something essential ('culture'), a coherent differential identity, vanishes." Culture may be actively resistant or more pliably resilient, but in any case it does not seem to be nearly as fragile as an earlier generation of anthropologists viewed it (e.g., Wilson and Wilson 1945), dissolving like the slug when the salt of an alien civilization is poured over it.

The very notion of "culture contact," seductive even now, must suppose that local groups had no truck at all with outsiders precolonially—and this is an unlikely situation indeed for any part of the world during any era (Marcus and Fischer 1986a:78). For even those few groups that aim to repel all outsiders must be aware of them, and must have prior well-developed notions of the Other that fuel their isolationism. To one degree or another, all human groups must have some relationship with their neighbors, if only an intellectual awareness of other ways of living and of other repertoires of objects. In the case of the Beng, obvious cultural influences (dances, sculptural styles, jewelry styles, and so on) from the neighboring Ando, Baule, Jimini, and Jula peoples initially made me wonder nervously if Beng culture as such existed at all. But expanding the notion of culture to include open borders, and the possibility of absorption or transformation of cultural influences, soon put my mind to rest on this score. Indeed, with such a perspective, the very term *culture contact* virtually loses its meaning, if one acknowledges that all societies have always been in some sort of contact, direct or indirect, with at least a neighboring group.

The notion of culture contact remains implicit in the classic and still useful model of commodification developed by Marx (1967). Despite the richly suggestive investigation into commodities and commodity fetishism that Marx inaugurated, commodification studies tend to rely implicitly on the problematic assumption that before the process of commodification, Third World societies existed in relatively isolated pockets and because of this isolation, when faced with abrupt contact with the powerful West, they have succumbed rapidly to cultural degradation. If we reject the initial assumption of social isolation implicit in the model, the hypothesized process of unavoidable cultural deterioration becomes questionable. Positing a far more open and flexible set of rural societies in the Third World, with regular interchange not only with one another but also internationally through a complex network of long-distance trade—which we know existed at least throughout Africa for many centuries before the European colonial period—leads us to question why such societies would instantly transform in deep and wholly destructive ways when faced with yet another set of imported goods.

Furthermore, the power differential between what is typically perceived dualistically as a donor society–recipient society relationship is frequently seen by Western scholars as producing only a one-way major cultural imposition by one society on the other. Thus the very notion of commodification often implies passivity and helplessness on the part of rural, village-level societies in the face of what is essentially conceived as a metropolitan cultural bulldozer. This, too, I find unacceptable on both theoretical and ethnographic grounds. Recent work in anthropology has done much to acknowledge that even people who appear by the standards of Western models of interpretation to be unavoidable victims of distant hegemonic systems can be in their own modest but inspirational ways active shapers of their own experience. The point here is certainly not to deny the force inherent in the world market or in the social and political relations that fuel the dominant world powers. In the late twentieth century, these are major components of the experience of virtually all peoples, no matter how seemingly remote (Thomas 1989). Rather, my intention is to turn the usual analytic gaze, from Western hegemonic nation to rural village, back on itself and instead, by focusing on the micro level, to allow for "indigenous agency" (ibid.:59) in a minority population, analyzing how the local impact of the world powers is interpreted and dealt with by one group of rural people who encounter them.[2] In this way, without denying global power inequalities, we might nevertheless go some way toward "collapsing the macro-micro distinction itself" (Marcus 1989:24) so as to recover a level of local experience. My initial assumption, then, is that the response of a rural, Third World people to foreign technologies is not fully predictable according to a universalist model, but must be investigated intensely in each case.

While questioning the inevitability of a linear sequence of invariable cultural destruction as posited by the commodification model, I remain interested in the basic issue at the heart of that model—what happens when a new set of objects makes its way into another society—while endeavoring to expand the sorts of questions we can ask when confronted with this issue. My aim will be to approach commodification as a process that is open-ended, subject to negotiation and conceptual redefinition by those first acquiring Western goods. Rather than assuming a priori what the effects of commodification should be, I hope to explore how rural people themselves perceive, and intellectually reappropriate, foreign objects by endeavoring to assign them a culturally appropriate space.

For when goods circulate, they never enter a cultural vacuum; rather, they insert themselves into a space already occupied by other physical objects and, more importantly, a space that is occupied by an intellectual set of suppositions about the relationship of material to moral culture (e.g., Mauss 1967; Douglas and Isherwood 1979; Goldberg 1986; Herf 1984; Miller 1987; Molohon 1984). Specific reactions to the new objects (and the political, economic, and symbolic structures that produced them) that come into the lives of previously marginalized populations may range from complete rejection (as in the extreme case of the Amish in America) to wary suspicion of alien customs and objects to enthusiastic experimentation and adoption of them. Yet even when goods appear superficially to be accepted eagerly into the local repertoire for the perceived technical advantages they offer, as envisioned by Western development planners and Third World politicians alike, their full incorporation at a structurally meaningful level may be accomplished only to the extent that the new objects are defined and redefined, sometimes quite creatively, to fit in conceptually to the local culture, such that villagers "appropriate that which they have not themselves created" (Miller 1988:370; cf. Sahlins 1981:70, Schneider 1984:122).

For example, for several decades anthropologists have investigated the efferves-cent "cargo cults" now famous in Melanesia for their imaginative categorization of Western commodities as "cargo" and their messianic prediction that the current political order will soon be reversed, overturning the near monopoly that Western-ers have on the majority of industrial commodities (and the ability to produce them). Conversely, in this vision Third World societies will no longer be excluded from the orbit of those attractive and labor-saving objects. While an earlier generation of scholars viewed the cargo cults through a functionalist lens, as desperate attempts to stabilize an unstable environment (e.g. Wallace 1956),[3] other observers have stressed more dynamic and interpretive approaches. Thus Wagner (1979:161) sees these cults as "interpretation[s] of interpretation[s]," writing that the movements "might best be considered as a dialogue carried on [by indigenous peoples] with themselves" (1979:142). The dialogue clearly concerns the nature of the Melanesians' own societies and their access to resources, both material and moral, when compared to the West. In a similar vein but in the Latin American context, Whitten has written (1985:252) that rural Third World people "discuss the events in which they participate, those they hear about, and those they imagine, just as do those who sit in board rooms and on planning councils to devise new schemes for 'development.'"

It is the sense of an inner dialogue constructed with respect to local forms of knowledge about the world that I will stress in my own treatment of contemporary cultural trends. If the Beng, and other apparently peripheral populations like them, are at one level the prey of a dominating system, we may still see them as using the very considerable conceptual forces available to them to shape these new influences to their own purposes. Rather than viewing the Beng as mindless victims of a coercive set of encompassing forces creating only a false consciousness, I will explore how the Beng are, as Jean Comaroff writes of the Tshidi (a chiefdom of the South African Tswana), "determined, yet determining, in their own history" (1985:1). Such an approach should have the virtue of acknowledging the existence of an enveloping world system, while emphasizing how that structure first impinges on, but is then reshaped by, people's own consciousness.

In other places, there have been quite spectacular and symbolically resonant forms of response and resistance to Western culture, reshaping colonial and postcolonial culture into local forms of counterhegemony. In Africa, syncretic religious movements have been one well-documented means of carrying on an inner dialogue about imported ideas and objects. Independent religious movements such as the Zionist churches of the South African Tswana, for example, have been described as occupying a "middle ground" between two religious systems, African and Western (Jean Comaroff 1985:153), evolving as a creative means of coming to terms with the contradictions between two previously disparate cultural systems.[4] More recently, the Comaroffs have written (Comaroff and Comaroff 1990:212) that the Tswana are also trying, through cattle, to insert themselves securely and comfortably into the "space between old and new commodities" (also see Comaroff and Comaroff 1987). In eastern Zaire, the Bashu people have utilized a traditional ideology of witchcraft to sort out the meanings of their new cash-based, village lives created in colonial times from a subsistence economy located in dispersed settlements (Packard 1980). But rather than somewhat mechanically inserting the new model of society into the old ideology, the Bashu have innovated on that ideology, with the result that they have produced "long-term conceptual change" (Comaroff and Comaroff 1990:241) working from a combination of traditional and modern elements.

In Oceania, subtle but significant linguistic changes signal a transformation in posited knowledge about the world. Among the West Futuna people of Vanuatu, as Keller and Lehman have described (n.d.:18), traditionally terms for "material essence" and "efficacious image" both took possessive pronouns that were used only for inalienable objects or properties. But when Christians adopted these terms to signify the body and soul, respectively, the West Futuna innovated on their linguistic usage and switched to the other set of pronouns available in their language—pronouns applicable to the category of objects that are considered by them to be alienable—as a means of adapting to, and commenting on, the Christian view of body and soul as dissociable from each other—and thus, perhaps, as the ultimate form of commodity.

Another dramatic form of creative synthesis of discrete traditions marks the Latin American workers studied by Taussig (1980). Among them, one finds indigenous critiques of the culture of capitalism in the form of pacts with the devil made by Colombian plantation workers and statues of mine owners' spirits made and then worshiped by Bolivian tin miners (also cf. Gose 1986, Ong 1987, Renshaw 1988). Such creative acts speak poignantly to the power, both symbolic and material, of the world capitalist system, coupled with the ability of people to fashion new but meaningful rituals reinterpreting their own encounter with that frequently life-suppressing system.[5]

In the Beng case the reaction to Western goods has not been single-stranded. Unlike the Colombian and Bolivian workers described by Taussig, the Beng have not unified their reactions into a major new ritual; unlike the Bashu farmers described by Packard, they have not permanently and structurally transformed their own ideology as a means of coming to terms with changing social circumstances; unlike the Tswana, the Fang, and many others in Africa and elsewhere, they have not embraced a new synthetic religion. Neither fully resistant nor fully accepting, the Beng response to industrial culture has been multilayered, revealing a deep ambivalence about particular objects: the Beng people find themselves both attracted to and repelled by the new objects increasingly available to them. This seemingly alien system of goods, which might appear to be imposed on a local population by a dominant force, is nevertheless being enthusiastically embraced by the Beng at least partially at the same time that it is being kept at a conceptual distance. And if Beng villagers are not wholly comfortable with all that the latest imported technology brings with it and represents, their deities are even less so. Indeed, as we shall see, the main spirits that the Beng worship are said to be profoundly disturbed by several aspects of Western technology.

In this chapter I will discuss the intellectual and moral dilemmas that newly introduced Western commodities pose for the Beng. As in the previous chapters, we will find the principles of identity and difference appearing and combining in multiple ways. What is at issue here is the very notion of ethnicity: what it means to be Beng. Can Beng culture exist as such only if it heightens identity by excluding the difference embodied in foreign material influences or can it stretch to incorporate difference, in the form of alien commodities and ways of living, without being culturally engulfed by that difference? In the pages that follow, we will find both impulses at work.

THE BENG IN THE WORLD

The earliest recorded European contact with the inland Beng dates only from the late nineteenth century. Indeed, many Beng professed ignorance to me concerning the transatlantic slave trade. It is certainly possible that, living as they did far from the coastal traders and deep in the forest away from major raiding routes, the Beng managed to escape the New World slave trade as well as all direct contact with Europeans until the late 1880s.[6] So the inundation of Western commodities into Bengland might well be relatively recent, affording us a good position from which to view the process of reinterpretation that must necessarily accompany such a technological shift—a reinterpretation that may be more obscure in other places because of a combination of earlier contact coupled with weak historical records.

Yet my description so far of the Beng in the world is misleading to some extent, as it suggests a relatively "undisturbed" culture before European contact. In fact, while Beng may have encountered whites only within the past century, the evidence suggests that they have a history of extensive precolonial trade networks with other Africans. Most notably, they had frequent contact with local and long-distance traders (mostly Julas but also some Jiminis, both living to the north) who came regularly to Beng villages to buy the regionally famous kola nuts produced by Beng farmers (Braulot n.d.: 38; Person 1968a:41, 103; Person 1968b:930; Person 1975:1580, 1686, 1745, 1757, 1763; Person 1971:n.p.; Tauxier 1921:374). Moreover, because they have taboos that forbid them from engaging in iron work, pottery, and weaving, the Beng were quite dependent on Julas and Jiminis living to the north, with whom they traded for iron hoe blades and guns (for hunting), ceramic water jars and cooking pots, and woven cloth (as well as salt) (Tauxier 1921:373). They either paid for these items with cowry shells—a local form of currency—or in some cases (for instance, with cloth and pots) traded karity butter or bark cloth mats, which men fashioned from local trees.

In addition to these locally imported goods, the Beng also remained open to regional religious influences. For instance, they used the services of itinerant healers and diviners who might come to the village. Other Beng sought out apprentice positions with well-known diviners of neighboring ethnic groups from whom they could learn an exotic variety of this specialty. Religious cults may well have circulated in the past too, as they have in recent times. For example, about twenty years ago, most of the families living in one Beng village adopted from the neighboring Jimini a medical cult that promised to protect cult members from all harm, including illness, witchcraft, and even bullets. The adepts washed daily with a decoction of imported herbs kept in a ceramic pot that was embedded in a mound of earth, the whole surrounded by a gate. But when most of the new cult members in the Beng village fell ill or even died from one disease or another, all but one household abandoned the cult. Such rapid adoption—often followed by subsequent rejection—of alien religious or healing traditions (which may take on decidedly political overtones in some places as well) is typical of many parts of Africa (e.g., Fuglestad 1975; J. Goody 1986:7; MacGaffey 1983:2; Maier 1983; Schloss 1988:16), and it is likely that such spiritual borrowing, like trading, went on actively in the Beng area well before the current era.

Despite this multistranded network of relations with surrounding groups, as a minority ethnic group of only some 10,000, the Beng have placed a decided emphasis on their ethnic autonomy. They insisted to me that until recently they had resisted regular intermarriage with the traders and neighbors with whom they were in regular contact. (The statistical reality of this assertion, I suggest, is less significant than the claim itself.) They learned the languages of the surrounding groups for trade purposes—as I stated earlier, most Beng are at least trilingual, speaking Beng, Baule, and Jula, and often Ando as well—but, while incorporating many foreign words into their lexicon (Charles Bird, personal communication), they have held onto their own minority language (Loucou 1984:76; cf. Clozel 1902:18, Delafosse 1904:146). Living in or near high tropical forest, they seem to have been content with existing on the fringes of the mainstream. As we have seen in chapter one, an avowed pacifism meant that when faced with enemies—in the past century, the Muslim crusader Samori and his army, and soon after him the French—the Beng response was twofold: to pray to their deities to be spared, and to flee into the forest. Thus, despite having regular commercial and religious ties (as well as occasional near skirmishes) with their neighbors, the Beng have tried to maintain themselves as a relatively isolated ethnic enclave.

While the Beng have been enveloped by the world system to some degree, they have remained subsistence farmers, growing virtually enough crops to feed themselves. Women continue to gather wild fruits and vegetables, while men still hunt to supplement the farm products. The Beng also now grow cash crops, mostly coffee but also cotton, rice, peanuts, and cocoa. Government traders come to the villages with cash to buy the crops, then transport them to Abidjan, where the produce is sold on the world market. With their cash the Beng buy mostly imports—clothes, soap, medicine, jewelry, liquor, and assorted luxuries. The amount of cash that a

given farmer earns varies wildly from year to year owing to a variety of unpredictable factors: meager harvests caused by local droughts or insect infestations; illnesses of the farmers or their children, who provide critical labor in the fields; and
erratic government policies and prices. In fall 1989, for example, government
traders were instructed to buy the farmers' crops on credit because of the severity of
the budget deficit, due in part to the decline in coffee prices on the world market.
That year the farmers had little income. Thus, remote as they are, the Beng feel
directly the effects of the international economy—and suffer from them. In some
cases, people are malnourished. This makes them more susceptible to diseases. In
turn, when they are ill, they are unable to buy the expensive medicines that the
dispensary doctor in town might prescribe, so they rarely bother to make the trip to
town to consult with him. Death rates must increase significantly during those
years. Nevertheless, the people's memory of a subsistence economy is still keen, and
they are able to survive—if barely—on their food crops.

Because of the difficulties of eking out a living in such conditions, subject as
they are not only to unpredictable natural disasters but also to sociopolitical
upheavals, an increasing number of young Beng men have been leaving the area to
engage in wage labor, either in the cities or on large plantations to the south. Still,
a large number of them view it as a temporary measure by which to obtain cash in
lean years (this was especially the case during the West African drought of 1983–
85). While more and more Beng are living permanently in the major cities and
towns of Côte d'Ivoire, many emigrés hope to (and do) return to their villages to
resume farming their own fields (for another case of "reverse migration" in Côte
d'Ivoire, see Yao 1989).

Those who do return to the villages inevitably bring with them news of urban
life-styles. And inevitably they bring with them urban objects that they were able to
buy that they think will prove useful back in the village. To understand Beng views
of such objects, we must first investigate how Beng see the people who are
responsible for those technological creations.

BENG VIEWS OF WHITE PEOPLE

Beng classify whites as people who are *kale*. This term can be translated roughly as
"powerful," given a metaphysical foundation to power. This form of power is itself
considered neutral but can be potentially either beneficial or harmful. The range of
African people, deities, and objects that the Beng consider *kale* is wide and
includes twins, witches, diviners, great hunters, medicinal plants, and political
leaders (village and clan chiefs, kings and queens, and country presidents), as well
as the forest spirits they worship. Indeed, most (though not all) *kale* people are said
to derive their *kale*-ness from an association with forest spirits.

Most Beng asserted this to be categorically the case for white people as a group.
Some Beng took this in its most negative possible aspect, further classifying whites
as witches (*brunā*). In this case, they specifically pointed to items of Western

technology made by whites that proved their capabilities of witchcraft. Who but a witch could invent a camera? A typewriter? An airplane?

Other Beng claimed that whites were themselves spirits. Here they cited their conviction that unlike blacks, white people do not experience digestive processes. Food is ingested but is not excreted. Yet those who asserted the spirit status of whites declined to speculate further whether whites are the malicious or beneficent type of spirit. In any case, the proof of the spiritual origin of whites was again that whites create those dazzling technological products. When my husband and I protested to a Beng friend that not only had we not manufactured our typewriter, camera, or tape recorder, but that we had no idea about their inner workings and always had to pay someone (inevitably an African) to fix them when they broke down, he explained patiently that this was irrelevant since our ancestors and countrymen had created and manufactured the items. The general cultural genealogy connecting us to the great inventors of our culture was sufficient to classify us as belonging to the same species, as it were. And that species may be a sort of spirit.

The word used here was *bɔŋzɔ*, as with the Beng forest spirits, but my informant qualified that whites are a different kind of spirit from those who inhabit the Beng region. For one thing, whites are visible with impunity, unlike the local spirits, which are normally invisible but would cause instant death if ever seen (though the destructive effects of French colonialism might here be considered as perhaps a metaphorical version of this belief). Moreover, whites do not inhabit the forest, as do the local spirits, but live in human areas. Because of these differences, and because the vast majority of whites reside quite far from the Beng territory, the Beng do not actively worship whites as they do their own forest spirits. But as with their own forest spirits, Beng remain deeply distrustful of whites whom they encounter, and they do endeavor to maintain their distance from them. In the case of my husband and myself, despite periodic bouts of dysentery, it was six months or more before many villagers tentatively removed us from the "spirit" category and into the "human" one; I am certain that other villagers never made this classificatory change (Gottlieb and Graham n.d.).

Because of their varying identity, wavering between the problematic categories of spirit and witch, most whites are not sought out for normal social interaction; indeed, village Beng tend to avoid whites as much as is feasible and are quite wary in their dealings with them. Thus while the Beng have classified whites as a group, they have not yet progressed beyond ethnic stereotypes to construct portraits— mocking or otherwise—of individual white people, as minorities and Third World groups elsewhere have done who have had longer contact with whites (e.g., for the Apache, see K. Basso 1979). Empowered, at the very least, with a form of *kalε*-ness that is quite distinct from that of, for example, Beng ritual specialists—who are also classified as *kalε*—white people remain at base unpredictable and impenetrable. Associated with this attitude toward white people is a mix of uneasiness and fascination concerning the wide range of products they bring with them.

SUSPICION OF WESTERN COMMODITIES
AND TECHNOLOGY

SPIRITS AND LOGGERS

As we saw in chapter 2, the Beng see the spirits of the forest as intimately involved in the affairs of humans, indeed as essential to the maintenance of human life and culture: the Earth spirits, in particular, are moral forces upholding just causes, punishing people who commit sins against them, and enforcing a large number of taboos that prescribe and proscribe behavior.

Other spirits are not attached directly to a named Earth but are said to live independently in their own forest enclaves. Such spirits (also called bɔŋzɔ) fall into three subcategories. One type, considered potentially malevolent, is avoided at all costs. Other forest spirits inhabit four species of trees (including the majestic iroko, an African teak), one of which may never be felled. The other three trees are only chopped down when their wood is to be used in carving statues, with which some diviners attract the forest spirits during certain divinations. Before chopping down one of these trees for a sculpture, the artist must first sacrifice a chicken to apologize to the indwelling spirits and ask them to find another abode.

The spirits that live in the forest trees are becoming increasingly perturbed by a direct incursion into their realm. For it is precisely their trees that are desired by Western countries, hence by the parastatal logging companies doing business in Côte d'Ivoire. Loggers now come into Bengland to chop down these trees for local processing in sawmills and in some cases for sale as timber on the international market. While the Beng have been meagerly compensated for some of their timber losses in loads of cement delivered to the villages that have agreed to the logging, in other cases they told me that loggers have simply come in without permission and chopped down forest trees without any payment whatsoever to the villagers. Many Beng are understandably outraged at the loss of potential revenue from the timber industry, seeing this as outright theft of their resources. Yet other Beng are opposed to the loggers' activities altogether, preferring to forgo the potential revenue in favor of what they consider a more important payoff: the contentment of the forest spirits.

For each time loggers chop down a tree, the spirits in that tree are angered at the destruction of their abode, and are forced to find other trees in which to live. A simple sacrifice to the resident spirits of a given tree before felling it would suffice to appease the spirits, but the loggers, as outsiders, are either ignorant or con-temptuous of local custom and never offer the required propitiatory sacrifices. The result has been stunning. In summer 1985, while I was in Bengland, one or two professional loggers were killed by a falling tree that they were chopping down. I heard many similar stories of episodes that had occurred in my absence. The loggers must circulate such stories among themselves, and I imagine the Beng region has a grim reputation in their circles; but the loggers must assess the financial rewards they reap from these enormous trees as great enough to justify the risk. As for the

Beng, they are certain that the "accidents" are all caused by the tree spirits, who are rebelling in this way against the destruction of their abodes.

Tree spirits killing poaching loggers: this is a potent image indeed. Here, we might say, is a sort of spiritual revenge that the Beng postulate is being taken on their behalf for the injustice being done them. As pacifists of a sort, the Beng would never consider doing actual physical harm to the encroaching loggers. And as a fairly disenfranchised minority, they feel helpless before the powerful and distant parastatal logging companies to protest their losses. But as believers in a religion that they consider powerful in its own way, populated by spirits that are fundamentally on their side so long as they treat them properly, the Beng have found their means of protection, one that, to be sure, may occasion sneers from skeptical Westerners but that is utterly reasonable for members of the circle of belief. In this case, the power of the Beng to resist unfair capitalist practice lies in their religious faith, and so far that has not failed them. If it should, it will be revealing to see what their next step will be: deeper faith via extra sacrifices to the tree spirits to apologize for the loggers' continuing encroachments and prayers for vengeance against them; political organizing to directly confront the logging companies and effectively demand compensation for (or cessation of) the logging activities; or some other form of rectification or revenge, as yet unimagined.

If the tree spirits in the forest have sided with the Beng against the depredations of ecologically and spiritually threatening capitalist activities in their realm, the Earth spirits that live in their own forest enclaves are believed to have a slightly different but equally conservative reaction to the presence of at least certain Western products. Indeed, as we shall see in the next section, the Beng assert that the Earth spirits' relationship to the twentieth century and all its technological innovations is seriously problematic. A clear sign of this, they say, is that the Earth spirits, considered by the Beng to be absolutely central to their own village lives, have begun to retreat deeper and deeper into the forest.

NOXIOUS, NOCTURNAL, AND FLYING COMMODITIES

In some parts of Africa the smell of gasoline, as well as the smell of other Western technological artifacts, is considered repulsive to traditional religious figures.[7] Among the Shona of Zimbabwe, for example, Lan (1985:70, 143–145, 196) notes that before independence, ancestors' mediums were obliged to avoid petrol fumes; hence they also avoided transportation by cars and buses, which were seen as polluting. The Beng similarly have been concerned with a number of odors that have begun to invade their land. But in their case, it is not human ritual specialists but spirits that are said to be offended.

One odor said to be displeasurable to the forest spirits is that of cigarette smoke. Significantly, tobacco itself does not appear to be a recent introduction. Old Beng men and women regularly grow tobacco and process the leaves by pounding them along with some potash into a powder that is then wetted with saliva and rolled in a ball along the lower lip. The forest spirits are said to enjoy this form of chewing tobacco. Indeed, in some myths, they are offered powdered tobacco as a sort of bribe by which humans seek to attain various ends. So the spirits' repulsion at the odor of cigarette smoke is a very specific response to a recent Western variation on a semi-traditional product.[8]

Cigarette smoke figures prominently in a Beng myth that accounts for the separation of the human and spirit domains. For the physical distance that now divides the two was not always present; and as this myth shows, it is cigarette smoke that partly generated the spirits' suspicion of humans, leading to further tests and ultimately to their spatial alienation from the human domain.[9]

Why the Spirits Are Invisible

A certain Man and a certain Spirit went to construct a village. Every day, they ate *foutou*, but there were always leftovers. They drank palm wine, but there was always some left. When they were done eating, the Man would roll a cigarette, every day he would roll a cigarette. One day, the Spirit said, "When we eat *foutou*, we always have leftovers, when we eat meat, we always have leftovers, when we drink our palm wine, we always have leftovers. In addition, when you 'eat your fire' [smoke cigarettes], I can't stay by your side." The Man asked, "Why is that?" The Spirit replied, "If the day comes that we don't find anything to eat or drink, you'll come and eat me!" Then the Spirit ran off into the forest.

The next morning, the Man said he was going to go hunting. The Spirit went on ahead to the spot where the Man would be coming. The Spirit asked him, "In your village, when women pound something, between the mortar and the pestle, which of their noises travels the farthest?" The Man replied, "It's the mortar whose noise travels farthest." The Spirit then asked him, "But if the pestle hadn't hit against the mortar. . . ?" The Man said, "Ah! It's the pestle whose noise travels farthest! It's true: if the pestle hadn't hit against the mortar. . . !" The Spirit then beat up the Man. The Man ran off, he ran off to his village.

Every day in the forest, the Spirit hit the Man when he was out hunting. Finally, his child said to him, "Papa, why haven't you killed anything the past five days when you've been out hunting?" He replied, "Little boy, it's not my fault. The Spirit that left went and waited for me in the forest. Every day he beats me up! In beating me up, he asks me, 'Between the noise of the mortar and the noise of the pestle, which travels the farthest?' When I don't know, he beats me up!" The child said, "Papa, tomorrow I'm going along too."

The next morning, the boy and his father went off to go hunting. As soon as they got there, they saw the Spirit right away. He came and asked the Man, "In your village, between the noise of the mortar and the noise of the pestle, which travels the farthest?" The child ran up to his father's side and went and smacked the Spirit on his cheek, *kpao*. Then he asked the Spirit, "Between my hand and your cheek, which one sounds the loudest?" The Spirit answered, "I beat up your father, beat him up, beat him up, and he wasn't able to ask me about it at all. You, just a child, you've come and hit me and you've asked me about my affairs, while I'm not able to do the same to you. This is a great source of shame to me. Therefore, from now on, I'll be able to see people, but people themselves will no longer be able to see me." Then he put darkness between us. And that's why we don't see spirits any more—there's the reason.

This myth chronicles how spirits and humans once lived together in villages but were separated when the spirits became offended at the humans' habit of smoking cigarettes, which apparently represented inappropriate gluttony to the spirits. For in spite of having an abundance of food, as demonstrated by the daily presence of leftovers, the man was still hungry enough after a full dinner to "eat fire" (smoke cigarettes), leaving the spirit to wonder if the man, if truly hungry one day, might try to eat him. Disgusted at the cigarettes and the insatiable appetite they implied, the spirits withdrew to the forest. The spirit then decided to test the man's intelligence by asking him a riddle, which the man continually answered incorrectly. But the man's son came to his father's aid and responded with a second riddle that demonstrated his understanding of the complex logical conundrum embodied in the original riddle. The spirit, now further offended that his intellectually superior position was being challenged—and, worse still, by a child—made himself invisible to the human eye. A gulf between spirit and human was thereby created.

In one sense, the myth reveals a conviction that humans are on a par with spirits. After all, a human proved himself the intellectual equal of a spirit, driving it and its colleagues away in humiliation. But another reading is that it is the spirits who were victorious, as it was they who took the decisive step in making themselves invisible to humans, yet still able to see the latter. This inequity in gaze can be seen as a metaphor for the wider imbalance of power between the two, with spirits now profoundly able to alter—and disrupt—humans' affairs, if not given the proper respect.[10]

In the myth, the spirits' initial withdrawal from the human environment was precipitated by their disgust with cigarettes, which were taken as a dangerous symbol of excessive gluttony. But the spirits' move to the forest did not occasion an unbreachable rupture—far from it. As we have seen in chapter 2, the Beng remain in intimate and regular contact with the spirits, despite the latters' invisibility and their separate habitats. Indeed, regular communication with the spirits is seen by the Beng as crucial to their daily well-being.

But in contemporary times it is said that the spirits have begun to withdraw even deeper into the forest. This is distressing to the Beng, for they see the postulated physical retreat as metaphoric of a psychological retreat as well—a decision by the spirits to begin to abandon the Beng. This is a prospect no people who believe in gods would greet with sanguinity.

This decision on the part of the spirits is said to be made on account of two specific imported commodities, gasoline and kerosene, that, like cigarettes in the myth just presented, take on negative symbolic import. Specifically, the odors of these products are considered offensive. With the Shona, it is the human mediums of the spirits that are offended, while among the Beng, the offense is to the spirits themselves.

For the Beng say that the forest spirits are quite disgusted with the gasoline fumes that are now pervasive even in the remoter and smaller Beng villages. Several cars and trucks drive by daily on roads that lead past, or within a kilometer of, most Beng villages, and the odor of passing vehicles is certainly noticeable. Worse, the odor of gasoline is seen as identical to the odor of kerosene, and the latter is likewise said to be noxious to the forest spirits. Nowadays, nearly every Beng household, no matter how poor, owns a small kerosene lantern, which is used to light the compound on all but full-moon nights. Between cars, trucks, and lanterns, then, gasoline and kerosene pervade the air that the spirits, even deep in the forest, must breathe, and these spirits are manifestly displeased with the scent.

These odors have several characteristics: they are boundless, incapable of being confined to a given spot; they are invisible, therefore all the more mysterious and frustrating; and of course they are unpleasant. In these ways they can be seen as an apt symbol for Western culture at large, which is likewise pervasive and yet in a sense invisible in its effects not only on the general culture but also on the individual psyche. Yet looking at the level of daily practice, it is the greatest irony that kerosene is in fact used by virtually every village Beng household (in contrast to cars, which are owned only by a few wealthy, urban Beng). Precolonially, the Beng, like some other African groups in the wider area (including the Fante of Ghana), had their own ingenious means of illuminating the night: with small iron lamps burning karity butter; from burning a certain flammable grass; and burning the dried-out seeds of the *kprɔkprɔ* fruit strung on a stick, manufactured regularly by children for the purpose. But when kerosene lamps came on the scene, the labor involved in making these various indigenous torches was judged excessive, and they were abandoned. Beng are poignantly aware of the resultant contradiction: daily use of an object that makes life easier, yet alienates their own dieties. And in alienating their deities, perhaps, as Janet Keller has suggested (personal communication), they alienate a part of themselves as well.

Automobiles are problematic in a further respect. Not only are their exhaust fumes a source of moral repulsion but their appearance at night is equally troublesome. Here, the connection with forest spirits is downplayed in favor of an association with witches. Put simply, when driven at night, cars are said to be the province of witches. As elsewhere, Beng witches are said to do their work at night, in contrast to benign humans, who labor during the day (Needham 1978:36–37). In order to transport themselves someplace at night, witches may transform themselves into forest animals and thereby travel more rapidly. Nocturnally driven automobiles have in a loose sense been added to the repertoire of "were-beings," but rather than an object of transformation, they are instead themselves transformed: the witch changes the victim into a car that she or he then rides at night to the cannibal feast at the desired destination. In this way, night-driven cars come to embody evil.

Another modern mode of transportation—airplanes—is likewise associated with witches. This fits in well with almost all African (perhaps universal) notions of witches as being capable of flight—in opposition to other people, whose mode of locomotion restricts them to the ground (Needham 1978:39–40). Throughout Africa, witchcraft has come to stand for immorality incarnate. Perhaps the Christian missionaries' misguided association of witches with the devil was at one level not so far off the mark, insofar as Africans do see witches as the embodiment of all that is antisocial, and this itself is associated with sin. In pairing night-driven cars as well as airplanes with witchcraft, then, the Beng are associating these forms of imported technology with their deepest understanding of immorality.

Not only are selected alien objects singled out as the embodiment of evil, but certain strangers are also accorded distrust. As we shall see in the next section, foreigners now living among the Beng are proving a problematic presence.

Because of a variety of ecological, political, economic, and social conditions in this region of West Africa, there is continued pressure on savanna populations living to the north of the Beng to move south to more fertile farm lands (e.g., Coulibaly, Gregory, and Piché 1980). The Beng region has been touched by this regional trend. There are now at least a few "foreigners" from the north—especially Jimini, Jula, and Mossi people from northern Côte d'Ivoire and southern Burkina Faso, and some Bamana migrants from Mali—living in most Beng villages, and the larger villages now have separate *quartiers*—some quite large indeed—to house these immigrants. Most farm in the forest, but some Julas also conduct petty trade locally, while some Jimini men practice as village blacksmiths. With few exceptions, these newcomers do not learn the Beng language; they communicate with the Beng in Jula, which virtually all Beng know (or occasionally in Jimini, which some Beng know).

Along with this refusal by the immigrants to learn the Beng language is a broader disinterest on their part in Beng customs. In particular, few if any of the "strangers" are aware of the six-day structure to the traditional Beng week, hence they are totally ignorant of the taboo against working in the forest one day per week. As a result, the immigrants violate a major Beng Earth taboo each week. The Beng told me that the Earth is angry at this, and that this is contributing to a declining fertility of the soil.

Moreover, in the larger villages with significant migrant populations, Beng themselves have begun to ignore the traditional taboos, presumably from the example of noncompliant foreigners surrounding them. For instance, the night before collecting kola nuts from the trees, men are required to refrain from sexual intercourse; and when actually collecting the nuts, men must either go totally nude to climb the tree, or they must wear nothing but the traditional bark cloth underwear; on days that one is working in the kola plantations, one must not touch fish. Nowadays, these ritual requirements are being widely ignored. Moreover, I was told that the Beng residents of the village of Bongalo no longer observe the weekly rest day dictated by the Earth, and menstruating women there likewise now work in the fields. These new developments have angered the Earth, which is making its dissatisfaction known in two ways: declining soil fertility and punishment of specific people held responsible. For an example of the latter, the chief of Bongalo was killed by a tree falling on him in the forest. This was interpreted as the Earth's punishment for his villagers' sins. Here, as with the killed loggers, we see the forest spirits looking to protect their interests and protesting in quite effective ways against what they consider to be violation of their rules and life-style by Western-influenced outsiders encroaching on their territory.

As I stated, the forest spirits are not only punishing the transgressors against their rules, or those considered responsible for upholding those rules; they are also letting their displeasure be known by causing a noticeable drop in the fertility of the soil in which the Beng grow their crops.

DECLINING SOIL FERTILITY

Ecological studies of the Beng farms might cite various causes of the distressing decline in soil fertility: introduction of monocropping to replace intercropping; a shorter fallow period (now five to seven years, reduced from fifteen to twenty years); and both unaccompanied for the most part by chemical fertilizers to replenish the newly lost minerals or by pesticides to ward off the new insects brought by monocropping. Government extension agents in the Beng region often sell at locally exorbitant prices the pesticides and fertilizers they are supposed to give away to the farmers, hence few Beng farmers can afford to buy these products. In short, here as elsewhere in the Third World, the Green Revolution has failed miserably.

But like many other Africans, Beng farmers look beyond ecological and other empirical factors, which they recognize, to a deeper metaphysical cause. For as with many Africans (e.g., see Schloss 1988 on the Ehing of Senegal), notions of productivity are deeply spiritual among the Beng. Crop fertility is seen as emanating from metaphysical harmony, while lack of crop productivity is due to a rupture in the desired balance between traditionally defined spiritual forces. The Beng see an intimate link between the rapidly declining crop fertility and the spirits' posited retreat from noxious odors to a more distant spot in the forest. Humans' abuse of their environment, broadly defined, is seen as the cause of both.

An interesting contrast can be drawn with the Colombian peasants studied by Taussig. With those farmers, it is precisely cash crops that in many cases show high productivity (perhaps because of the regular and successful application of pesticides and fertilizers). Interestingly, in such cases, the farmers view impressive cash-crop productivity as resulting from a pact that the successful farmers made with the devil. In other words, they maintain that capitalist success is achieved only by acts of immorality. The Beng have developed the flip side to this logic. They see a lack of crop fertility as the result of a moral decline: religious taboos no longer being observed by outsiders and Beng alike and spirits being repelled by invasive foreign odors. Specifically, Beng interpret crop failures as a sign that the Earth and its spirits have begun to punish them, perhaps even to abandon them, because of overzealous embracing of migrants and imported commodities. The obnoxious odors serve them and their spirits as an apt metaphor for the omnipresence of Western imports and of Western culture more generally.

To what extent might the Beng vision of Western commodities be seen as an indigenous critique of capitalism itself? Taussig, for example, has shown that such is the case for the tin miners of Bolivia and the plantation workers of Colombia (and cf. Gose 1986 on Andean mine workers and Ong 1987 on Malaysian factory workers). In a general sense, this interpretation may indeed be relevant to the Beng case. The spirits' disgust at the odors entering Bengland may well be a metaphor for the pervasive, unavoidable, and often noxious spread of the capitalist model itself. But such an indigenous critique would be partial at best. For as uncomfortable as the Beng spirits are said to be with certain aspects of Western technology, Beng people themselves are quite intrigued with a good many imported commodities. Here we encounter another side of their reaction to Western goods, revealing profound ambivalence in their overall assessment and understanding of commodities.

THE REINTERPRETATION OF WESTERN COMMODITIES

> [W]hat anthropology often discovers within meetings of less developed societies with industrialization . . . is less likely to be tradition's obliteration and more its persistence, whether as indelible idioms of kinship or worship or as the syncretisms of daily practices.
>
> Constance Perin, "Speaking of Tradition and Modernity"

We have seen how the Beng have incorporated Western technology and its makers into their collective mental repertoire, but only by assigning it a dangerous space, one that embodies a profound symbolic risk. Yet I would draw an unbalanced picture if I were to end my account here. For in other cases the Beng have endeavored, with varying degrees of success, to move the cognitive risks posed by imported commodities and styles of living into a more morally neutral space. I conclude this chapter by discussing three Western imports that, while not technically commodities, nevertheless serve as important forms of foreign material culture with significant sociological and cultural overtones: architectural forms, schooling, and medicinal products.

HOUSING

In 1960, following President Houphouët-Boigny's initiative, the Ivoirian government "undertook a vigorous propaganda offensive to regroup small villages into unified villages . . . in order to manage them according to modern *lotissement* plans . . . for the modernization of rural housing construction plans" (DuPrey 1970:59; my translation). In 1965, the president declared ambiguously that "all slums" should be eliminated (Cohen 1974:29). Some local city and town governmental officials interpreted this as a mandate to destroy all village houses built in a vernacular architectural style. In the Beng area, around 1965–68, this mandate began to be carried out, and the process of lotting began in some villages (Nguessan Kwame, personal communication): a rectangular pattern of paths was set down along which the new houses would be built—as J. Goody describes it, a "grid of civilization" (1977:148ff.). As the urban planner Kevin Lynch has observed (1960:99), a simple grid pattern is an easy means for providing "imageability"—the ability to produce a readily accessible and describable image of a city's structure in the mind's eye and use this image to get around it—and this is a key ingredient in people feeling comfortable in a city. Undoubtedly the French planners in Abidjan who helped design the new Ivoirian villages were steeped in the specific vision of the popular Western rectilinear grid as a readily "imageable" form for a town, and unhesitatingly transferred this to the small, rural villages. Accordingly, in the Beng region, local representatives of the national government informed the Beng that their traditional houses—large, round, thatched-roof structures housing an extended patrilocal family (see figure 2)—would have to be destroyed, to be replaced by smaller, rectangular buildings with tin roofs.

Some villages resisted this program entirely. And in the villages that elected to adopt the new plan, some old people independently resisted these developments, especially the house replacement, to the last. I was told of elders who died within weeks or even days of witnessing the destruction of their old round houses, with their powerful religious icons crushed inside. The symbolism must have been too much to bear.

But many other Beng—virtually all the young people, but also many old people—were not so affected and seemed to accept the new architectural forms and town plans with grace. Yet that does not mean that a new world view entirely replaced the old. The Beng, like people elsewhere, have in many cases accepted new structures and commodities into their world in such a way as to modify the intent of the creators and remold the products into ones they could live with comfortably. It is not surprising, then, that the inhabitants of most of the new compounds I studied in one of the recently reorganized villages had managed in effect to reconstitute the original household. The newly introduced housing style— presumably meant to stress the autonomy of the nuclear family (cf. Côte d'Ivoire 1968:19)—while being embraced at a visual level, had effectively been subverted by the Beng at a structural level. It is true that the nuclear components of the traditional patrilocal extended family were broken down and were living separately. But they now reside in houses that are only a few feet apart and are located in the same compound. In one case I observed, a row of houses sheltered a group of three adult brothers and a male patrilateral parallel-cousin, with their wives and children. These people, once under one round roof, were now distanced by separate, lineally related roofs; but living as very near neighbors, they still maintained a high level of propinquity and daily interaction. In ways such as this, local populations such as the Beng have managed to adapt to and, to some extent, benefit from introduced technologies and their accompanying new aesthetic standards, while retaining their fundamental family structures.[11]

SCHOOL

Another initial rejection of the West followed by later reevaluation is evident in the Beng response to the colonially introduced school system. When faced in midcentury with mandatory recruitment of a small proportion of their children to local elementary schools, elders in most villages vowed to resist this attempt at what they saw as forced alienation of their young people from their own cultural traditions (and undoubtedly from their agricultural labor pool as well). They offered a prayer to a powerful shrine and its spirits, asking that their newly enrolled children fail at school and thereby return quickly to the village. This apparently brought the intended results: for a long time, the vast majority of Beng children who attended primary school left after only a year or two, rarely being promoted to junior high school, let alone high school.

In the late 1970s, elders began to question the earlier decision. They observed successful students from other ethnic groups (especially Baule and Anyi to the south) gaining well-paying jobs in town and sending back cash to the villages for modest improvement projects. Other villages seemed to be prospering while Beng villages were at best remaining stagnant, at worst declining. In particular, as we have seen, crop yields were decreasing noticeably and soil fertility was weakening. We have already considered one set of explanations that the Beng are offering for this distressing state of affairs: an unwelcome influx of Western products polluting the air of the indignant spirits (as well as foreigners inhabiting their villages). But another explanation that some Beng are now offering runs counter to that one. According to these Beng, declining crop yields are due to a *lack of access* to Western technologies and to cash that might be brought into the villages by educated young people. The contrast to the prior argument could not be greater; but notice that both explanations focus on Western goods and external influences, either as excess or as insufficiency.

The latter variety held sway in a sense, for in 1980 a group of elders commenced a series of sacrifices to the Earth shrine that had been appealed to earlier. But this time they requested a nullification of the prior prayer that had doomed Beng schoolchildren to failure. This instituted a new era: formal acceptance of crucial elements of Western culture.

As might be imagined, that acceptance was not without ambivalence. Parents now often allow their children to attend school, but they produce prodigious amounts of guilt in them over the decision to "leave the family." When they return to the villages, the students are ridiculed for their new ways: wearing Western clothes; sleeping late; failing to formally greet relatives, neighbors, and friends every morning and evening; and worst of all, lacking eloquence in their natal language (which they may rarely or even never speak while living away from Bengland). The elders now see the results of their reversal of their recent prayer, and they are becoming somewhat dismayed. Still, they keep sending their children to school, and they keep sacrificing chickens to the Earth so that the students may pass their tests and be promoted to the next grade. And, like Africans elsewhere, they expect these children, when they finally gain paying jobs out in the world, to send back a good proportion of their salaries to their village relatives. An individual's success is still seen as a communal achievement; accordingly, responsibility to the family does not end with emigration.

When Beng schoolchildren living in town fall sick, they often return to the village for treatment. Even if they come to embrace certain intellectual values of the urban West that they are being taught, they generally continue to define their bodies as a creation of the African village. In the next section we explore how the Beng medical system has reacted to Western influences.

MEDICINE

Like other indigenous populations, the Beng have a comprehensive system of medicine based on both herbs and ritual cures. Almost every Beng adult knows at least a few herbal cures, but there are also specialist healers (who usually work as farmers by day) who may be familiar with hundreds of medicinal herbs. Despite this impressive indigenous pharmacopoeia, Beng are open-minded about trying alien styles of cures for a given disease. While I lived among the Beng, if an herbal cure did not work in a particular case, villagers often asked my husband and myself for Western medicines that we had available. Like people elsewhere in Africa, the Beng often see two levels of cure possible for a given ailment: a ritual or social action required to treat the ultimate cause of the disease, and an herbal remedy to treat the symptoms. Western medicines often easily replace or supplement the herbal component of this dual system. But as we shall see, even this aspect of medicine is defined in a culturally meaningful way beyond mere chemistry.

Herbs and Pills

With some medicines, the Beng in fact remain quite conservative. For example, there are many traditional remedies that require leaves to be heated in a pot, with the decoction then used as a body rinse in the bath. For some of these herbal recipes, the healer specifies that the patient must cook the decoction in a locally produced ceramic pot, not an imported steel one, and that he or she must pour the rinse over the body from a locally grown gourd, not an imported metal cup. Such instructions reveal a fierce determination to retain literally the shape as well as the ingredients of traditional medicines.

In other instances, Beng patients are more open-minded about foreign cures. Undoubtedly the most popular pill my husband and I had to offer was aspirin, which people wanted for a variety of aches and pains. While aspirin, like other pills, was a foreign remedy, it became incorporated into the traditional system of understanding medicines. I watched this occur during a conversation I had with a friend, Mokro:

> Mokro: I have a headache, could you give me an aspirin?
> Amwe: Sure, here's one.
> Mokro: Thanks; what are the taboos that go with it?
> Amwe: Taboos? I don't know of any.
> Mokro: Are you sure?
> Amwe: Well, probably you shouldn't take the pills with alcohol.
> Mokro: Isn't it also taboo to have lemons while taking this pill?
> Amwe: Lemons? No, I never heard that about this pill.
> Mokro: Well, I'm pretty sure that's the case, so I'd better just avoid lemons today.

Despite my initial resistance to the suggestion that taboos accompany aspirins, Mokro revealed her own conception of the situation. I believe that the explanation of the taboo she proposed is dual.

First, in the indigenous system of herbal medicine, all treatments are explicitly associated with one or more taboos. These include eating certain foods of particular symbolic characteristics and engaging in certain activities, including sex. Thus the sought-after aspirin taboo may have been Mokro's innovation in this particular case, but the logic behind the innovation was part of a wider system of traditional medical practice. The patient was simply incorporating a foreign item into a familiar system of thought.

More specifically, after my conversation with Mokro, I started observing other people's behavior in relation to pills and noticed that people tended to avoid ingesting lemons when taking any pills—quinine derivatives, antibiotics, and so on. Although no villager ever explained this recently created taboo in this way, I offer the following interpretation. All the above-mentioned pills tend to taste mildly to markedly bitter (cécé). Lemons likewise are said by the Beng to be bitter. Now, the Beng medical system contains, among other principles, the notion that two similar substances, even if valued positively as separate entities, will cancel each other out when combined. I believe this partially explains the innovated taboo on ingesting (bitter) lemons while under treatment with imported (bitter) pills (for another example of this principle at work among the Beng, see Gottlieb 1990; for a similar case among Brazilian Indian populations, see Menget 1982:201, 203).

In addition, the Beng use lemons in a variety of contexts as a personal ritual to prevent mystically induced harm. For example, mothers attach a whole lemon, strung onto a cord, to a newborn's wrist, and farmers plant a stake with a whole lemon attached to it in their fields, to protect against "Mouth," a disease of withering brought about, paradoxically, by a compliment paid by an admirer (of infant or field). Additionally, a leaf or stick from the lemon tree may be chewed to protect against witchcraft unleashed at a king's funeral (Gottlieb 1989) or, as we saw in chapter 5, against retribution by the soul of a sick dog whom a young man might kill to put it out of its misery. Keeping in mind both these aspects of lemons—their bitterness and their protective qualities—we can see how Mokro was able to conceptually expand the indigenous herbal system to encompass imported medicines in pill form.

Powder
It is not only humans who have accommodated alien commodities. While the forest spirits, as we have seen, are repelled by the odors of cigarettes, cars, and kerosene lamps and are angry about the encroachments on their territory by loggers and immigrants who ignore their taboos, those same spirits are nevertheless attracted to another recently introduced product: talcum powder. Traditionally the Beng daubed white kaolin on their bodies when they wanted to attract spirits for protection; this was true of infants (Gottlieb 1981), brides, singers, and especially diviners. The latter, operating in the village, seek metaphysical sources of knowledge about human affairs. In daubing white clay, which they classify as medicine, on their bodies, diviners temporarily seduce the forest spirits into the village. There, the spirits whisper to them their knowledge of human affairs, and the

diviners pass on this information to their clients. But the kaolin deposits are far away, and talcum powder, which is sold in the village markets, produces the same white, powdery results. The spirits are said not to notice any difference.

After a century of Western goods' being used in Beng villages, one might expect a corresponding major shift in understanding of the world, even an erosion in faith in the local gods, the forest spirits. But this has not occurred, at least not in any massive way. Certainly there has been somewhat of a realignment of the axes of faith. But this realignment has not taken the form of abandonment of traditional systems of thought and ritual action, with nothing but alcohol to replace them, as has occurred in many other places, especially in the New World (e.g., see Crapanzano 1972, Mead 1932); nor has it resulted in an embracing of new religious cults blending local and "universal" traditions. Instead, the Beng continue to retain faith in their own spirits while cautiously adopting new commodities and life-styles, some of which they know offend those gods—who themselves may be losing some faith in the humans who created them.

My argument in this chapter has been that religion and the general "belief system" inevitably underlying it remain not only relevant but even central in a changing ("modernizing") world. Other recent works on Africa provide compelling case studies of this assertion. For example, Lan's (1985) analysis of the Rhodesian guerrilla war against white rule in Zimbabwe (then Rhodesia) stresses the crucial role played by spirit mediums in the popular acceptance of the guerrillas. Without integration into the indigenous religious structure, the guerrillas would have lacked any basis for legitimacy. Moreover, Lan (1985:xv) makes it clear that the guerrillas themselves were, or came to be, "believers" in the system into which they were incorporated.

By asserting the relevance of local religions in a modernizing world, I do not imply that such religions remain a static, conservative force. This may indeed be the case in some instances, but by no means in all. "Rapid change" in the form of exposure to foreign technologies may produce any of several reactions on the part of indigenous peoples. In the Zimbabwean example, traditional religious structures in fact provided a conceptual framework for radical change, effecting fundamental sociopolitical transformations.

To return to the issues that I raised at the opening of this work, now seen in light of the relationship between the Beng and the West: in spite of the obvious and extreme power imbalance between a rural minority population and an urban-based, hegemonic, international system, any meaningful understanding of the "impact" of commodities on a local culture leads us to consider a two-way relationship between the two sets of participants. As Ferguson has written in a general, programmatic statement (1988:491),

> With the realization that culture is historical and history cultural, "symbolic" cultural analysis and "political-economic" historical analysis can no longer be credibly opposed. . . . [I]t is not a question of whether to ignore culture and focus on political

economy or to ignore political economy and dwell on culture; it is a matter of grasping political and economic realities in a culturally sensitive way, and grasping culture in a way that convincingly relates it to political economy.

My own treatment of commodities in Beng life has aimed for such a balanced account of the impinging effects of Western products, coupled with the Beng perspective on those products. What we have found is that both resistance and incorporation are present as contrary Beng reactions to new stimuli. On one hand, certain Beng deities have begun to retreat before Western technology, threatening to reduce further the already declining soil fertility. I interpret this as a metaphorical resistance on the part of the Beng themselves against Western commodification. On the other hand, people do adopt specific new products not only into their technological repertoire but also into their conceptual repertoire. Surprisingly, the spirits too accept certain objects—notably, talcum powder—as part of their meaningful universe, finding themselves drawn back by diviners to the villages that otherwise house those modern noxious fumes. The ambiguity of foreign goods is highlighted by the association of Western technology with witchcraft (or at least ambiguous spiritual power) and white people with witches, spirits, and spirit allies who manufacture those goods by illegitimate means.

The contradiction that emerges in considering Beng reactions to Western commodities points to a hesitation in taking a final stand on those influences. The pragmatic uses of such imports as Western medicines seem convincing, yet there is the danger that they will make too strong inroads into the culture, replacing central traditional practices. Ascribing skepticism about certain new commodities and techniques to the forest spirits is one means of objectifying a nagging discomfort with foreign goods; yet the forest spirits themselves are so fundamental to Beng culture that the displeasure attributed to them must be reckoned with. Even so, the spirits themselves are attracted to other imported commodities, making their reaction to Western imports complex. In short, the reconstruction of desire itself is ambivalent (Appadurai 1986:29).

To follow the theme we have pursued through this work now seen in an expanded sphere: Beng maintenance of identity—ethnic identity itself—wavers between exclusivity and incorporation of difference. We have seen how the spirits hover around the human world, inserting themselves into the intimate crevices of human life yet living at a distance; how the descent system embraces two distinct models for clanship—models that emphasize both proximity and distance at sociological and symbolic levels; how the alliance system likewise includes two models that stress in effect marrying the self and marrying the other; and how the mythic, ritual, and daily treatment of dogs and hyenas similarly includes both aspects of the self and of the other in their relationships to humans. So, too, the contemporary Beng understanding of Western imports hovers between inclusion and exclusion.

Here we can take the range of reaction to urban housing style as paradigmatic. If some of the elders of the "modernized" Beng villages were devastated by the changes to their living space, others were resigned; still other Beng (especially but not exclusively the young people) were enthusiastic. If housing embodies an intimate space through which the self is projected, this range of reactions to new architectural form indeed shows the variation in attitudes to impinging and structurally meaningful difference.

Beng thought shows consistency in its inconsistency. That is, in all the spheres of social life we have explored in this work, we have seen a consistent wavering between identity and difference. Rather than committing itself firmly to a single principle, as some cultural systems seem to do, Beng thought—like individual Beng—maintains an active oscillation between the two principles we have been exploring. And so it is not surprising that the Beng seem to be suspending final judgment on Western commodities. Or perhaps there is no final judgment, as the Beng continually reevaluate their stance toward their own culture and the new influences that continually, and inevitably, surround them.

Notes

1. THE BENG IN THE WORLD OF IDEAS

1. In older literature, the Beng have been referred to by other groups' terms for them: "Gan" (the Jula term) and "Ngan" or "Ngen" (the Baule term). "Beng" is the auto-ethnonym.

2. I recorded this song in Asagbe as part of a Unity Dance. Pascal Kouadio Kouakou transcribed it and helped me translate it into French; I have retranslated it into English.

3. The figure includes only those Beng—the great majority—who live in the *préfecture* of M'Bahiakro, where I did my work; there are also some Beng, but far fewer, in the neighboring *sous-préfecture* of Prikro.

4. While I have no reason to doubt their self-description as pacifists, some published accounts have alluded to military deeds of the Beng. Rey-Hulman (1978:76) mentions in passing that the Beng had warrior expeditions. Person (1975:1712 n. 8) mentions two Beng war leaders in the 1890s, though he also characterizes the Beng as "peaceful" (ibid.:1686). Additionally, an offshoot of the Beng who are now living assimilated among the Anyi are reputed to have been "fierce soldiers" (Ekanza 1983:160; my translation). It is likely that any such warlike groups of Beng must have broken off from the rest, who insisted on remaining pacifist, with the warriors migrating elsewhere. Further work among these various Beng subgroups is sorely needed to confirm or disprove this and other murky spots in Beng history.

5. Four Beng informants told Person (1968a:41; 1968b:930, 1002 n. 148; 1975:1686, 1712 n. 6, 1745) that Samori conquered and extracted kola tribute from the Beng. All Beng whom I questioned about this scenario denied it vehemently, but it is possible that they have suppressed an unpleasant memory. Further field research on this point remains to be done.

6. For a very useful summary and overview of these recent trends in literary criticism, see Culler (1982). In psychology, a work by the existentialist psychologist Kirk Schneider (1990) on "the paradoxical self," which develops ideas of Kierkegaard (1954), suggests that an acknowledgment that human beings are rooted in contradiction at a psychological level can enable individuals to lead more productive and creative lives. The poet Robert Bly has developed similar ideas in a Jungian tradition, in a series of essays on the "human shadow" (1988).

7. The theory was first laid out in a series of articles (Lévi-Strauss 1963a, 1963b, and 1963d); for a critique of Lévi-Strauss's use of linguistics, see Mounin (1974).

8. Bateson's brilliant double-bind theory of schizophrenia (1972) was a logical development from this early work. For another early exposition of a position that in some ways resembles my own, see Nadel (1957).

9. Some authors have been inspired by Turner's work (1969) on communitas as a ritual form providing an alternative mode of consciousness to that offered by ordinary life (societas). For example, Handelman (1984) analyzes Newfoundland outport society as generally revolving around sociality, with an intensification of social ties in a face-to-face community. But an annual "mumming" ritual reverses this model, turning the close insider into a stranger and thus symbolically representing the demise of the community, which is thereby "deconstructed" (259). A related framework is offered in a few recent works presenting a "spare" folk ideology that is held to serve as a "reserve" to be "activated" in times of crisis or change (political or ecological), as Salzman (1978:68) has suggested was the case for the Bedouin of

Cyrenaica. For other examples that, in one way or another, employ perspectives compatible with my own, see Bloch (1985) on the Merina of Madagascar; Gibson (1985) on the Buid of the Philippines; Hugh-Jones (1979) on the Piri-Parana of Northwest Amazonia; Karp (1980) on the Iteso of Kenya; Sapir (1977b) on the Diola of Senegal; Shore (1978) on Samoa; Sillitoe (1988) on the Wola of the Papua New Guinea Highlands; and Bauer (1989) on the Tigray of Ethiopia.

10. However, in daily life, mediators are important for the Beng in the form of actual people, who serve as individual mediators on a wide array of social and ritual occasions. I hope to develop this theme in a future work.

11. Indeed, Tyler (1987:12) characterizes Derrida's position as giving priority to difference—a position Tyler challenges for his own reasons.

12. Some anthropologists have taken up this recent surge of philosophical interest in identity and difference by seeing their operations in ethnographic contexts. For example, Drummond (1981:653ff) analyzes myth among the Arawak as well as in the Trobriand Islands as providing a transformation from sameness (in the form of asexual reproduction) to difference (as sexual reproduction). In Australia, Myers (1986b) looks at Pintupi meetings as occasions for mediating "between two dialectically related values that are central to any political identity for Pintupi: relatedness and autonomy" (1986b:432). Myers sees the tension between these two values, which approximate to what I am terming for the Beng "identity" and "difference," as constituting "the central dilemma for Pintupi life" (434; also see Myers 1986a:159–179). Schloss (1988) also focuses on the relations between sameness and difference, in the context of intergender relations. The Ehing of Senegal go to great lengths to ritually separate men and women and in so doing to bestow certain advantages upon men. Yet they also recognize the inevitable futility of this continuing endeavor owing to the nature of reproduction and marriage as well as the undeniable "powers and value of women" (Schloss 1988:157). While separation for the Ehing is an ideal, identity is nevertheless at some levels unavoidable. For another treatment of separation and identity in relation to gender, see Strathern (1987b); on separation and identity in relation to kinship, see Héritier (1982:166ff). For a discussion of difference at the heart of Nuer thought, see Evens (1989:344–345 n. 9). A recent ethnographic use of Derridean perspectives on *différance* is in Fischer and Abedi (1990:150–221). In contemporary developmental psychology there is also a strong interest in the related issues of identity and difference. Stern (1985) offers an exciting synthesis of current research suggesting that infants endeavor to differentiate themselves from their mothers from their first moments out of the womb. This line of analysis would accord with both Beng thought and Derrida's work, all emphasizing the centrality of difference right at the heart or beginnings of social life. Much recent work in literary criticism has also explored the significance of the principle of difference, especially in regard to gender, ethnicity, and race (e.g., Johnson 1987).

13. For a related discussion of how the Western polarity of spiritual and material domains is likewise profoundly rooted in a specific cultural ideology that may be irrelevant elsewhere, see Nandy's discussion (1983) of India.

2. OF KAPOKS AND THE EARTH

1. The Beng term *pɔ gbali* translates as "giver of things" and the alternative term *ba gbali* as "giver to the Earth," but I follow common usage among West Africanist anthropologists by referring to this traditional priest who worships the Earth as "Master of the Earth."

2. In addition to the various forest spirits, Beng also recognize and pray to ancestors. However, they give ancestors considerably less ritual attention than do Africans in some other parts of the continent, and "ancestor worship" is far more a private and sporadic affair, often confined to the nuclear family, than a public one of value to the village, clan, or even lineage. This may well be, as Jackson's discussion of the topic would predict (1977c:134–136), because Beng villages are not organized around a single clan or lineage, hence clan

ancestors, who would by their nature be divisive (and, in relation to the village, somewhat irrelevant), are not emphasized.

3. Compare, for example, the Greek mythological figure of Gaia, or Ceres, and the Navajo figure of Changing Woman (Witherspoon 1977:91–94)—both female earth deities.

4. While the term *fetish* might be appropriate here (Ellen 1988), I refrain from using it because of its overwhelmingly condescending usage by an older generation of travelers to West Africa.

5. Beng conversion to any denomination of Christianity is still much less than their conversion to Islam: many villages have no Christians, while a few villages have a small number. Moreover, the depth of conversion is quite variable. While some Christians do indeed attenuate their relationship to Earth worship, others merely add on to their own pantheon the new deity or deities from the imported religions, while continuing to worship the Earth. In this sense their embracing of Christianity might be better termed an "accretion" than a "conversion."

6. Within two to three days after anyone dies, some family members of the deceased consult a diviner to determine the cause of death, which is then announced publicly. Diviners are said to have knowledge of the Earth's affairs, in effect serving as their translators. A skeptical observer might suggest that diviners must have prodigious memories, keeping track of all sacrifices performed at least by his or her fellow villages and often by those living in other villages as well (see Shaw 1985). If this is indeed the case, it is all the more striking that many Beng decide to consult a diviner in another village (compare Colson 1966), precisely to minimize the possibility that the diviner has knowledge of the affair from human gossip networks rather than from communication with spirits (also, not all villages have a diviner).

7. There are at least four such named Earths for the entire Beng region of M'Bahiakro. The Earths are ranked by seniority and, as with human kinship, the oldest Earth is more respected; it is also worshiped more infrequently, only for truly important matters. Following Beng wishes, I refrain from printing the proper names of these Earths.

8. The Beng region straddles the transitional area between two very different ecological zones: dense forest to the south and open savanna to the north. In recognition of this situation, the Beng have divided their cultural space into two political regions, which they have named Forest (*kleŋ*) and Savanna (*bao*). While the densest forest is indeed found in the Forest region and the largest wooded savannas are found in the Savanna region (France 1970), since the entire area is an ecologically mixed one, the designations "Forest" and "Savanna" are, however, better seen as political rather than strictly ecological markers.

9. There are several eligibility requirements for the priesthood: the candidate must be male (though I documented one exception to this rule); must not have been circumcised (until recently, circumcision was a mark of Islam, but it is now a general sign of modernity); must not be a practicing member of another religion; must be the child of an arranged marriage (see chapter 4); and must be right-handed. In addition, the post is hereditary. Each Earth is owned by a matriclan, and its Masters of the Earth are accordingly selected within that matriclan. Within the matriclan, however, succession seems to be irregular: given an ideal of matriclan endogamy (see chapter 4), a son may in some cases succeed his father as Master of the Earth, as well as a younger brother his older brother, or a nephew his uncle.

10. There is no Beng word whose sole meaning is the English "mystical" or "spiritual," but in some of its uses the word *grégré* takes on this sense. The word is used commonly in Ivoirian French (spelt *gris-gris*) as a noun to refer to any type of spiritually charged object. As used in Beng, the word's meanings range from "strong" in a quite secular sense (as in muscular power) to "strong" in what we might call a more mystical or spiritual sense.

11. Although the speaker may only refer to *ba* without invoking the name of that Earth, it is clear from the context that it is not the unified Earth but rather one of his or her village's named Earths that is being invoked in this way. (If an individual's village is associated with two or three named Earths, one should invoke the Earth associated with his or her matriclan.)

12. On the association of auspiciousness with cold (and inauspiciousness with heat), see Gottlieb (1990a).

13. While the spirits proper (bɔŋzɔ ti pɔ) are invisible, there is a certain kind of spirit that may be seen by humans with impunity. Called alufyā (or alufya), these spirits are said to be short and they whistle or squeak to communicate with each other. But they are "not the real spirits" (of the Earth), and they live scattered through the forest rather than concentrated in their own forest-based villages.

14. The average adult's knowledge of forest plants is impressive, and a healer's knowledge is truly encyclopedic. In exploring rather unsystematically the topic of affliction, I collected ninety-eight tree names and twenty-three liana names, and I have no doubt that these represent a small proportion of known and named plants. Further study of this topic is needed.

15. The particular day of worship in the six-day week varies between the two Beng regions: in the Forest region it is the fourth day of the week (Po Fē), while in the Savanna region it is the sixth day (Ba Fē Bɛ) that is so designated. Actually, the spatial boundaries of each calendrical system are a bit more subtle than this gross characterization, as they depend on the course of a local river. Separating the forests and fields of the villages in the two political regions is the Baya River, an offshoot (in Beng terms, a "little finger") of the Be River, itself an offshoot of the Nzi River. As a rule, the villagers whose farms are located in the Forest region and are said by the Beng to be located "behind" the Baya River observe a rest day and worship the Earth on the fourth day of the week, while those villagers whose farms are located in the Savanna regions and are said to be "in front of" the Baya River observe a rest day on the sixth and last day of the week. However, if a villager happened to be living in the Forest region but farming a field located in the Savanna region "in front of" the Baya River, she or he would observe the Savanna region rest/Earth worship day (and vice versa). More recently, a seven-day calendar has also been adopted by the Beng; for a discussion of how the two calendrical systems intersect, see Gottlieb (1986).

16. On the first day of a wedding to an arranged-marriage groom, a bride undergoes a brief but significant ritual, called "being washed" (ŋa ʒroa). One or two kinswomen who are related to her agnatically come and dump water over her head and give her a short speech: "Today we washed your thighs. From now on, you must respect Earth Day. When you're menstruating, stay in the village." A crowd of children may be present, shouting "Hó hò hó hò." If a young woman is not to be wed in an arranged marriage (see chapter 4), the ritual is performed at some point during late adolescence when she would have been married. Despite the absence of a husband, in a sense she is said to be married, and she may now choose her own husband.

17. The wife's maternal half-brother died suddenly after developing a headache and fainting; two or three days after his death, one of this man's daughters died of chickenpox; about a month later, the wife's matrilateral parallel-cousin, who was nine months pregnant, developed heart pains and died the same day without having gone into labor; the couple's own daughter died of a snake bite in the forest; the husband's sister's daughter lost a great deal of weight and died; and the house of the husband's patrilateral cross-cousin caught fire and all the possessions inside as well as the house itself were ruined.

18. A village chief told me that neighboring peoples who share the same Earth with the Beng would also be affected by such a drought, as would the Beng if someone of those ethnic groups had likewise polluted the Earth. The ethnic groups he mentioned were Ando, Baule, Jamala and Jimini. He also insisted that the cause of all droughts is always a case of forest sex. Other informants mentioned additional possible reasons for drought: the patriclan that is in charge of the rain (Krilɛŋ) is lacking a queen, who alone is empowered to perform the most powerful of the rainmaking ceremonies (see chapter 3); the sacred goats that are kept in one of the Beng villages and are dedicated to the Earth are hungry and must be fed with a villagewide sacrificial meal; and whites (i.e., myself and my husband) are living in the area. During my fieldwork the first and third of these explanations were joined to the more usual one of forest sex in trying to explain the drought of that year. Fortunately for my husband and

myself, the drought ended after a couple who were guilty of committing forest sex were punished, and the theory that we might be to blame for the drought was forgotten.

19. Significantly, most of these forest sex cases are also cases of rape. In these instances, the rape is blamed on madness, which is itself caused by witchcraft. In one case I recorded, a well-known healer was bewitched and attempted to rape his wife in the forest. She escaped, and when he came out of his temporary insanity within a few hours, he hanged himself in the forest, from shame. It seems appropriate that the act of forest sex, itself utterly immoral, is associated with a further act of immorality.

20. The cost of a cow is approximately $150 to $300. It is bought by the guilty man or, if he is young and unmarried, by his father; in either case, his own matriclan members help contribute. The average yearly income of a Beng nuclear family nowadays ranges from $300 to $1,000 (the exchange rate fluctuates between about 200 and 400 CFA = $1 U.S.). My consultant did not know what the king would do with the couple's polluted clothes, but in any case the intent is clear: separate the guilty man and woman from the pollution to cleanse them as well as the Earth. The fact that it is the king who is given the clothes serves to affirm his ultimate "ownership" over the Earth (see Gottlieb 1989).

21. Two Beng—one woman and one man—offered me the same explanation for the prohibition against females eating Earth meat. If one will be eating Earth meat on a given day, they explained, one must refrain from sexual activity the night before. In the past, women ate Earth meat along with men; but once, a woman had falsely claimed that she had not had sex the night before eating the meat. As she lied about this, she soon died. Henceforth, women are no longer trusted to tell the truth about their sexual activities and are no longer permitted to eat Earth meat. What this says about gender relations among the Beng is complex but can be summarized here. First, it speaks to a considerable bias toward men in participation in the religion. Second, it reveals a suspicion that women's speech is not to be trusted. Nevertheless, this apparent religious and linguistic disenfranchisement of women is at least partially counterbalanced by other factors that make it difficult to characterize Beng society overall as male-dominated. For one thing, women participate in Beng religion in many other ways: they may offer sacrifices to the Earth; they may be diviners and healers; they apply paint and jewelry to their infants daily that attract or propitiate spirits (Gottlieb 1981); in exceptional circumstances they may even be Masters of the Earth. As for social life, women's ascribed unreliable speech can work in their favor. All marital disputes should always be concluded by a formal apology—via a mediator—by the husband to his wife because without this it is said that the woman would be resentful and likely divorce her husband. The subject of gender relations must await another forum for fuller discussion.

22. This rule in theory applies to all other Beng, male and female, but it is not so rigorously followed by these others, probably because no specific punishment seems to result from violating the taboo if one is not pregnant.

23. In one case, this consisted of a plate of mashed yams dyed red with palm oil and topped with a new egg (this dish is used in other sacrifices in a variety of circumstances by the Beng; variations of this are also used as a sacrifice by the Asante—see Rattray 1927:60, 72, 151; it may be widely used by other groups in West Africa). In other cases, the "snake-person" is given an herbal mixture to drink.

24. One informant told me that as a girl of about eight to ten years she had witnessed the ritual transformation described here and claimed that it "really" happened to the extent that should I ever see the ritual, I would be able to capture the transformation on film. Unfortunately the opportunity never presented itself.

25. See Davis-Floyd (n.d.) for a similar analysis of the role of liminality in American pregnancy and childbirth beliefs and practices.

26. Traditionally the spot for delivering children was a few meters from the village into the forest, but Beng classify this space as belonging to the village.

27. See Sapir (1981) for an analogous argument concerning the "natural symbolism" of hyenas.

28. It is, however, invoked in gift-giving in a manner that indicates a distant responsibility for human affairs.

29. Compare the Kuranko of Sierra Leone, a Northern Mande–speaking group, who—presumably because they are now Muslim—specifically refrain from sacrificing palm wine "because it intoxicates" (Jackson 1977c:125).

30. My sources on this question were in their late twenties. Although they had grown up in round houses, the structures had been destroyed during their adolescence, and it is possible that as children, they had not noticed or thought about the visual similarity between field and house design.

31. Another informant asserted that the spirits cannot understand French, the official language of Côte d'Ivoire, since "they have never been to school." This would signal a contemporary alienation of the spirits from the human world, indicating an increasing unwillingness to participate in village affairs (for further treatment of this theme, see chapter 6).

32. For a comparable example also from West Africa, compare J. Lubbock (1871:166), cited in Ellen (1988:228); also, cf. Lévi-Strauss (1963c).

3. DOUBLE DESCENT AS A SYSTEM OF THOUGHT

1. The Beng system of double descent parallels that of the linguistically related Gban (formerly known as the Gagou) of western Côte d'Ivoire (Chauveau and Richard 1975), but is in marked contrast to the other Southern Mande groups to which the Beng are also related, which have patrilineal but no matrilineal clans. It is possible to speculate that the Beng began with patriclans from Northern Mande culture before they split off over 2,000 years ago and then at some unknown point added matriclans as an influence from the Gur- and Akan-speaking groups who eventually became their neighbors (Jimini; Baule, Anyi, Ando) (see Loucou 1984:76), whose kinship systems are matrilineal (for the Ando, see Deniel 1976) or at least matrifocal (for the Baule, see, e.g., Etienne and Etienne 1967). However, this hypothesis awaits confirmation (or rejection) by a historian. For this reason, my analysis focuses on the main features of the descent system as it is found today.

2. Janet Keller (personal communication) has suggested "home" as an alternative translation of the Beng *wla*. This term has the virtue of evoking feelings of personal attachment, but I have decided in favor of "house" partly because it stresses the physical locus, which is important in the Beng conception, and partly because of anthropological convention.

3. Note that such substitutions are still subject to a pervasive gerontocratic bias: clan elders would send junior relatives, but not the reverse.

4. Individuals also inherit plantations through the matriclans. Traditionally these were kola tree plantations, but nowadays coffee trees have virtually replaced kola trees as the economic mainstay. Palm wine trees continue to be passed down matrilineally, as before. However, in contrast to clan gold, none of these plantations belonged or now belong to the matriclan as a collectivity: an individual could sell off a part of the plantation (or even all of it) without having to consult other clan members.

5. An exception is due to infant mishandling: if a newborn is not washed properly with homemade black soap soon after birth, it is said he or she will grow up to have a strong body odor, regardless of matriclan affiliation.

6. Unlike many other matrilineal regimes in which succession, while specified as adelphic, is otherwise open and thus conducive to competition (Douglas 1969:129), Beng matriclans specify the heir to valuable property as the eldest among brothers. This tends to rule out competition between brothers for clan-transmitted property. It does, however, reveal an acknowledgment of hierarchy within the matriclan, which might on occasion produce its own competition. In a sense, the rule of lateral inheritance—which also governs succession to political offices, which are also occupied by reference to matriclan membership—embod-

ies a contradictory combination of identity and competition, a contradiction that, as we shall see, characterizes witchcraft as well.

7. This is also true for the matrilineal Asante (Fortes 1950:275). The Baule, whose social organization is decidedly matrifocal, also bewitch only uterine kin (Etienne and Etienne 1967:59).

8. In fact, it is the king of the region who ultimately "owns" all the Beng. Theoretically he is obliged to protect his citizens from all ravages, including witchcraft. However, it is said that every night witches beleaguer him with powerful demands to victimize their matrikin. He uses his own occult powers to refuse them, but occasionally, from exhaustion, he capitulates. Thus any successful act of witchcraft is said to have been preauthorized by the king. This fact is, however, spoken about only rarely (see Gottlieb 1989).

9. Witchcraft within the matriclan takes on a political dimension as well: a newly installed king, queen, or village chief must bewitch two or three matrikin within a year of assuming office. In this case, two of the victims are somewhat specified by genealogical relationship (Gottlieb 1989). In addition, while my Beng friends denied any specific patterns in relation to age concerning bewitching, my own observations revealed that victim and witch were always either approximate agemates, or else the witch was older than the victim—never the reverse. If the many witchcraft stories I recorded are indeed representative, this would be a reflection of the general gerontocratic principle that defines much of Beng social life. Still, it is significant that no Beng pointed it out to me.

10. In the distantly related (Northern Mande) Kuranko language, the word for patriclan is sie (Jackson 1974:401).

11. For a somewhat similar case in Melanesia, see Harrison (1988).

12. One exception occurs with the patriclan Somosóliŋlεŋ. The taboo food of this clan is honey (somo), and the claimed personality trait of its members is cowardice. Now, collecting honey requires a certain amount of bravery because the gatherer is subject to the attack of bees. It may be that Somosóliŋlεŋ members are viewed as cowardly because they will not collect and eat honey—or, conversely, that their taboo food became honey as a symbol of their inherent cowardice. In either case, there seems to be a close relationship between the taboo food of honey and the clan members' attributed personality trait of cowardice. Another patriclan whose food taboos are not entirely arbitrary (by Western anthropological standards) is Krilεŋ. Huge black mushrooms and a large black bird called kri kɔkɔ are taboo to clan members because of their color. This patriclan, which in some ways is ranked as royalty (the name includes one of the words for king, kri), uses white objects in several of its rituals as a symbol of purity, and in this context (though not all contexts) black would seem anathema to its members as a symbol of defilement. In addition, the crocodile is taboo as food to clan members for another reason: it inhabits the water. Kri members are buried in water and they are ritual rainmakers, and this is seen as being incompatible with eating meat from the water-dwelling crocodiles—perhaps because among all large creatures, Kri members should have a monopoly on water. I collected analogous stories concerning the origins of food taboos for two other patriclans as well.

13. I originally came to suspect this accidentally, through interviewing. Often people who did not know me well were reluctant to divulge the name of their patriclan—names being commonly a secret topic in Beng affairs—but if they felt sympathetic toward my inquiry, they responded by mentioning their food taboos as an indirect means of telling me their clan affiliations.

14. Exceptions would include foster children and miscellaneous short- and long-term guests. The same logic for women observing their husbands' food taboos is given by the Kuranko, a patrilineal, Mande-speaking people of Sierra Leone (Jackson 1974:408). Among the matrilineal Asante, women adopt their husbands' ntoro (matriclan) taboos either on marriage or at their first pregnancy (Rattray 1927:52).

15. There are a few exceptions to this general rule. Regional kings and matriclan chiefs, no matter what their patriclan affiliations, are buried in the middle of their courtyards or

behind their houses. Possibly this is a symbolic statement of how central they were to village affairs. Victims of violent or accidental deaths (including homicides and suicides and women who died in childbirth) are always buried in the forest.

16. For a discussion of this situation among the Kuranko, see Jackson (1974).

17. Not all healers are members of this clan, nor are all Bolaleŋ members healers. But significantly, I observed that the most successful and renowned healers do invariably belong to Bolaleŋ.

4. THE MARRIAGES OF COUSINS

1. In fact, Article I of the Civil Code refers only to marriages that are registered officially with the government. Since few, if any, of the marriages that village-dwelling Beng arrange are registered, technically they would not be considered illegal, insofar as they are not recognized as marriages at all. (Cf. Launay 1982:140 for a similar point as regards the Jula of northern Côte d'Ivoire.)

2. A woman is given an arranged-marriage husband only once in her life. Though theoretically she does not have the right to refuse him, in practice this does happen from time to time, in which case she may or may not be offered another choice. If she divorces or is widowed by her first husband, a woman is free to choose any subsequent partners (for a similar case among the Bobo of Burkina Faso, see Şaul 1989:60). In contrast, a man may be given two or, occasionally, even three arranged-marriage wives. Though theoretically he has the right to refuse her, a man rarely exercises this option. There are a few situations in which marriages would not be arranged; especially, a child with a severe physical or psychological incapacity and the last child or children in a large family (for demographic reasons that I explore below) might not be offered arranged-marriage spouses.

3. Though Lévi-Strauss (1969a) contests the utility of a distinction between "preference" and "prescription," I find it to be of some use in explaining the Beng system of marriage (cf. Muller 1973; and see Rossi 1982:52–56 for a review of this controversy). I take a "preferred" rule to be an ideal sought by many but not all individuals of a given society, and a "prescribed" rule to be one that is technically obligatory for all.

4. Compare Van Baal (1975:94–96), who sees only disadvantages to this variety of marriage.

5. I adopt this pair of terms because of entrenched anthropological usage while noting the unwarranted masculine perspective they assume.

6. For an analogous case among the Bobo of Burkina Faso, see Şaul (1989).

7. A similar ritual is done by the neighboring Baule (see P. Etienne and M. Etienne 1971:179, n. 2), for the same infraction (Mona Etienne, personal communication).

8. For a symbolically informed logic concerning a related marriage prohibition among the Samo of Burkino Faso, see Héritier (1989:163).

9. For more recent treatments of relative age in Kuranko kinship and mythology, see Jackson (1977a, 1978); for a Kabre (Togo) case of the first two children being sent to live with grandparents, see Piot (1985). Other mentions of the importance of relative age include Muller's analysis of the complicated marital alliance system of the Rukuba of Nigeria (1973:1569) and Geertz's discussion (1973c) of the Balinese system of four birth-order slots into which all children are at least nominally put.

10. One informant stated it thus: "The first daughter belongs to the father; the next one who follows her belongs to the mother; she who comes next belongs to the father; the next one who follows her once more belongs to the mother" (leŋ doile, de pɔe, nya fē bi a mana, da pɔe. A su a li le, de pɔe. Nyǎ, fē bi a ma múŋ de, da ŋo pɔe). While Beng speak of the individual mother or father having rights to the child, in practice the parent's entire sibling set must agree to the proposed match and in theory all the elders of the parent's matriclan must be in accord as well. In fact, the bride's maternal grandmother or paternal grandfather

must first be asked about a proposed match before the parent's siblings are asked for their approval. Nevertheless, I think the Beng spoken emphasis on the single parent as actor is significant and so I adopt the same usage.

11. This marriage of two sisters to two brothers would seem to violate the rule, stated earlier in this chapter, against such repeated alliances between this category of affines. The likeliest explanation is that since the first marriage was, so to speak, annulled because of the groom's impotence—indeed, it may never have been consummated—the next sister marrying this man's brother would not be considered as "doubling" the alliance pattern, since the first match never really "counted" as a marriage. It is certainly curious that two brothers should be impotent. If the disorder in their cases was psychologically based, it may be related to the personality problems of their father, an Ando man who is an alcoholic and considered to be a social blunderer. Their mother is deceased, and I had no reports about her mental health; the other siblings of the impotent brothers seemed to be "normal," both mentally and physically.

12. A similar theme has been noted among the Wan—who, of all the southern Mande groups, may be linguistically the most closely related to the Beng (Philip Ravenhill, personal communication). Ravenhill (1976) also discusses an oscillation among the Wan between consolidation and extension of marital ties, though the Wan use different methods. In contrast, the Baule, who neighbor the Beng to the south and west, do not have any type of elementary alliance system. They do not practice cross-cousin marriage (unlike the Asante, to whom they are historically related); they forbid marriage with all first cousins and, in principle, with all uterine kin (P. Etienne and M. Etienne 1971:179–80) (indeed, there are no distinct kin terms for cross- and parallel-cousins; P. Etienne and M. Etienne 1967:56); and they prohibit the duplication of matrimonial ties between kin groups. Nevertheless, there are two forms of Baule marriage that contradict the intent of these rules. First, individuals may marry their own slaves, and, since the slave status was transmitted matrilaterally, slaves might marry close patrilateral relatives who would normally be forbidden (M. Etienne 1976:6; M. Etienne 1986: 154–5, n. 11). Second, when it comes to remarriage of widows, the Baule again contradict their own rules and seek remarriage of the widow with a kinsman—but not too close a kinsman—of the deceased man, thereby revealing, as with the Beng and the Wan, an ambivalence about marrying "close" (M. Etienne 1986). It is possible that such an ambivalence about marrying close and marrying far, which we find in varying forms among the Beng, the Wan, and the Baule, may be more widespread in Africa, and perhaps elsewhere as well, than has thus far been reported (Mona Etienne, personal communication).

5. HUNTING DOGS AND LAUGHING HYENAS

1. For a use of terms parallel to mine for Africa, see Okpewho (1983); for a compatible discussion of "minor genres" as the locus of serious issues among the Chamula of Mexico, see Gossen (1972).

2. This myth was told to me by Yacouba Kouadio Ba and Kouassi Tolo. Yacouba Kouadio Ba and I translated it into French and then, as with the other myths to be presented in this chapter, I retranslated it into English.

3. Given the wide variety of animals that have been inserted into this myth, I suspect that the kind of analysis offered here for the Beng might be relevant for other societies that offer variants. That is, what are the wider roles (in both mythology and daily life) of Insect and Hare among the Khoikhoi, Dog and Goat among the Yaka, and so on? An interesting comparative analysis might come of an intensive exploration of the specific mythologies of the individual societies in question.

4. In contrast to dogs, there are very few cats in Beng villages, and they are in no way viewed as pets. They are not named, are not fed as kittens, are not the object of ritual taboo

or attention, and are generally disdained. They seem to have caught the sociological imagination of the Beng to a far less extent than have dogs.

5. This myth was told to me by Kouassi Tolo. Yacouba Kouadio Ba and I translated it into French.

6. The Minyanka of Mali, with whom the Beng are very distantly connected at least linguistically, tell a myth that relates Dog's betrayal of Monkey in order to reveal cultic secrets to humans (Colleyn, cited in de Heusch 1985:176). This mythic theme of Dog's betrayal of fellow animals in favor of humans may be more widespread in Africa and elsewhere and certainly bears further comparative study.

7. As I am interpreting it, the Beng dog bears some resemblance to the classical animal trickster in West Africa (Pelton 1980) and elsewhere. Like the trickster, the Beng dog is unreliable and represents contradictory principles. Yet unlike the typical trickster, the Beng dog is not a prankster—he does not poke fun at or play tricks as such on humans or other animals—and he is certainly not sexy. I view him as a serious component and an adversary of human society; for this reason I think the classification of him as the alter ego of humans is more appropriate.

8. Why dogs should be viewed by the Beng in this way is an open question, but it is surely related to the long history of their domestication by humans. Dogs originated in the Western Hemisphere (Olsen 1985:3) but may have been first domesticated in China (ibid.:41). The oldest known remains of domesticated dogs date to approximately 11,000 B.P. in North America (ibid.:31), to 7,000 B.P. in mainland East Asia (ibid.:48), and possibly to 5,000 B.P. in Western Europe (ibid.:71). Unfortunately the early history of the domesticated dog in sub-Saharan Africa is, as yet, wholly unknown (Stanley Ambrose, personal communication).

9. Such an approach to naming pets is by no means universal. An article on American customs reports that in a sample of 12,000 dog names, the largest category was that of human names, many in English or Anglicized (Safire 1985). This is in direct contrast to the Beng system of naming dogs and may indicate an American view of pet dogs closer to the British attitude (Leach 1964), which emphasizes the more positive, human aspects of dogs but none of the ambivalence that characterizes the Beng view of dogs. Elsewhere in Africa, available data indicate still other approaches to naming dogs. The Yoruba of Nigeria, for example, in addition to using proverbs as dog names, often name their dogs either for deities worshiped by their owners or for other characteristics describing their owners or themselves (Beier 1959:31–33), while the Kujamaat Diola of Senegal name their dogs "only very rarely" (Sapir 1981:534). Further comparative study of dog names might provide a basis for systematic comparison (see n. 3).

10. Here I follow the usage of W. D. Halls, in his translation of Hubert and Mauss' work on sacrifice (1964). Halls uses "sacrifier" to refer to the person on whose behalf a sacrifice is conducted, and "sacrificer" to refer to the person who is actually conducting the sacrifice (e.g., a priest).

11. All domesticated animals, not only dogs, are said to produce ghosts (wrú) that can afflict humans. However, the Beng say that the ghosts of dogs are far more potent and potentially malicious than are the ghosts of sheep, goats, and chickens, and there are correspondingly far more beliefs and practices concerning dogs and their ghosts than there are for the other domesticated animals. Domesticated sheep, goats, and chickens may be seen as a mild version of dogs in terms of the cosmological and social roles I see them playing in relation to humans.

12. Elsewhere in Africa, the burial of dogs may carry quite a different connotation. Among the Tabwa of Zaire, dogs are routinely buried in a fairly perfunctory way, and the graves are treated rather casually, as are the graves of humans. There the regular act of burying dogs does not serve to heighten ritually the perceived relationship between canine and human (Christopher Roberts, personal communication).

13. It is unclear how widely dog sacrifices are performed in Africa. The Minyanka of Mali

are reported to sacrifice these animals more regularly than do the Beng. Approximately ten to thirty dogs are sacrificed by them semi-annually as part of the Nya cult, and the dogs are clearly seen as a substitute for human sacrifice in this instance (de Heusch 1985:174–183, 203–204). Among the Yoruba, certain cults likewise demand dog sacrifices (Beier 1959:34–36).

14. I am grateful to Janet Keller (personal communication) for this point.

15. The ambivalence Beng feel toward dogs may be generalized to a view of these animals as occupying a mediatory position. This more general theme seems more commonly found in Africa. For instance, Thompson writes of the Kongo of Central Africa (1983:121): "Between the village of the living and the village of the dead there is a village of dogs. . . . A dog or doglike . . . [charm] is often used by Kongo mystics to see beyond our world." There dogs are seen as interstitial, between living humans and their ancestors, and are used as ritual mediators between the two realms. While they do not play this precise role among the Beng, the two cultures share a more general view of dogs as an in-between category; for the Beng, it is Self and Other in a more general sense than for the Kongo.

Outside of Africa, cf. Tambiah (1969) and Bulmer (1967) for cases of ambivalent or mediatory views of dogs.

16. This myth was recounted to me by Kouakou ("L'Aji") Kouassi. Pascal Kouadio Kouakou and I translated it into French.

17. This myth was recounted to me by Koffi ("Kanya") Kouassi. Véronique Amlan Akpoueh and I translated it into French.

18. These red and black feathers are considered by the Beng to be very pretty; they are used in making necklaces for children and adults, to bring good luck and wealth. Such necklaces, called *yɔŋ pu baŋ*, are one variety of "animist" jewelry seen as offering magical protection to the wearer.

19. In the scientific literature, their recorded speed is up to 65 km (33 miles) per hour (Grzimek 1975:189).

20. Recounted to me by Koffi ("Kanya") Kouassi. Véronique Amlan Akpoueh and I translated it into French.

21. The nocturnal habits of hyenas may account for their being assigned as witches' familiars in other parts of Africa, as for example among the Shona of southern Africa (Lan 1985:36), the Kujamaat Diola of Senegal (Sapir 1981), and several Western Sudanic peoples (Calame-Griaule and Ligers 1961).

22. Hyena meat is commonly taboo throughout Africa, but exceptions have been documented, as with the Kujamaat Diola of Senegal (Sapir 1981:531). Among the Beng, as we saw in chapter 3, most other food taboos are inherited from the father and belong to the patriclan. In addition, some people may have individual food taboos diagnosed by a diviner. Apart from hyena meat, the only other meat that is taboo to all Beng is that of the vulture—like the hyena, a carrion eater (but see below, n. 28). Apart from meat, the only other use that might be made of a hyena carcass would be to sell the skin in town to whites—who are well outside the moral universe of the Beng and therefore considered appropriate customers.

23. Recounted to me by Komena Kwame. Véronique Amlan Akpoueh and I translated it into French.

24. This recent exodus of the hyenas from the Beng region to the other side of the Mbe River (the western border of the Beng territory) is explained in two myths. Consistent with Hyena's other mythic escapades, both myths blame the move on the immoral behavior of Hyena, specifically in relation to female affines (wife, mother-in-law). In one myth ("Hyena and Hare at Their Mother-in-Law's Funeral"—recounted by Komena Kwame and translated into French by Véronique Amlan Akpoueh and myself), instead of bringing the proper animals to his mother-in-law's funeral to be sacrificed in her honor, Hyena shows up empty-handed. He is made to feel so ashamed by the other mourners that he runs to the other side of the Mbe River in humiliation. In the other myth ("Rabbit and Hyena Kill Their Wives"—recounted by Koffi "Kanya" Kouassi and translated into French by Véronique Amlan Ak-

poueh and myself), Hyena is tricked by Hare into killing his wife and is forced to cross the Mbe River to avoid being beaten by an outraged crowd.

25. Cf. Calame-Griaule and Ligers (1961), who highlight the village-bush distinction that characterizes human-hyena relations among Western Sudanic peoples.

26. On medicinal uses of hyena feces by the Kaguru of Tanzania, compare Beidelman (1986:39 and n. 14).

27. Hyenas' sound is also problematic. They howl an eerie cry that one scientist has described as *whoo-oof* (Walker 1964:1263). The Beng reproduce one of their sounds as *wruuuuuu*. In shortened form this is also the Beng word for a human ghost (*wrú*), which in some circumstances is likewise said to howl eerily late at night. While I am not claiming an etymological relationship between the two words, the similarity in sound may cause Beng speakers to make an unspoken association between hyenas and human death.

28. It is a "ritual of sorts" because, as we shall see, unlike a ritual properly speaking, it does not effect complete transformation in the practitioner (Turner 1967a:95, 1985:171) but, rather, prevents a transformation that is threatening to occur. Yet if the viewer of the newly dead hyena does not follow this procedure, the transformation she or he undergoes will indeed be permanent. Beng say that the organ of another animal moves independently after death, and that this is also detestable. When either of the two local kinds of tortoise dies, the Beng say its heart continues to beat. Because of this anatomical anomaly, the tortoise heart is taboo to all. An individual who eats it would not really succumb when it came time to die, just as the tortoise never really dies (the beating heart being seen as a vital sign of life); the person would just rot, and no one would know of the "death." A respectable funeral would be out of the question.

29. Dried corncobs are used for one's ablutions after defecation and are readily available in the forest. Given this use, they would also be appropriate in the present instance. Schumacher noted (personal communication) that it is quite rare to stumble upon forest animals as they lie dying. He suggested that any observer of a newly dead hyena would most likely be a hunter and would in fact have caused the animal's demise. In this case, the irony would be more potent: the dead hyena achieves revenge not only for the human's mocking of his mythical counterpart but for the hunter's killing of him as well. This scenario awaits confirmation from further field investigation.

30. A variation on the conjoined triple theme of hyena, laughter, and mother is found in a Kuranko myth (Jackson 1982:100–101). In this narrative, Hyena punishes all who laugh during a commemorative ceremony for his deceased mother, yet he himself joins in the collective laughter when provoked by a participant in the ceremony. A comparative study of other associations of hyena and laughter might yield interesting results.

31. The hyena is not the only animal to produce contaminating excretions in the village. If a partridge defecates in the village, it is likewise said that there will be many deaths in the village that year. Thus any partridge seen in the village is immediately killed. However, if a partridge were to excrete in the village, the village would not be "broken" as it is with hyena feces, nor would it be permanently evacuated. I should add that other hyena fecal processes figure in the Beng mythological corpus. In one myth the plot revolves around Hyena passing wind. Another myth ("Spirit, Hyena, Cow, and the Division of Labor") features a Spirit putting a finger up Hyena's rectum and hurling him far into the distance. (This myth was told to me by Koffi "Kanya" Kouassi. Véronique Amla Akpoueh and I translated it into French.) It is clear that the subject of Hyena's anus in all its manifestations—defecating, passing wind, serving as a receptacle for objects other than feces, and apparently trembling after death—are of intense interest to the Beng, who have taken them as symbolic markers of various levels of societal disgust.

32. The works cited in support of this point are themselves part of a broader perspective that focuses on the power of language—for example, see Ahern (1979) and Crapanzano (1980:79).

33. There is an interesting contrast with the role of death and the hyena among the

Kujamaat Diola. Of the latter, Sapir writes (1981:538): "It is as though Kujamaat thought tolerates the ambiguity of . . . [the] hyena (their decidedly unexemplary positions) during their lives only to void the ambiguity at death," by bringing hyena corpses into the village and giving them a humanlike funeral. By contrast, the Beng amplify the ambiguity of hyenas at their deaths, but this ambiguity is symbolically dangerous and, unless dealt with swiftly by a ritual, ultimately proves fatal in a bizarre manner. The Beng emphasis on the link between hyenas and mortality emerges in a linguistic connection. As we have seen, by excreting in human territory, a hyena is said to destroy the village. The verb used by my informant in describing this to me was *wi* (lit., "to break"). Significantly, this same verb was being used by Beng in describing the military depredations that Samori perpetrated on some nearby villages and towns at the end of the nineteenth century in his effort to create an Islamic empire. So the locution describing the forced abandonment of a Beng village because of the presence of hyena feces resonates with local military history. In both cases, the destroyer is in reality, or is often depicted mythically as, a Muslim threatening the integrity of Beng religion. The question of why the Beng should negatively value hyenas, and the subversion they symbolize, must be put off for another forum, but I note only briefly a tentative solution by way of comparison. The Bamana of Mali, whose Northern Mande language is distantly related to Beng, revere hyenas as sacred, using their representations in the masculine *kore* initiation ritual as symbols of wisdom. It may be that for the Bamana the hyena's subversive character is respected, in keeping with the general respect accorded by the Bamana to heroic humans, who are themselves in some ways strikingly subversive (Bird and Kendall 1980). In contrast, the Beng have no developed role for the hero and thus, perhaps, no serious place for positively valued subversion. Charles Bird, Martha Kendall and I hope to pursue this comparative analysis further.

34. For another critique of this position, see E. Basso (1985:309–311).

35. In other societies one may find an alternate view of the society kept at the implicit level; in such systems, as da Matta (1984) proposes, what is not stated in cultural forms may be as significant as what is stated, the two (of which one half may be silent) revealing the total range of social values. The Beng system, by contrast, makes two alternative, even competing, views explicit through the two "readings" in myth and ritual.

6. COMMODITIES

1. While I refer to "Western culture," I do not assume homogeneity across national boundaries. Rather, I am adopting implicitly the viewpoint of village Beng, who associate industrial technology with white people and who perceive all whites as existing within a single cultural tradition. Specifically, as the colonial rulers of Côte d'Ivoire, the French have been taken as the prototype for all whites (including Lebanese and Asians) with whom Beng villagers have had contact.

2. For an early and inspirational example of this approach at the ideological level, see MacGaffey's compelling account (1972) of how the Kongo people have inserted Westerners into their cosmology.

3. A pungent critique of this line of analysis is offered by Wagner (1979:164), who writes: "While it seems likely that both the disruption and the re-establishment [of local village life] will be perceived and accomplished in cultic terms, it is also evident that cults themselves frequently bring about as much disruption as any outside influence." This echoes earlier critiques of functionalist analyses of witchcraft, which pointed out that witchcraft may introduce as much "tension" as it "relieves" (Douglas 1970).

4. For a similar analysis of the Bwiti cult of the Fang people of Gabon, see Fernandez (1982); on the Kimbanguist Church in Zaire, see MacGaffey (1983); on the Harris Church in Côte d'Ivoire, see Augé (1975) and Augé et al. (1975).

5. Other authors have focused on the sociological waters through which goods must navigate. Gell (1986), for instance, analyzes the ways that social relations have—and have

not—been transformed by the Muria Gonds of India as a result of newly acquired wealth. In this chapter, I provide a complementary focus. I leave aside the sociological question of how new commodities have affected social and political structures of Beng life, instead concentrating on the encompassing symbolic framework through which these commodities have had their meanings defined (cf. Babcock 1986:318).

6. The French colonial officer Louis-Gustav Binger visited the Beng region in 1889; his impressions are noted in Binger (1892:224–230). A medical doctor, Maclaud, visited in 1893–94; a very brief vocabulary list he collected is reprinted in Delafosse (1904:149). Also in 1893, Cpt. Braulot was sent up-country by Binger and stayed briefly with the Beng (Braulot n.d.).

7. For a welcome plea for anthropologists to consider the sensual components of daily life, including odors, see Stoller (1989).

8. I was told by one friend that long ago Beng (men?) smoked their own tobacco in handmade wooden pipes, but I was not able to confirm this. Assuming it is true, it would emphasize the fine nature of the distinctions that the forest spirits make between their own and foreign technologies. Elsewhere in Africa, cigarettes are also said to be distasteful to traditional spirits, for example, among the Igbo (Fagunwa 1982:17).

9. This story was told to me in Beng by "Baa" Hubert Kouadio Akpoueh and was translated into French jointly by the storyteller, his sister Véronique Amla Akpoueh, and myself.

10. Diviners are able to see the spirits, but only blurrily. During their divinatory sessions, they attract the spirits with such items as statues, eggs, kaolin, and cowry shells, and the spirits then speak to them.

11. In fact, some touted advantages of the new houses are dubious. The tin roofs and cement walls do keep out snakes and rodents and rule out dry-season fires and wet-season leaks. However, the new roofs also heat the interiors to almost intolerable temperatures in the dry season. Moreover, the grid pattern of the village streets requires greater distance between the houses than was previously the custom. This often brings with it greater presence of grasses, hence more snakes in the villages. Moreover, the cost of buying the roofs and the cement with which to plaster the walls puts pressure on rural farmers to increase cash-crop production, which can take time from cultivation of subsistence crops or hunting—in essence, requiring the intensification of the cash economy at the cost of the subsistence economy, a common problem in the Third World today now beginning to be recognized as such by Third World governments and Western development planners and scholars alike.

References

Abrahamsson, H.
    1977   The Origin of Death: Studies in African Mythology. New York: Arno Press
          (reprint). (Orig. pub., Uppsala: Alquist & Wiskell, 1951.)
Ahern, Emily
    1979   The problem of efficacy: Strong and weak illocutionary acts. Man 14(1):1–17.
Albera, Dionigi
    1988   Open systems and closed minds: The limitations of naivety in social an-
          thropology—a native's view. Man 23(3):435–452.
Appadurai, Arjun
    1986   Introduction: Commodities and the politics of value. In The Social Life of
          Things: Commodities in Cultural Perspective. Arjun Appadurai, ed. Cambridge:
          Cambridge University Press, pp. 3–63.
    1988   Putting hierarchy in its place. Cultural Anthropology 3(1):36–49.
Apte, Mahadev L.
    1985   Humour and Laughter: An Anthropological Approach. Ithaca: Cornell Univer-
          sity Press.
Arens, William
    1975   The Waswahili: The social history of an ethnic group. Africa 45(4):426–438.
    ———, and Ivan Karp
    1989   Introduction. In Creativity of Power: Cosmology and Action in African So-
          cieties. W. Arens and Ivan Karp, eds. Washington, D.C.: Smithsonian Institution
          Press, pp. xi–xxix.
    ———, eds.
    1989   Creativity of Power: Cosmology and Action in African Societies. Washington,
          D.C.: Smithsonian Institution Press.
Augé, Marc
    1975   Théorie des pouvoirs et idéologie: Étude de cas en Côte-d'Ivoire. Paris: Her-
          mann.
    1982   The Anthropological Circle: Symbol, Function, History. New York: Cambridge
          University Press. Martin Thom, trans. (Original: Symbole, fonction, histoire.
          Paris: Hachette, 1979.)
    ———, et al.
    1975   Prophétisme et thérapeutique: Albert Atcho et la communauté de Bregbo. Paris:
          Hermann.
Austin, J. L.
    1962   How To Do Things with Words. Oxford: Oxford University Press.
Babcock, Barbara
    1986   Modeled selves: Helen Cordero's "Little People." In The Anthropology of
          Experience. Victor W. Turner and Edward M. Bruner, eds. Urbana: University of
          Illinois Press, pp. 316–343.
Bakhtin, Mikhail M.
    1981   Discourse in the Novel. In The Dialogic Imagination: Four Essays by M. M.
          Bakhtin. Michael Holquist, ed. Caryl Emerson and Michael Holquist, trans.

Austin: University of Texas Press, pp. 259–422. (Original: Voprosy Literatury i Estetiki. Moscow: Khudozhestvennaia literatura, 1975. Essay orig. written, 1934–35.)

1984   Rabelais and His World. Hélène Iswolsky, trans. Bloomington: Indiana University Press. (Original: Tvorchestva Fransua Rable. Moscow: Khudozhestvennaia literatura, 1965.)

Barth, Fredrik

1975   Ritual and Knowledge among the Baktaman of New Guinea. New Haven: Yale University Press.

Bascom, William

1965   The forms of folklore: Prose narratives. Journal of American Folklore 78(1):3–20.

Basso, Ellen

1985   A Musical View of the Universe. Philadelphia: University of Pennsylvania Press.

Basso, Keith

1979   Portrait of "The Whiteman": Linguistic Play and Cultural Symbols among the Western Apache. Cambridge: Cambridge University Press.

1984   "Stalking with stories": Names, places, and moral narratives among the Western Apache. In Text, Play, and Story: The Construction and Reconstruction of Self and Society. 1983 Proceedings of the American Ethnological Society. Edward M. Bruner, ed. Washington, D.C.: American Ethnological Society, pp. 19–55.

1988   "Speaking of names": Language and landscape among the Western Apache. Cultural Anthropology 3(2):99–130.

Bateson, Gregory

1936   Naven. Stanford: Stanford University Press.

1972   Toward a theory of schizophrenia. In Steps to an Ecology of Mind. New York: Ballantine/Chandler, pp. 201–227. (Essay orig. pub.: Behavioral Science 1(4) [1956].)

Bauer, Dan

1989   The Sacred and the Secret: Order and Chaos in Tigray Medicine and Politics. In Creativity of Power: Cosmology and Action in African Societies. W. Arens and Ivan Karp, eds. Washington, D.C.: Smithsonian Institution Press, pp. 225–243.

Beidelman, T. O.

1961   Hyena and Rabbit: A Kaguru representation of matrilineal relations. Africa 31(1):61–74.

1963   Further adventures of Hyena and Rabbit: The folktale as a sociological model. Africa 33(1):54–69.

1975   Ambiguous animals: Two theriomorphic metaphors in Kaguru folklore. Africa 45(2):183–200.

1986   Moral Imagination in Kaguru Modes of Thought. Bloomington: Indiana University Press.

Beier, Ulli

1959   The Yoruba attitude to dogs. Odò: A Journal of Yoruba and Related Studies 7(March):31–37.

Bellman, Beryl

1984   The Language of Secrecy: Symbols and Metaphors in Poro Ritual. New Brunswick, N.J.: Rutgers University Press.

Binger, Louis-Gustav

1892   Du Niger au Golfe de Guinée par le pays de Kong et le Mossi (1887–1889). 2 vols. Paris: Hachette.

1895a   [Letter to Emile Chautemps, Minister of the Colonies, April 13, 1895.] France. Archives Nationales, Section Outre-Mer. Côte d'Ivoire V. Dossier 3. Unnumbered folder.

1895b [Letter to Administrateur A. Nebout, April 6, 1895.] France. Archives Nationales, Section Outre-Mer. Côte d'Ivoire IV. Dossier 3. Folder b.

Bird, Charles, and Martha Kendall
1980 The Mande hero. *In* Explorations in African Systems of Thought. Ivan Karp and Charles Bird, eds. Bloomington: Indiana University Press, pp. 13–26.

Bleek, W. H.
1864 Reynard the Fox in South Africa: or Hottentot Fables and Tales. . . . London: Tubner & Co.

Bloch, Maurice
1983 Marxism and Anthropology: The History of a Relationship. New York: Oxford University Press.
1985 Almost eating the ancestors. Man 20(4):631–646.

———, and Jonathan Parry
1982 Introduction: Death and the regeneration of life. *In* Death and the Regeneration of Life. Maurice Bloch and Jonathan Parry, eds. Cambridge: Cambridge University Press, pp. 1–44.

Bly, Robert
1988 A Little Book on the Human Shadow. San Francisco: Harper and Row.

Boggs, Carl
1976 Gramsci's Marxism. London: Pluto Press.

Bourdieu, Pierre
1977 Outline of a Theory of Practice. Richard Nice, trans. Cambridge: Cambridge University Press. (Original: Esquisse d'une théorie de la pratique. Geneva: Droz, 1972.)

Braulot
N.d. [Report on 1893 voyage in Côte d'Ivoire.] France. Archives Nationales, Section d'Outre-Mer. Côte d'Ivoire III. Document 3.

Bruner, Edward M.
1984 Introduction: The opening up of anthropology. *In* Text, Play, and Story: The Construction and Reconstruction of Self and Society. 1983 Proceedings of the American Ethnological Society. Edward M. Bruner, ed. Washington, D.C.: American Ethnological Society, pp. 1–16.
1986 Ethnography as narrative. *In* The Anthropology of Experience. Victor W. Turner and Edward M. Bruner, eds. Urbana: University of Illinois Press, pp. 139–155.

———, and Phyllis Gorfain
1984 Dialogic narration and the paradoxes of Masada. *In* Text, Play, and Story: The Construction and Reconstruction of Self and Society. 1983 Proceedings of the American Ethnological Society. Edward M. Bruner, ed. Washington, D.C.: American Ethnological Society, pp. 56–79.

Buckley, Thomas, and Alma Gottlieb
1988 A critical appraisal of theories of menstrual symbolism. *In* Buckley and Gottlieb, eds. 1988, pp. 1–50.

———, eds.
1988 Blood Magic: The Anthropology of Menstruation. Berkeley: University of California Press.

Bulmer, Ralph
1967 Why is the cassowary not a bird? A problem in zoological taxonomy among the Karam of the New Guinea Highlands. Man 2(1):5–25.

Calame-Griaule, G., and Z. Ligers
1961 L'Homme-hyène dans la tradition Soudanaise. L'Homme 1(2):89–118.

Carrier, James G.
  1987 History and self-conception in Ponam society. Man 22(1):111–131.
Cassirer, Ernst
  1944 An Essay on Man: An Introduction to a Philosophy of Human Culture. New Haven: Yale University Press.
  1955 The Philosophy of Symbolic Forms. 3 vols. Ralph Mannheim, trans. New Haven: Yale University Press. (Original: Philosophie der Symbolischen Formen. Berlin: Bruno Cassirer, 1921.)
Chauveau, Jean-Pierre, and Jacques Richard
  1975 Organisation socio-économique Gban et économie de plantation. Abidjan: O.R.S.T.O.M., Sciences Humaines 8(2). Centre de Petit Bassam.
Chiappelli, Fredi, ed.
  1976 First Images of America. 2 vols. Berkeley: University of California Press.
Ciardi, John
  1965 An Alphabestiary. Philadelphia: J. B. Lippincott.
Clay, Brenda
  1977 Pinikindu: Maternal Nurture and Paternal Substance. Chicago: University of Chicago Press.
Clifford, James
  1986a Introduction: Partial truths. In Writing Culture: The Poetics and Politics of Ethnography. James Clifford and George E. Marcus, eds. Berkeley: University of California Press, pp. 1–26.
  1986b On ethnographic allegory. In Writing Culture: The Poetics and Politics of Ethnography. James Clifford and George E. Marcus, eds. Berkeley: University of California Press, pp. 98–121.
Clozel, Marie François-Joseph
  1902 Les coutumes indigènes de la Côte d'Ivoire. Paris: A. Challamel.
Cohen, Michael
  1974 Urban Policy and Political Conflict in Africa: A Study of the Ivory Coast. Chicago: University of Chicago Press.
Colie, Rosemary
  1966 Paradox Epidemica. Princeton: Princeton University Press.
Colson, Elizabeth
  1966 The alien diviner and local politics among the Tonga of Zambia. In Political Anthropology. Marc J. Swartz, Victor W. Turner, and Arthur Tuden, eds. Chicago: Adine, pp. 129–139.
Comaroff, Jean
  1985 Body of Power, Spirits of Resistance: The Culture and History of a South African People. Chicago: University of Chicago Press.
———, and John L. Comaroff
  1990 Goodly beasts, beastly goods: Cattle and commodities in a South African context. American Ethnologist 17(2):195–216.
Comaroff, John L.
  1980a Bridewealth and the control of ambiguity in a Tswana chiefdom. In The Meaning of Marriage Payments. John Comaroff, ed. London: Academic Press, pp. 161–196.
  1980b Introduction. In The Meaning of Marriage Payments. John Comaroff, ed. London: Academic Press, pp. 1–47.
  1987 Sui genderis: Feminism, kinship theory, and structural "domains." In Gender and Kinship: Essays toward a Unified Analysis. Jane Fishburne Collier and Sylvia Junko Yanagisako, eds. Stanford: Stanford University Press, pp. 53–85.
———, and Jean Comaroff
  1987 The madman and the migrant: Work and labor in the historical consciousness of a South African people. American Ethnologist 14(2):191–209.

Côte d'Ivoire
   1968   Town Planning and Rural Housing Modernization in the Ivory Coast. Abidjan: Ministry of Information, Republic of Ivory Coast.
   1971   Atlas de Côte d'Ivoire. Abidjan: Ministère du Plan de Côte d'Ivoire.
   1984   [Census of 1984.] Préfecture—Bouaké. Département—Bouaké. Sous-préfecture—M'Bahiakro. Canton—Abbeys.

Coulibaly, Sidiki, Joel Gregory, and Victor Piché
   1980   Les migrations voltaiques. Vol. I: Importance et ambivalence de la migration voltaique. Ouagadougou: Centre Voltaique de la Recherche Scientifique.

Crapanzano, Vincent
   1972   The Fifth World of Forster Bennett: Portrait of a Navaho. New York: Viking.
   1980   Tuhami: Portrait of a Moroccan. Chicago: University of Chicago Press.

Crocker, J. Christopher
   1969   Reciprocity and hierarchy. Man 4(1):44–58.
   1977   The mirrored self: Identity and ritual inversion among the Eastern Bororo. Ethnology 16(2):129–145.
   1985   Vital Souls: Bororo Cosmology, Natural Symbolism, and Shamanism. Tucson: University of Arizona Press.

Culler, Jonathan
   1982   On Deconstruction: Theory and Criticism after Structuralism. Ithaca: Cornell University Press.

Cultural Anthropology
   1988   Special issue, vol. 3, no. 1. Place and Voice in Anthropological Theory.

Cunnison, Ian
   1956   Perpetual kinship: A political institution of the Luapula peoples. Journal of the Rhodes-Livingstone Institute 20:28–48.

da Matta, Roberto
   1984   On carnaval, informality, and magic: A point of view. In Text, Play, and Story: The Construction and Reconstruction of Self and Society. 1983 Proceedings of the American Ethnological Society. Edward M. Bruner, ed. Washington, D.C.: American Ethnological Society, pp. 230–246.

Davis-Floyd, Robbie
   N.d.   American Childbirth as a Rite of Passage. Berkeley: University of California Press. In press.

de Certeau, Michel
   1980   On the oppositional practices of everyday life. Frederic Jameson and Carl Lovitt, trans. Social Text 3(Fall):3–43.

de Heusch, Luc
   1985   Sacrifice in Africa: A Structuralist Approach. Linda O'Brien and Alice Morton, trans. Bloomington: Indiana University Press.

Delafosse, Maurice
   1904   Vocabulaires comparatifs de plus de 60 langues ou dialectes parlés à la Côte d'Ivoire et dans les régions limitrophes. Paris: Leroux.

Deniel, Raymond
   1976   Une société paysanne de Côte-d'Ivoire: Les Ano, tradition et changements, Abidjan: I.N.A.D.E.S.

Derrida, Jacques
   1973   Differance. In Speech and Phenomena and Other Essays on Husserl's Theory of Signs. David B. Allison, trans. Evanston: Northwestern University Press, pp. 129–160. (Article orig. pub., Bulletin de la Société française de philosophie 62[3][1968]:73–101.)

Dieterlen, Germaine
   1973   A contribution to the study of blacksmiths in West Africa. In French Perspectives in African Studies: A Collection of Translated Essays. Pierre Alexandre, ed.

162 *References*

Robert Brain, trans. London: International Institute for Oxford University Press, pp. 40–61. (Article orig. pub., Annuaire de l'E.P.H.E. 73[1965–66]:12–28.)

Douglas, Mary
1966 Purity and Danger. London: Tavistock.
1968 The social control of cognition: Some factors in joke perception. Man 3:361–376.
1969 Is matriliny doomed in Africa? In Man in Africa. Mary Douglas and Phyllis M. Kaberry, eds. London: Tavistock, pp. 123–137.
1970 Introduction: Thirty Years after Witchcraft, Oracles and Magic. In Witchcraft Confessions and Accusations. Mary Douglas, ed. London: Tavistock, pp. xiii–xxxviii.
————, and Baron Isherwood
1979 The World of Goods. New York: Basic Books.

Dozon, Jean-Pierre
1987 L'Ethnie: Une notion à réevaluer. Kasa Bya Kasa: Revue Ivoirienne d'Anthropologie et de Sociologie 9:3–15.

Dresch, Paul
1986 The significance of the course events take in segmentary systems. American Ethnologist 13(2):309–324.

Drummond, Lee
1981 The serpent's children: Semiotics of cultural genesis in Arawak and Trobriand myth. American Ethnologist 8(3):633–660.

Dumont, Louis
1979 The anthropological community and ideology. Social Science Information 18(6):785–817. Alan McDonnell Duff and Louis Dumont, trans. (Essay orig. pub.: L'Homme 18[1978].)

Dundes, Alan
1972 Folk ideas as units of worldview. In Toward New Perspectives in Folklore. Americo Paredes and Richard Bauman, eds. Austin: University of Texas Press, pp. 93–103.

du Prey, Pierre
1970 La Côte d'Ivoire de A à Z. Abidjan: TEXTU.

Eickelman, Dale
1976 Moroccan Islam: Tradition and Society in a Pilgrimage Center. Austin: University of Texas Press.

Ekanza, Simon-Pierre
1983 Mutations d'une société rurale: Les Agni du Moronou, 18e siècle à 1939. Doctoral diss., University of Aix—Marseilles I (Université de Provence).

Ellen, Roy F.
1988 Fetishism. Man 23(2):213–235.

Etienne, Mona
1976 Women and slaves: Stratification in an African society. Paper presented at the 75th Annual Meeting of the American Anthropological Association, Washington, D.C.
1979 The case for social maternity: Adoption of children by urban Baule women. Dialectical Anthropology 4:237–242.
1985 Structures sociales, transformations économiques et rapports des sexes chez les Baoulé de Côte d'Ivoire. Doctoral diss., University of Paris V (Ecole des Hautes Etudes en Science Sociales).
1986 Contradiction, constraints and choices: Widow remarriage among the Baule of Ivory Coast. In Widows in African Societies: Choices and Constraints. Betty Potash, ed. Stanford: Stanford University Press, pp. 241–282.

Etienne, Pierre, and Mona Etienne
1967 Terminologie de la parenté et de l'alliance chez les baoulé (Côte d'Ivoire). L'Homme 7(4):50–76.

1971 "A qui mieux mieux" ou le mariage chez les Baoulé. Cahiers O.R.S.T.O.M., série Sciences humaines 8(2):165–186.

Evans-Pritchard, E. E.
1950 Kinship and Marriage among the Nuer. Oxford: Oxford University Press.

Evens, T. M. S.
1989 The Nuer incest prohibition and the nature of kinship: Alterlogical reckoning. Cultural Anthropology 4(4):323–346.

Fagunwa, D. O.
1982 Forest of a Thousand Daemons: A Hunter's Saga. Wole Soyinka, trans. New York: Random House. (Original: Ogbuju ode ninu Igbo irunmale. Apapa Lagos: Thomas Nelson Ltd. Nigeria, 1950.)

Fardon, R.
1984 Sisters, wives, wards and daughters: A transformational analysis of the political organization of the Tiv and their neighbours. I. The Tiv. Africa 54(4):2–21.

Feher, Michael, with Ramona Naddaff and Nadi Tazi, eds.
1989 Zone: Fragments for a History of the Human Body, Parts 1–3. New York: Urzone.

Feldmann, Susan, ed.
1963 African Myths & Tales. New York: Dell.

Ferguson, James
1988 Cultural exchange: New developments in the anthropology of commodities (review essay of *The Social Life of Things: Commodities in Cultural Perspective,* ed. Arjun Appadurai). Cultural Anthropology 3(4):488–513.

Fernandez, James
1974 The mission of metaphor in expressive culture. Current Anthropology 15:119–133.
1982 Bwiti: The Religious Imagination in Africa. Princeton: Princeton University Press.

Finnegan, Ruth
1970 Oral Literature in Africa. Oxford: Clarendon Press.

Fischer, Michael M. J., and Mehdi Abedi
1990 Debating Muslims: Cultural Dialogues in Postmodernity and Tradition. Madison: University of Wisconsin Press.

Fish, Stanley
1980 What makes an interpretation possible? In Is There a Text in This Class? Cambridge: Harvard University Press, pp. 338–355.

Fortes, Meyer
1950 Kinship and marriage among the Ashnati. In African Systems of Kinship and Marriage. A. R. Radcliffe-Brown and C. Daryll Forde, eds. Oxford: Oxford University Press for the International African Institute.

Foucault, Michel
1980 Truth and power. In Power/Knowledge: Selected Interviews and Other Writings, 1972–1977. Colin Gordon, ed. Colin Gordon et al., trans. New York: Pantheon, pp. 109–133. (Original in Michel Foucault, Microfisica del Portere. Turin, 1977.)

France, Institut Géographique National
1970 [Map.] République de Côte d'Ivoire. Dressé par l'Institut Géographique National. Dakar: Centre en Afrique Occidentale.

Fried, Morton
1975 The Notion of Tribe. Menlo Park: Cummings.

Fuglestad, Finn
1975 Les Hauka: Une interprétation historique. Cahiers d'Etudes Africaines 15(2):203–216.

Gaines, Atwood D.
1982 The twice-born: "Christian psychiatry" and Christian psychiatrists. Culture, Medicine and Psychiatry 6:305–324.

Garro, Linda
  1988 Explaining blood pressure: Variation in knowledge about illness. American
         Ethnologist 15(1):98–119.
Geertz, Clifford
  1973a Deep play: Notes on the Balinese cockfight. In The Interpretation of Cultures.
          New York: Basic Books, pp. 412–453. (Orig. pub.: Daedalus 101 [1972].)
  1973b The Interpretation of Cultures. New York: Basic Books.
  1973c Person, time, and conduct in Bali: An essay in cultural analysis. In The
          Interpretation of Cultures. New York: Basic Books, pp. 360–411. (Orig. pub.: New
          Haven: Yale University, Southeast Asian Studies, Cultural Report Series no. 14.)
  1973d Thick description. In The Interpretation of Cultures. New York: Basic Books,
          pp. 3–30.
  1980 Negara: The Theatre State in Nineteenth-Century Bali. Princeton: Princeton
         University Press.
Gell, Alfred
  1986 Newcomers to the world of goods: Consumption among the Muria Gonds. In
         The Social Life of Things: Commodities in Cultural Perspective. Arjun Ap-
         padurai, ed. Cambridge: Cambridge University Press, pp. 110–138.
Gellner, Ernest
  1969 Saints of the Atlas. Chicago: University of Chicago Press.
Gibson, Thomas
  1985 The sharing of substance versus the sharing of activity among the Buid. Man
         20(3):391–411.
Giddens, Anthony
  1976 Functionalism: Après la lutte. Social Research 43(2):325–366.
Goldberg, Margaret
  1986 God realms and spiritual technology: Tibetan attitudes towards modern tech-
         nology. Paper presented at the 85th Annual Meeting of the American Anthropo-
         logical Association, Philadelphia.
Goody, Esther
  1982 Parenthood and Social Reproduction: Fostering and Occupational Roles in West
         Africa. Cambridge: Cambridge University Press.
Goody, Jack
  1959 The mother's brother and the sister's son in West Africa. Journal of the Royal
         Anthropological Institute of Great Britain and Ireland 89(1):61–88.
  1961 The classification of double descent systems. Current Anthropology 2(1):3–25.
  1977 The Domestication of the Savage Mind. Cambridge: Cambridge University
         Press.
  1986 The Logic of Writing and the Organization of Society. Cambridge: Cambridge
         University Press.
Gordon, Robert
  1988 Apartheid's anthropologists: The genealogy of Afrikaner anthropology. Amer-
         ican Ethnologist 15(3):535–553.
Gose, Peter
  1986 Sacrifice and the commodity form in the Andes. Man 21(2):296–310.
Gossen, Gary
  1972 Chamula genres of verbal behavior. In Toward New Perspectives in Folklore.
         Americo Paredes and Richard Bauman, eds. Austin: University of Texas Press, pp.
         145–167.
Gottlieb, Alma
  1981 Beng baby decoration: The efficacy of symbols and the power of women. Paper
         presented at the 24th Annual Meeting of the African Studies Association, Bloom-
         ington, Ind.

1983   Village Kapok, Forest Kapok: Separation, Identity and Gender among the Beng of Ivory Coast. Ph.D. diss., University of Virginia.

1986   Changing the calendar: Economics and religious innovation among the Beng of Côte d'Ivoire. Paper presented at the 29th Annual Meeting, African Studies Association, Madison, Wis.

1988   Menstrual cosmology among the Beng of Ivory Coast. In Blood Magic: The Anthropology of Menstruation. Thomas Buckley and Alma Gottlieb, eds. Berkeley: University of California Press, pp. 55–74.

1989   Witches, kings and the sacrifice of identity: Or, the power of paradox and the paradox of power among the Beng of Ivory Coast. In Creativity of Power: Cosmology and Action in African Societies. W. Arens and Ivan Karp, eds. Washington, D.C.: Smithsonian Institution Press, pp. 245–272.

1990a   Rethinking "female pollution": The Beng case (Côte d'Ivoire). In Beyond the Second Sex: New Directions in the Anthropology of Gender. Peggy Reeves Sanday and Ruth Gallagher Goodenough, eds. Philadelphia: University of Pennsylvania Press, pp. 115–138.

1990b   A Society of Secrets: The Beng of Côte d'Ivoire. Paper presented at the 33rd Annual Meeting of the African Studies Association, Baltimore.

N.d.   Beng-English Dictionary. With the assistance of M. Lynne Murphy. Bloomington: Linguistics Club, Indiana University. Forthcoming.

———, and Philip Graham

N.d.   A Parallel World. New York: Crown Publishers. Forthcoming.

Gough, Kathleen

1971   The Nuer: A re-examination. In The Translation of Cultures. Thomas Beidelman, ed. London: Tavistock, pp. 79–121.

Graham, Philip

1989   A writer in a world of spirits. Poets and Writers Magazine (May–June):29–38.

Gramsci, Antonio

1971   Selections from the Prison Notebooks of Antonio Gramsci. Quintin Hoare and Geoffrey Nowell Smith, trans. New York: International Publishers. (Original: Quaderni del Carcere. Turin: Einaudi, 1948–51.)

Griaule, Marcel

1965   Conversations with Ogotommeli. Ralph Butler et al., trans. London: Oxford University Press for the International African Institute. (Original: Dieu d'eau: Entretiens avec Ogotommêli. Paris: Editions du Chêne, 1948.)

Grzimek, Bernhard

1975   The spotted hyena. In Grzimek's Animal Life Encyclopedia. Bernhard Grzimek, ed. New York: Van Nostrand Reinhold Co., pp. 185–191.

Hall, Stuart

1985   Religious ideologies and social movements in Jamaica. In Religion and Ideology. R. Bocock and K. Thompson, eds. Manchester: Manchester University Press, pp. 269–296.

1986   Gramsci's relevance for the study of race and ethnicity. Journal of Communication Inquiry 10(2):5–27.

Handelman, Don

1977   Play and ritual: Complementary frames of metacommunication. In It's a Funny Thing, Humour: International Conference on Humour and Laughter. Antony J. Chapman and Hugh C. Foot, eds. Oxford: Pergamon Press, pp. 185–192.

1984   Inside-out, outside-in: Concealment and revelation in Newfoundland Christmas mumming. In Text, Play, and Story: The Construction and Reconstruction of Self and Society. 1983 Proceedings of the American Ethnological Society. Edward M. Bruner, ed. Washington, D.C.: American Ethnological Society, pp. 247–277.

Haraway, Donna

1988 Situated knowledges: The science question in feminism and the privilege of partial perspective. Feminist Studies 14(3):575–599.

Harrison, Simon
1988 Magical exchange of the preconditions of production in a Sepik River village. Man 23(2):319–333.
1989 Magical and material politics in Melanesia. Man 24(1):1–20.

Hastrup, Kirsten
1990 The ethnographic present: A reinvention. Cultural Anthropology 5(1):45–61.

Heidegger, Martin
1969 Identity and Difference. New York: Harper and Row. Joan Stambaugh, trans. (Original: Identitat ünd differenz. Pfüllingen: Günther Neske, 1957.)

Herf, Jeffrey
1984 Reactionary Modernism: Technology, Culture, and Politics in Weimar and the Third Reich. Cambridge: Cambridge University Press.

Héritier, Françoise
1981 L'Exercise de la parenté. Paris: Le Seuil.
1982 The symbolics of incest and its prohibition. In Between Belief and Transgression: Structuralist Essays in Religion, History, and Myth. Michel Izard and Pierre Smith, eds. Chicago: University of Chicago Press, pp. 152–179. (Original: La fonction symbolique. Paris: Gallimard, 1979.)
1989 Semen and blood: Some ancient theories concerning their genesis and relationship. Tina Jolas, trans. Zone 5, special issue on Fragments for a History of the Human Body, part 3, 159–175. (Original: Nouvelle revue de psychanalyse 32 [Fall 1985].)

Hoffman, Daniel
1972 Poe Poe Poe Poe Poe Poe Poe. Garden City, N.Y.: Doubleday.

[Holquist, Michael]
1981 Introduction. In The Dialogic Imagination: Four Essays by M. M. Bakhtin. Austin: University of Texas Press, pp. xv–xxxiv.

Hubert, Henri, and Marcel Mauss
1964 Sacrifice: Its Nature and Function. W. D. Halls, trans. Chicago: University of Chicago Press. (Original: L'Année sociologique II [1899]:29–138.)

Hugh-Jones, Christine
1979 From the Milk River: Spatial and Temporal Processes in Northwest Amazonia. Cambridge: Cambridge University Press.

Hunt, Alan
1985 The ideology of law: Advances and problems in recent applications of the concept of ideology to the analysis of law. Law and Society Review 19(1):11–37.

Hymes, Dell
1979 Foreword. In Keith Basso, Portrait of "The Whiteman." Cambridge: Cambridge University Press, pp. ix–xviii.

Jackson, Michael
1974 The structure and significance of Kuranko clanship. Africa 44(4):397–415.
1977a Birth-order position. In The Kuranko: Dimensions of Social Reality in a West African Tribe. New York: St. Martin's Press, pp. 161–180.
1977b Sacrifice and social structure among the Kuranko, Parts I and II. Africa 47(1):41–49.
1977c Sacrifice and social structure among the Kuranko, Part III. Africa 47(2):123–139.
1978 Ambivalence and the last-born: Birth order position in convention and myth. Man 13:341–361.
1982 Allegories of the Wilderness: Ethics and Ambiguity in Kuranko Narratives. Bloomington: Indiana University Press.

Johnson, Barbara
1987 A World of Difference. Baltimore: Johns Hopkins University Press.
Jordan, Brigitte
1983 Childbirth in Four Cultures. Montreal: Eden Press.
Karp, Ivan
1978 Fields of Change among the Iteso of Kenya. London: Routledge and Kegan Paul.
1980 Beer drinking and social experience in an African society: An essay in formal sociology. In Explorations in African Systems of Thought. Ivan Karp and Charles Bird, eds. Bloomington: Indiana University Press, pp. 83–119.
1987 Laughter at marriage: Subversion in performance. In Transformations of African Marriage. David Parkin and David Nyamwaya, eds. Manchester: Manchester University Press for the International African Institute, pp. 137–155.
Keesing, Roger
1987 Anthropology as interpretive quest. Current Anthropology 28: 161–176.
Keller, Janet, and Kris Lehman
N.d. Complex concepts. Cognitive Science. In press.
Kertzer, David I., and Jennie Keith, eds.
1984 Age and Anthropological Theory. Ithaca: Cornell University Press.
Kessler, Evelyn S.
1976 Women: An Anthropological View. New York: Holt, Rinehart and Winston.
Kierkegaard, Søren [Anti-climacus]
1954 Despair viewed under the aspects of finitude and infinitude. In Fear and Trembling and Sickness unto Death. W. Lowrie, trans. Princeton: Princeton University Press. (Original: Sygdommen til Doden, by A. Climacus, ed. S. Kierkegaard. Copenhagen: Paa Universitetboghandler C. A. Reitzels Forlag, 1849.)
Kiernan, J. P.
1988 The other side of the coin: The conversion of money to religious purposes in Zulu Zionist churches. Man 23(3):453–468.
Kirby, Vicki
1990 Feminisms, readings, postmodernisms. Paper presented at the 89th Annual Meeting of the American Anthropological Association, New Orleans.
Kittel, D. W. W.
1975 Passing like Flowers: The Marriage Regulations of the Tugen of Kenya and Their Implications for a Theory of Crow-Omaha. Ph.D. diss., University of Illinois.
Kopytoff, Igor
1986 The cultural biography of things: Commoditization as process. In The Social Life of Things: Commodities in Cultural Perspective. Arjun Appadurai, ed. Cambridge: Cambridge University Press, pp. 64–91.
1987 The internal African frontier: The making of African political culture. In The African Frontier: The Reproduction of Traditional African Societies. Igor Kopytoff, ed. Bloomington: Indiana University Press, pp. 3–84.
——— , ed.
1987 The African Frontier: The Reproduction of Traditional African Societies. Bloomington: Indiana University Press.
Kruuk, Hans
1972 The Spotted Hyena: A Study of Predation and Social Behavior. Chicago: University of Chicago Press.
Kuper, Adam
1982a Lineage theory: A critical retrospect. Annual Review of Anthropology 11:71–95.
1982b Wives for Cattle. London: Routledge and Kegan Paul.
1983 Anthropology and Anthropologists: The Modern British School. Rev. ed. London: Routledge and Kegan Paul. (Orig. ed., 1973.)

1988 Comments on session, "Rethinking Kinship in Africa." Presented at the 87th Annual Meeting of the American Anthropological Association, Phoenix.

Lan, David
1985 Guns and Rain: Guerrillas and Spirit Mediums in Zimbabwe. Berkeley: University of California Press.

Laqueur, Thomas
1986 Orgasm, generation, and the politics of reproductive biology. Representations 14:1–41.

Larrain, Jorge
1979 The Concept of Ideology. Athens: University of Georgia Press.

Launay, Robert
1982 Traders without Trade: Responses to Change in Two Dyula Communities. Cambridge: Cambridge University Press.

Leach, Edmund
1964 Anthropological aspects of language: Animal categories and verbal abuse. In New Directions in the Study of Language. Eric H. Lenneberg, ed. Cambridge: MIT Press, pp. 23–63.
1976 Culture and Communication: The Logic by Which Symbols Are Connected: An Introduction to the Use of Structuralist Analysis in Social Anthropology. Cambridge: Cambridge University Press.

Lehman, F. K.
1967 Ethnic categories in Burma and the theory of social systems. In Southeast Asian Tribes, Minorities, and Nations. Peter Kunstadter, ed. Princeton: Princeton University Press, pp. 93–124.
1979 Who are the Karen, and if so, why? Karen ethnohistory and a formal theory of ethnicity. In Adaptation and Identity: The Karen on the Thai Frontier with Burma. Charles F. Keyes, ed. Philadelphia: ISHI Press, pp. 215–253.
1983 Review of Françoise Héritier, L'Exercise de la Parenté. American Ethnologist 10(2):378–380.

Le Saoût, Joseph
1976 Etude descriptive du Gban, Côte d'Ivoire. Phonétique et phonologique. Paris: Societe d'Etudes Linguistiques et Anthropologiques de France/C.N.R.S.

Levasseur, A.
1971 The modernization of Africa with particular reference to family law in Ivory Coast. In Ghana and the Ivory Coast: Perspectives on Modernization. Philip Foster and Aristide Zolberg, eds. Chicago: University of Chicago Press, pp. 151–166.

Lévi-Strauss, Claude
1963a Language and the analysis of social laws. In Structural Anthropology, vol. 1. Claire Jacobson and Brooke Grundfest Schoepf, trans. New York: Basic Books, pp. 55–66. (Essay orig. pub. American Anthropologist 53(2) [1951]:155–163.)
1963b Linguistics and anthropology. In Structural Anthropology, vol. 1. Claire Jacobson and Brooke Grundfest Schoepf, trans. New York: Basic Books, pp. 67–80. (Essay orig. pub. International Journal of American Linguistics, supplement, 19(2) [1953]:1–10.)
1963c The sorcerer and his magic. In Structural Anthropology, vol. 1. Claire Jacobson and Brooke Grundfest Schoepf, trans. New York: Basic Books, pp. 167–185. (Essay orig. pub. Les Temps Modernes 41 [1949].)
1963d Structural analysis in linguistics and in anthropology. In Structural Anthropology, vol. 1. Claire Jacobson and Brooke Grundfest Schoepf, trans. New York: Basic Books, pp. 31–54. (Essay orig. pub. Word 1(2)[1945].)
1963e Totemism. Rodney Needham, trans. Boston: Beacon Press. (Original: Le totémisme aujourd'hui. Paris: Presses Universitaires de France, 1962.)

1966a   The future of kinship studies. Proceedings of the Royal Anthropological Institute 1965:13–22.

1966b   The Savage Mind. Anon. trans. Chicago: University of Chicago Press. (Original: La Pensée sauvage. Paris: Plon, 1962.)

1967   The story of Asdiwal. In The Structural Study of Myth and Totemism. Edmund Leach, ed. London: Tavistock. (Essay orig. pub. Ecole pratique des Hautes Etudes, Section des Sciences religieuses, Extrait annuaire, 1958–59 [1958].)

1969a   The Elementary Structures of Kinship. James Harle Bell et al., trans. Boston: Beacon Press. (Original: Les Structures elémentaires de la Parenté. Paris: Presses Universitaires de France, 1949.)

1969b   The Raw and the Cooked: Introduction to a Science of Mythology, vol. 1. John and Doreen Weightman, trans. New York: Harper and Row. (Original: Mythologies 1: Le cru et le cuit. Paris: Plon, 1964.)

1973   From Honey to Ashes: Introduction to a Science of Mythology, vol. 2. John and Doreen Weightman, trans. New York: Harper and Row. (Original: Mythologies II: Du miel aux cendres. Paris: Plon, 1966.)

1976   Jean-Jacques Rousseau, founder of the sciences of man. In Structural Anthropology, vol. 2. Monique Layton, trans. New York: Basic Books, pp. 33–43. (Essay orig. pub. in Jean-Jacques Rousseau. Neufchâtel: La Baconnière, 1962.)

1978   The Origin of Table Manners: Introduction to a science of Mythology, vol. 3. John Weightman and Doreen Weightman, trans. London: Cape. (Original: Mythologies III: L'Origine des manières de table. Paris: Plon, 1968.)

1981   The Naked Man. John and Doreen Weightman, trans. New York: Harper and Row. (Original: Mythologies IV: L'homme nu. Paris: Plon, 1971.)

Lévy-Bruhl, Lucien

1966   The "Soul" of the Primitive. Lilian A. Clare, trans. Chicago: Henry Regnery. (Original: L'âme primitive. Paris: Alcan, 1927.)

1985   How Natives Think. Lilian A. Clare, trans. Princeton: Princeton University Press. (Original: Les fonctions mentales dans les sociétés inférieures. Paris: Alcan, 1919.)

Limon, Jose F.

N.d.   The return of the Mexican ballad: Americo Paredes and his anthropological text as persuasive political performances. In Creativity in Anthropology. Smadar Lavie, Kirin Narayan, and Renato Rosaldo, eds. Ithaca: Cornell University Press. In press.

Littleton, L. Scott

1985   Introduction: Lucien Lévy-Bruhl and the Concept of Cognitive Relativity. In Lucien Lévy-Bruhl, How Natives Think. Lilian A. Clare, trans. Princeton: Princeton University Press, pp. v–lviii.

Loucou, Jean-Noël

1984   Histoire de la Côte d'Ivoire: 1. La formation des peuples. Abidjan: C.E.D.A.

Lubbock, John

1871   The Origin of Civilisation and the Primitive Conditions of Man: Mental and Social Condition of Savages. New York: D. Appleton & Co.

Lubbock, Percy, ed.

1920   The Letters of Henry James. Vol. 2. New York: Charles Scribner's Sons.

Lynch, Kevin

1960   The Image of the City. Cambridge: MIT Press.

MacGaffey, Wyatt

1972   The West in Congolese experience. In Africa and the West: Intellectual Responses to European Culture. Philip D. Curtin, ed. Madison: University of Wisconsin Press, pp. 49–74.

1983 Modern Kongo Prophets: Religion in a Plural Society. Bloomington: Indiana University Press.

McNaughton, Patrick
1982 The shirts that Mande hunters wear. African Arts 15(3):54–58, 91.

Maier, D. J. E.
1983 Priests and Power: The Case of the Dente Shrine in Nineteenth Century Ghana. Bloomington: Indiana University Press.

Maine, Henry James Sumner
1864 Ancient Law. London, 5th ed.

Malinowski, Bronislaw
1948 Myth in Primitive Psychology. *In* Bronislaw Malinowski, Magic, Science and Religion and Other Essays. New York: Free Press, pp. 93–148. (Essay orig. pub. New York: Norton, 1926.)

Manuel, Frank E., and Fritzie P. Manuel
1972 Sketch for a natural history of paradise. Daedalus 101:83–128.

Marchand, Jean-Baptiste
1894 [Télégramme n° 43 to the Paris Colonies.] 25 September 1894. France. Archives Nationales, Section d'Outre-Mer. Côte d'Ivoire, Carton III, dossier 3.

Marcus, George
1989 Imagining the whole: Ethnography's contemporary efforts to situate itself. Critique of Anthropology 9(3):7–30.

Marcus, George E., and Michael M. J. Fischer
———, and Dick Cushman
1982 Ethnographies as texts. Annual Review of Anthropology 11:25–69.
1986a Anthropology as Cultural Critique: An Experimental Moment in the Social Sciences. Chicago: University of Chicago Press.
1986b Introduction. *In* Anthropology as Cultural Critique: An Experimental Moment in the Human Sciences. Chicago: University of Chicago Press, pp. 1–6.

Martin, Emily
1987 The Woman in the Body. Boston: Beacon Press.

Marx, Karl
1967 Capital. Vol. 1. London: Lawrence and Wishart. (First German ed., 1867.)

Marx, Leo
1964 The Machine in the Garden: Technology and the Pastoral Ideal in America. London: Oxford University Press.

Mauss, Marcel
1967 The Gift: Forms and Functions of Exchange in Archaic Societies. Ian Cunnison, trans. New York: Norton. (Original: *In* L'Année Sociologique, n.s. 1 [1923–24].)

Mead, Margaret
1932 The Changing Culture of an Indian Tribe. New York: Columbia University Press.

Meggitt, M. J.
1964 Male-Female relationships in the Highlands of Australian New Guinea. American Anthropologist 66(4,2):204–224.

Menget, Patrick
1982 Time of birth, time of being: The couvade. *In* Between Belief and Transgression: Structuralist Essays in Religion, History, and Myth. Michel Izard and Pierre Smith, eds. John Leavitt, trans. Chicago: University of Chicago Press, pp. 193–209. (Original: La fonction symbolique. Paris: Gallimard, 1979.)

Milan Women's Bookstore Collective
1990 Sexual Difference: A Theory of Social-Symbolic Practice. Bloomington: Indiana University Press.

Miller, Daniel
    1987   Material Culture and Mass Consumption. London: Basil Blackwell.
    1988   Appropriating the state on the council estate. Man 23(2):353–372.
Molohon, Kathryn T.
    1984   Responses to television in two Swampy Cree communities on the west coast of
           James Bay. Kroeber Anthropological Society Papers 63 and 64. Special Issue:
           Opportunity, Constraint, and Change: Essays in Honor of Elizabeth Colson (Jack
           Glazier et al., eds.), pp. 95–103.
Monteil, Parfait Louis
    1895   [Letter to Louis-Gustav Binger, Governor of Côte d'Ivoire.] March 30, 1895.
           France. Archives Nationales, Section d'Outre-Mer. Côte d'Ivoire IV, Dossier 3,
           folder b.
Moore, Sally Falk
    1975   Epilogue: Uncertainties in situations, indeterminacies in culture. In Symbol and
           Politics in Communal Ideology: Cases and Questions. Sally Falk Moore and
           Barbara G. Myerhoff, eds. Ithaca: Cornell University Press, pp. 210–239.
    1986   Social Facts and Fabrications: "Customary" Law on Kilimanjaro 1880–1980.
           Cambridge: Cambridge University Press.
Mouëttet
    1896   [Letter to Jean-Baptiste Chaudie, Governor-General of French West Africa.]
           July 26, 1896. France. Archives Nationales, Section d'Outre-Mer. Côte d'Ivoire
           IV, Dossier 5, folder d.
Mounin, Georges
    1974   Lévi-Strauss' use of linguistics. In The Unconscious in Culture: The Struc-
           turalism of Claude Lévi-Strauss in Perspective. Ino Rossi, ed. New York: Dutton,
           pp. 31–52.
Muller, Jean-Claude
    1973   On preferential/prescriptive marriage and the function of kinship systems: The
           Rukuba case (Benue-Plateau State, Nigeria). American Anthropologist 75:1563–
           1576.
Myers, Fred
    1986a Pintupi Country, Pintupi Self: Sentiment, Place, and Politics among Western
           Desert Aborigines. Washington: Smithsonian Institute Press/Canberra: Australian
           Institute of Aboriginal Studies.
    1986b Reflections on a meeting: Structure, language, and the polity in a small-scale
           society. American Ethnologist 13(3):430–447.
Nadel, S. F.
    1957   The Theory of Social Structure. New York: Free Press.
Nandy, Ashis
    1983   The uncolonized mind: A post-colonial view of India and the West. In The
           Intimate Enemy: Loss and Recovery of Self under Colonialism. Delhi: Oxford
           University Press, pp. 64–113.
Nebout, A.
    1895a [Letter to Louis-Gustav Binger, Governor of Côte d'Ivoire.] March 29, 1895.
           France. Archives Nationales, Section d'Outre-Mer. Côte d'Ivoire IV, Dossier 3,
           folder b.
    1895b [Letter to Louis-Gustav Binger, Governor of Côte d'Ivoire.] March 30, 1895.
           France. Archives Nationales, Section d'Outre-Mer. Côte d'Ivoire IV, Dossier 3,
           folder b.
Needham, Rodney
    1961   Genealogy and category in Wikmunkan society. Ethnology 1:223–264.
    1971   Remarks on the analysis of kinship and marriage. In Rethinking Kinship and
           Marriage. Rodney Needham, ed. London: Tavistock, pp. 1–34.

1972   Belief, Language, and Experience. Chicago: University of Chicago Press.
1978   Synthetic images. *In* Primordial Characters. Charlottesville: University of Virginia Press, pp. 23–50.

Newman, Katherine S.
1986   Symbolic dialectics and generations of women: Variation in the meaning of post-divorce downward mobility. American Ethnologist 13:230–252.

Nurse, Derek, and Thomas Spear
1985   The Swahili: Reconstructing the History and Language of an African Society, 800–1500. Philadelphia: University of Pennsylvania Press.

Okpewho, Isidore
1983   Myth in Africa: A Study of Its Aesthetic and Cultural Relevance. Cambridge: Cambridge University Press.

Olsen, Stanley J.
1985   Origins of the Domesticated Dog: The Fossil Record. Tucson: University of Arizona Press.

Ong, Aihwa
1987   Spirits of Resistance and Capitalist Discipline: Factory Women in Malaysia. Albany: State University of New York Press.

Onians, Richard Broxton
1951   The Origins of European Thought about the Body, the Mind, the Soul, the World, Time, and Fate. Cambridge: Cambridge University Press.

Ortner, Sherry B.
1973   On key symbols. American Anthropologist 75:1338–1346.
1974   Is female to male as nature is to culture? *In* Woman, Culture, and Society. Michelle Zimbalist Rosaldo and Louise Lamphere, eds. Stanford: Stanford University Press, pp. 66–87.
1984   Theory in anthropology since the sixties. Comparative Studies in Society and History 26(1):126–66.

Packard, Randall M.
1980   Social change and the history of misfortune among the Bashu of Eastern Zaire. *In* African Systems of Thought. Ivan Karp and Charles S. Bird, eds. Bloomington: Indiana University Press, pp. 237–267.

Pelton, Robert D.
1980   The Trickster in West Africa: A Study of Mythic Irony and Sacred Delight. Berkeley: University of California Press.

Perin, Constance
1986   Speaking of tradition and modernity. Cultural Anthropology 1(4):425–446.

Person, Yves
1968a   Samori: Une Révolution Dyula. Vol. 1. Dakar: Mémoires de l'I.F.A.N. 80.
1968b   Samori: Une Révolution Dyula. Vol. 2. Dakar: Mémoires de l'I.F.A.N. 80.
1971   Groupes culturels et ethniques. Les Mande (B2A). *In* Atlas de Côte d'Ivoire. Abidjan, Côte d'Ivoire: Ministère du plan de Côte d'Ivoire, unnumbered pages.
1975   Samori: Une Révolution Dyula. Vol. 3. Dakar: Mémoires de l'I.F.A.N. 89.

Peters, Larry G.
1982   Trance, initiation, and psychotherapy in Tamang shamanism. American Ethnologist 9(1):21–46.

Piot, Charles
1985   Marriage, production, and symbolic forms. Paper presented at the 84th Annual Meeting of the American Anthropological Association, Washington, D.C.

Poe, Edgar Allen
1894   William Wilson. *In* The Works of Edgar Allan Poe in Ten Volumes. Vol. II, Tales of the Grotesque and Arabesque. Chicago: Stone & Kimball, pp. 5–32.

Poyer, Lin

1988 Maintaining "otherness": Sapwuahfik cultural identity. American Ethnologist 15(3):472–485.

Pratt, Louise
1986 Fieldwork in common places. In Writing Culture: The Poetics and Politics of Ethnography. James Clifford and George Marcus, eds. Berkeley: University of California Press, pp. 27–50.

Przybylowicz, Donna, Nancy Harstock, and Pamela McCallum, eds.
1989 Cultural Critique 13(Fall), special issue: The Construction of Gender and Modes of Social Division, vol. 1.
1990 Cultural Critique 14(Winter), special issue: The Construction of Gender and Modes of Social Division, vol. 2.

Quine, W. V.
1962 Paradox. Scientific American, April:84–96.

Rabinow, Paul
1986 Representations are social facts: Modernity and post-modernity in anthropology. In Writing Culture: The Poetics and Politics of Ethnography. James Clifford and George Marcus, eds. Berkeley: University of California Press, pp. 234–261.

Radcliffe-Brown, A. R.
1950 Introduction. In African Systems of Kinship and Marriage. A. R. Radcliffe-Brown and Daryll Forde, eds. London: Oxford University Press for the International African Institute, pp. 1–85.
1952 The study of kinship systems. In Structure and Function in Primitive Society. New York: The Free Press, pp. 49–89. (Essay orig. pub. Journal of the Royal Anthropological Institute 71 [1941].)

Raglan, Lord
1958 Myth and ritual. In Myth: A Symposium. Thomas A. Sebeok, ed. Bloomington: Indiana University Press, pp. 122–135. (Orig. pub. American Folklore Society, Bibliographical and Special Series, v. 5 [1951].)

Rank, Otto
1971 The Double: A Psychoanalytic Study. Harry Tucker, Jr., trans. Chapel Hill: University of North Carolina Press. (Original: Der Doppelganger: Eine psychoanalytische Studie. Leipzig: Internationaler Psychoanalytischer Verlag, 1925.)

Rattray, R. S.
1927 Religion and Art in Ashanti. Oxford: Clarendon Press.

Ravenhill, Philip Leonard
1976 The Social Organization of the Wan, a Patrilineal People of Ivory Coast. Ph.D. diss. New School for Social Research.

Renshaw, John
1988 Property, resources and equality among the Indians of the Paraguayan Chaco. Man 23(2):334–352.

Rey-Hulman, Diana
1978 L'or et les différenciations sociales dans l'Anno, ou la création de l'espace politique de l'Anno. Journal des Africanistes 48(1):71–88.

Robertson, Claire C., and Martin A. Klein, eds.
1983 Women and Slavery in Africa. Madison: University of Wisconsin Press.

Rosaldo, Michelle Zimbalist
1980 Knowledge and Passion: Ilongot Notions of Self and Social Life. Cambridge: Cambridge University Press.

Rosaldo, Renato
1986 Ilongot Hunting as Story and Experience. In The Anthropology of Experience. Victor W. Turner and Edward M. Bruner, eds. Urbana: University of Illinois Press, pp. 97–138.
1989 Culture and Truth: The Remaking of Social Analysis. Boston: Beacon Press.

1990   Comments on session, "Anthropology's Interlocuters: Joan Scott on History and Experience." Presented at the 89th Annual Meeting of the American Anthropological Association, New Orleans.

Rosen, Lawrence
1979   Social identity and points of attachment: Approaches to social organization. *In* Clifford Geertz, Hildred Geertz, and Lawrence Rosen, Meaning and Order in Moroccan Society. London: Cambridge University Press, pp. 19–111.

Rossi, Ino
1982   Lévi-Strauss' theory of kinship and its empiricist critics. An anti-Needham position. *In* The Logic of Culture: Advances in Structural Theory and Methods. Ino Rossi, ed. S. Hadley, MA: Bergin & Garvey, pp. 42–67.

Roth, Paul A.
1989   Ethnography without tears. Current Anthropology 30(5):555–569.

Sacks, Karen
1974   Engels revisited: Women, the organization of production, and private property. *In* Woman, Culture, and Society. Michelle Zimbalist Rosaldo and Louise Lamphere, eds. Stanford: Stanford University Press, pp. 207–222.

Safire, William
1985   Name that dog. New York Times Magazine, December 22, 1985, sec. 6:8, 10.

Sahlins, Marshall
1976   Culture and Practical Reason. Chicago: University of Chicago Press.
1981   Historical Metaphors and Mythical Realities: Structure in the Early History of the Sandwich Islands Kingdom. Ann Arbor: University of Michigan Press.

Salamone, Frank
1975   Becoming Hausa: Ethnic identity change and its implications for the study of ethnic pluralism and stratification. Africa 45(4):410–425.

Salverte-Marmier, Philippe de, and M. A. de Salverte-Marmier
1966   Les étapes du peuplement. *In* Etude régionale de Bouaké. Vol. 1, Le Peuplement. Abidjan: Côte d'Ivoire, Ministère du Plan; Bureau de Conception, de Coordination et d'Exploitation des Etudes régionales de la République de Côte d'Ivoire.

Salzman, Carl Philip
1978   Does complementary opposition exist? American Anthropologist 80(1):53–70.

Sapir, J. David
1977a   The anatomy of metaphor. *In* The Social Use of Metaphor. J. Christopher Crocker and J. David Sapir, eds. Philadelphia: University of Pennsylvania Press, pp. 3–32.
1977b   Fecal animals: An example of complementary totemism. Man 12(1):1–21.
1981   Leper, hyena, and blacksmith in Kujamaat Diola thought. American Ethnologist 8(3):526–543.

Şaul, Mahir
1989   Corporate authority, exchange, and personal opposition in Bobo marriages. American Ethnologist 16(1):57–74.
1991   The Bobo "house" and the uses of categories of descent. Africa 61(1):71–97.

Schieffelin, Edward L.
1981   Evangelical rhetoric and the transformation of traditional culture in Papua New Guinea. Comparative Studies in Society and History 23:150–156.

Schloss, Mark R.
1988   The Hatchet's Blood: Separation, Power, and Gender in Ehing Social Life. Tucson: University of Arizona Press.

Schneider, David M.
1968   American Kinship: A Cultural Account. Englewood Cliffs, N.J.: Prentice-Hall.
1984   A Critique of the Study of Kinship. Ann Arbor: University of Michigan Press.

Schneider, Kirk J.
  1990 The Paradoxical Self: Toward an Understanding of our Contradictory Nature. New York: Plenum.
Schultz, Emily
  1984 From pagan to Pullo: Ethnic identity change in northern Cameroun. Africa 54(1):46–64.
Schwartzman, Helen
  1984 Stories at work: Play in an organizational context. In Text, Play, and Story: The Construction and Reconstruction of Self and Society. 1983 Proceedings of the American Ethnological Society. Edward M. Bruner, ed. Washington, D.C.: American Ethnological Society, pp. 80–93.
Shapiro, Warren
  1988 Ritual kinship, ritual incorporation and the denial of death. Man 23(2):275–297.
Sharp, Lauriston
  1952 Steel axes for stone age Australians. In Human Problems in Technological Change: A Case Book. Edward H. Spicer, ed. New York: Russell Sage Foundation, pp. 69–90.
Shaw, Rosalind
  1985 Gender and the structuring of reality in Temne divination: An interactive study. Africa 55(3):286–303.
Shore, Bradd
  1978 Ghosts and government. Man 13(2):175–199.
Sillitoe, Paul
  1988 From head-dresses to head-messages: The art of self-decoration in the Highlands of Papua New-Guinea. Man 23(2):298–318.
Simmel, Georg
  1950 The secret and the secret society. In The sociology of Georg Simmel. Kurt H. Wolff, trans. and ed. New York: Free Press, pp. 307–376. (Original: Soziologie unter Suchungen über die Formen der Vergesellschaftung. Leipzig: Duncker und Hamblot, 1908.)
Stern, Daniel N.
  1985 The Interpersonal World of the Infant: A View from Psychoanalysis and Developmental Psychology. New York: Basic Books.
Stoller, Paul
  1989 The Taste of Ethnographic Things: The Senses in Anthropology. Philadelphia: University of Pennsylvania Press.
Strathern, Marilyn
  1987a Out of context: The persuasive fictions of anthropology. Current Anthropology 28(3):251–281.
  1987b Producing difference: Connections and disconnections in two New Guinea Highland kinship systems. In Gender and Kinship: Essays toward a Unified Analysis. Jane Fishburne Collier and Sylvia Junko Yanagisako, eds. Stanford: Stanford University Press, pp. 271–300.
Stromberg, Peter G.
  1986 Symbols of Community: The Cultural System of a Swedish Church. Tucson: University of Arizona Press.
Sumner, Colin
  1979 Reading Ideologies: An Investigation into the Marxist Theory of Ideology and Law. London: Academic Press.
Suttles, Gerald D.
  1970 Friendship as a Social Institution. In Social Relationships. George J. McCall et al., eds. Chicago: Aldine, pp. 85–135.

Tambiah, Stanley J.
   1969   Animals are good to think and good to prohibit. Ethnology 8(4):423–459.
Taussig, Michael T.
   1980   The Devil and Commodity Fetishism in South America. Chapel Hill: University of North Carolina Press.
Tauxier, Louis
   1921   Le noir de Bondoukou. Paris: Larose.
Thomas, Nicholas
   1989   Taking people seriously: Cultural autonomy and the global system. Critique of Anthropology 9(3):59–69.
Thompson, Robert Farris
   1983   Flash of the Spirit: African and Afro-American Art and Philosophy. New York: Random House.
Thornton, Robert
   1988   The rhetoric of ethnographic holism. Cultural Anthropology 3(3):285–303.
Trawick, Margaret
   1988   Spirits and voices in Tamil songs. American Ethnologist 15(2):193–215.
Turner, Victor W.
   1957   Schism and Continuity in an African Society. Manchester: Manchester University Press.
   1967a Betwixt and between: The liminal period in *rites de passage*. *In* The Forest of Symbols. Ithaca: Cornell University Press, pp. 93–111. (Essay orig. pub. Proceedings of the American Ethnological Society [1964].)
   1967b The Forest of Symbols. Ithaca, N.Y.: Cornell University Press.
   1967c Ritual symbolism, morality, and social structure among the Ndembu. *In* The Forest of Symbols. Ithaca: Cornell University Press, pp. 48–58. (Essay orig. pub. in African Systems of Thought. Meyer Fortes and Germaine Dieterlen, eds. London: Oxford University Press, 1965.)
   1969   The Ritual Process. Chicago: Aldine.
   1985   Process, system, and symbol: A new anthropological synthesis. *In* On the Edge of the Bush: Anthropology as Experience. Tucson: University of Arizona Press, pp. 151–176. (Essay orig. pub. Daedalus; Discoveries and Interpretations: Studies in Contemporary Scholarship, v. 1 [1977].)
Tyler, Stephen A.
   1987   The Unspeakable: Discourse, Dialogue, and Rhetoric in the Postmodern World. Madison: University of Wisconsin Press.
Van Baal, J.
   1975   Reciprocity and the Position of Women: Anthropological Papers. Assen: Van Gorcum.
Vansina, Jan
   1965   Oral Tradition: A Study in Historical Methodology. H. M. Wright, trans. London: Routledge and Kegan Paul. (Original: De la tradition orale: Essai de méthode historique, annales du Musée de l'Afrique Centrale, 1961.)
Vellenga, Dorothy Dee
   1983   Who is a wife? Legal expressions of heterosexual conflicts in Ghana. *In* Female and Male in West Africa. Christine Oppong, ed. London: George Allen & Unwin, pp. 144–155.
Wagner, Roy
   1972a Incest and identity. A critique and theory on the subject of exogamy and incest prohibition. Man 7(4):601–613.
   1972b Misreading the metaphor: "Cross-cousin" relationships in the New Guinea Highlands. Paper presented at the 71st Annual Meeting of the American Anthropological Association, Toronto.

1974   Are there social groups in the New Guinea Highlands? *In* Frontiers of Anthropology. Murray J. Leaf, ed. New York: Van Nostrand, pp. 95–122.

1975   The Invention of Culture: Englewood Cliffs: Prentice-Hall.

1978   Lethal Speech: Daribi Myth as Symbolic Obviation. Ithaca: Cornell University Press.

1979   The talk of Koriki: A Daribi contact cult. Social Research 46(1):140–165.

Walker, Ernest R., ed.

1964   Mammals of the World. Baltimore: Johns Hopkins University Press.

Wallace, Anthony F. C.

1956   Revitalization movements. American Anthropologist 58:264–281.

Weber, Max

1976   The Protestant Ethic and the Spirit of Capitalism. Talcott Parsons, trans. New York: Scribner's. (Original: Die protestantische Ethik und der Geist des Kapitalismus, Archiv für Sozialwissenschaft und Sozialpolitik XX and XXI [1904–5].)

Weiskel, Timothy

1976   L'histoire socio-économique des peuples baulé: Problèmes et perspectives de recherche. Cahiers d'Etudes Africaines 16, 61–62(1–2):357–395.

1978   The precolonial Baule: A reconstruction. Cahiers d'Etudes Africaines 18, 72(4):503–560.

1980   French Colonial Rule and the Baule Peoples: Resistance and Collaboration, 1889–1911. Oxford: Oxford University Press.

Welmers, William E.

1960   The Mande languages. *In* Report of the Ninth Round Table Meeting on Linguistics and Language Study: Anthropology and African Studies. William M. Austin, ed. Georgetown University Institute of Languages and Linguistics, Monograph Series on Languages and Linguistics, #11, pp. 19–24.

1971   Niger-Congo, Mande. *In* Current Trends in Linguistics. Vol. 7, Linguistics in Sub-Saharan Africa, ed. Thomas Sebeok. The Hague: Mouton.

White, Hayden

1972   The forms of wilderness: Archaeology of an idea. *In* The Wild Man Within: An Image in Western Thought from the Renaissance to Romanticism. Edward Dudley and Maximillian E. Novak, eds. Pittsburgh: University of Pittsburgh Press, pp. 3–38.

Whitman, Walt

1968   Song of myself. *In* Leaves of Grass. Harold W. Blodgett and Sculley Bradley, eds. New York: W. W. Norton & Co., pp. 28–89.

Whitmore, T. C.

1981   Trees of the tropics. *In* The Oxford Encyclopedia of Trees of the World. Bayard Hora, ed. Oxford: Oxford University Press, pp. 263–269.

Whitten, Norman E., Jr.

1985   Sicuanga Runa: The Other Side of Development in Amazonian Ecuador. Urbana: University of Illinois Press.

Williams, George H.

1962   Wilderness and Paradise in Christian Thought: The Biblical Experience of the Desert in the History of Christianity and the Paradise Theme in the Theological Idea of the University. New York: Harper.

Wilson, Godfrey, and Monica Wilson

1945   The Analysis of Social Change, Based on Observations in Central Africa. Cambridge: Cambridge University Press.

Winter, E. H.

1963   The enemy within: Amba witchcraft and sociological theory. *In* Witchcraft and Sorcery in East Africa. John Middleton and E. Winter, eds. New York: Praeger, pp. 177–199.

Witherspoon, Gary
    1977   Language and Art in the Navajo Universe. Ann Arbor: University of Michigan Press.
Yanagisako, Sylvia Junko
    1987   Mixed metaphors: Native and anthropological models of gender and kinship domains. In Gender and Kinship: Essays toward a Unified Analysis. Jane Fishburne Collier and Sylvia Junko Yanagisako, eds. Stanford: Stanford University Press, pp. 86–118.
Yao, Elizabeth Annan
    1989   Impact of economic crisis and adjustment on urban-rural resource flows and food production in Divo. Paper presented at the Farming Systems Research and Extension Symposium, Fayetteville, Ark.
Young, Frank W.
    1965   Initiation Ceremonies: A Cross-Cultural Study of Status Dramatization. Indianapolis: Bobbs-Merrill.
Zilberg, Jonathan
    1989   Zimbabwean Stone Sculpture: Ethnic Dimensions. M.A. paper in lieu of thesis, University of Illinois.

Index

Abortions, 39. *See also* Childbirth
Abrahamsson, H., 99
Adoption, 52, 61. *See also* Foster parenting
Africa: fluidity of ethnic groups in, 1; relevance of ethnicity in, 1–2
Agni (ethnic group). *See* Anyi (ethnic group)
Agriculture. *See* Crops; Fertility, of the soil; Fields; Monocropping
Alliance systems. *See* Marriage
Ancestor worship, 144–145n.2
Ando: ethnic group, 3–4, 120, 146–147n.18; language, 3, 125
Anyi (ethnic group), 143n.4
Architecture. *See* Grid design of villages; Houses; Space; Villages
Arranged marriages, 72–73, 145n.9; rebellions against, 87–95
Arts traditions, 8, 124, 128
Asagbe (village), 19–20
Asante (ethnic group), 73, 99, 147n.23, 149nn.7, 14, 151n.12
Aspirin, 138
Australia: Pintupi (ethnic group), 144n.12; Wikmunkan (ethnic group), 83; Yir Yoront (ethnic group), 119

Babies: and body odor, 148n.5; body painting on, 8, 139, 147n.21; illegitimate, 39, 90; medicine for, 102; replaced with snakes, 37–38; and timing of lovemaking, 26; watched by dogs, 103. *See also* Breast milk; Childbirth
Bakhtin, Mikhail, 13–14, 114
Bamana (ethnic group), 108, 133, 154–155n.33
Baoulé (ethnic group). *See* Baule
Bark cloth, 30, 124, 133
Barth, Fredrik, 47, 49
Bashu (ethnic group), 123
Bateson, Gregory, 12
Bathing, 36, 146n.16
Baule: Beng identification with, 2, 3, 146–147n.18; ethnic group, 7, 91, 120, 149n.7, 150n.7, 151n.12; language, 2, 3, 50, 125
Bedouin (of Cyrenaica), 143–144n.9
Belief, and faith, 23, 31, 44–45
Beng (ethnic group): annual income among, 147n.20; arts tradition among, 8, 124, 128; definition of, 1–8, 124, 141–142; gender relations among, 147n.21; history of, 4–8, 47–48,

124–126; immigrants among, 133–134; as mediators, 8, 144n.10; migration to Côte d'Ivoire, 5–6, 7; other terms for, 143n.1; as pacifists, 5–8, 23, 125, 129; population of, 3; power differences among, 16–17; reaction to Western goods among, 3, 119, 123–124, 135–142; as refugees, 5, 7, 23; relations with neighboring ethnic groups, 2, 3, 120, 124–125, 133–134; views of White people, 126–127
Beng (language): as criterion for ethnic identity, 2–3, 125, 137; dictionary for, 3, 156n.6; songs composed among, 2; as understood by spirits, 41–42
Binger, Louis-Gustav, 28, 156n.6
Bird, Charles, 5
Bird feathers, 109, 111, 153n.18
Birds, 149n.11
Bloch, Maurice, 69, 117
Blood, 56–57, 59, 69. *See also* Menstrual blood
Body painting, of babies, 8, 139, 147n.21
Bonde Como (king), 54
Bongalo (village), 133
Bozo (ethnic group), 108
Breast milk, 55–56, 64
Bruner, Edward M., 11
Bubu (gown), 111

Calendar: days of the week, 29, 133; and reckoning of days, 30, 36; rest days, 29–31, 133. *See also* Day-night dichotomy
Cargo cults, 122
Case studies: Afwe's Insolence, Her Father's Curse, and the Spirits' Revenge, 26–27; Akissi and the Chicken, 22; Akissi and the Snails, 63; Akissi in the Yam Field, 32–33; Amwe and the Spitting Cobra, 33; Bernard and the Two Cows, 22; The Case of the Sold Gold, 54; The Case of the Stolen Gold, 54; Co-wives' Fight on Earth Day, 30–31; A Family of Three Daughters, 90–91; Forest Sex and Witchcraft, 34–35; A Former Slave's Memories, 58–59; The Jealous Cousin, 93–95; The Liana and the Soul, 55; A Man Meets a Spirit, 26; Marriages of a First Wife's Children, 86–87; Matriclan Exchange, 81; The Nephew and His Pregnant Aunt, 50–51; Planting a New Kapok Tree, 20; Refusing a Polluted Co-wife, 35; The Reluctant Mourner, 51; The Reluctant Mourner, Revisited, 55; Second Wife's Six Daughters' Marriages, 87; The

179